My Path to Peace and Justice

SHOULD WE TEACH LIFE + LOVE OR DEATH + HATE?

AN AUTOBIOGRAPHY

Richard T. McSorley, S.J.

FORTKAMP PUBLISHING / ROSE HILL BOOKS
MARION, SOUTH DAKOTA

Copyright © 1996 by Richard T. McSorley, S.J.

Published by *FORTKAMP PUBLISHING*

ROSE HILL BOOKS
28291 444th Avenue Marion, South Dakota 57043

Printed at Pine Hill Press, Inc., Freeman, South Dakota

International Standard Book Number: 1-879175-19-3

Library of Congress Catalog Card Number: 96-061672

Cover art and design by Beth Preheim

Unless otherwise credited, photos provided courtesy of Richard T. McSorley, S.J.

Second Printing 1997

Printed in United States of America

PINE HILL PRESS, INC.
Freeman, S. Dak. 57029

✣ Acknowledgments
with Gratitude

Many thanks to the following good people for their assistance along the path to completion of this autobiography:
John Dear, S.J. for suggestions and ideas; Sondra O'Shea for typing;
William Byron, S.J., Tara Duffy, Pat Blasius, Charles Gonzalez, S.J.
and Winifred Allen (my sister) for their encouragement; Beth Preheim and Michael Sprong of Fortkamp Publishing / Rose Hill Books for editing and production of this volume.

✤ *Contents*

— ❖ ❖ ❖ —

✤ Foreword

Everyone loves a good story, we're told. Now at more than eighty years of age, Richard McSorley, S.J. has a long, interesting life's journey to share with readers. Right from the beginning Dick McSorley found himself "off the beaten path." He was born and raised in Philadelphia, one of the fifteen sons and daughters of a faith-filled Irish American couple.

As a Jesuit Scholastic, he was interned from 1941 to 1945 in the Philippines by Japanese occupation forces. In 1945 MacArthur returned as he had promised. Dick, along with countless others, was liberated, and he returned to the United States to complete his theological studies in preparation for ordination to the priesthood. Later that year, the Bomb was dropped on Hiroshima and Nagasaki. As he writes in this account, little did he know how much this event would change his life, and indeed all our lives.

In the nearly fifty years since his first pastoral assignment as a priest to a mission church in Ridge, Maryland, Dick has been involved in a very immediate, "hands-on" way in the struggle to establish the just, peaceful reign of God in our midst. During this five-decade struggle, Father McSorley learned from remarkable mentors like John LaFarge and Horace McKenna; marched with Martin Luther King, Jr.; stood with Dan and Phil Berrigan; confronted the powers-that-be at Georgetown on the presence of ROTC units at the university; and shared the struggle, the long haul, with a multitude of people from all walks, states and styles of life.

I consider myself fortunate to have been a fellow traveler with Dick McSorley for the last half of this fifty-year span. I still recall the day on which I heard Father McSorley insist it is the willingness of our national leaders to use nuclear weapons that is the source and ultimate explanation for the mounting level of violence that threatens to destroy us as a nation and as a people. I am convinced that this analysis is profoundly true. It has in the past, and continues today, to inspire my own commitment to peacemaking.

Dick McSorley, in his autobiography, does not rate himself among the most talented of Jesuit confreres. When he was ordained, his provincial assigned him to minister in Ridge, rural Southern Maryland where expectations of him were modest indeed. A few years later, when he responded to a call from the Father General of the Jesuits for volunteers to serve in Japan, he received the following reply: "In the opinion of some grave and pious fathers of the Maryland Province, you would do better to use your talents in the United States rather than in Japan." From Ridge, Dick was transferred to Scranton University and assigned to teach philosophy. After a couple of years in this ministry, Dick requested time off to work for a Ph.D. in philosophy (certainly not an unusual request for a U.S. Jesuit), but the request was denied. Yet Dick overcame these obstacles to become one of the great peacemakers of the Twentieth Century.

I would spoil your enjoyment of this well-told tale if I gave away any more of the story line. Dick McSorley is an ordinary Christian who has made extraordinary accomplishments during his lifetime.

The life of Dick McSorley described in this engrossing autobiography is a constant reminder that as Mother Teresa repeats over and over again: "God doesn't call us to be successful, but to be faithful."

To those who know Dick McSorley, not only has he been a faithful witness to the gospel, but a successful witness as well.

—*Walter T. Sullivan*
Bishop of Richmond

I

The Philippines

1 ✤ *Pearl Harbor Day*

It was 7:30 a.m. and I was seated in the waiting room of the only dentist in Naga, a small town located seventy-five miles south of Manila. One of the few Americans in town, I was a Jesuit seminarian from Philadelphia and a teacher (?) at an all boys high school. After three years in the Philippines — two in Manila and one in Naga — I was preparing to head back to the United States where I would study theology.

A woman sitting next to me in the dentist's office asked, "Did you open your radio this morning?" I thought of what a luxury it would be to have time to listen to the radio in the morning. "The Japanese have bombed Pearl Harbor and Davao," she said. I remained silent, thinking that the old lady must be confused about geography; didn't she know that Pearl Harbor is eight thousand miles from Davao? (Davao is an island in the Philippines.)

She probably could sense my skepticism. "If you don't believe me then just look out the window." I pulled back the curtains and saw a crowd on the street below. They were gathered around a radio that was blaring loud enough for me to hear, "the United States of America has declared war on Japan."

So much for my dental appointment. I ran downstairs and on to one side of the plaza, the center of town, which was swarming with activity. "Did you hear the news about Davao being bombed?" I asked one of the people near the radio. "Yes, and Clark field." Clark, the American airfield north of Manila, was on this very island of Luzon.

A group of ten or more constabulary — police in khaki uniforms with rifles and bayonets — moved through the bazaars looking for merchants of Japanese descent. As the gathering crowd watched, the police lined up ten Japanese with their faces to the wall, bayonets at their backs. A Filipino approached me, "Can't you do something about this?" Apparently he thought an American dressed in a priest's white cassock would have some authority. "Speak to the captain. Tell him these people aren't enemies. The bayonets a few inches from their backs might go into them if anybody slips."

I walked over to the constabulary officer who seemed to be in charge. "Can't you move your men back a little from the Japanese so there won't be any accident here? They aren't trying to escape. They are known to everybody here in the town." My interference only angered the captain, and he replied, "We have orders to round them up." Frustrated and confused, I abruptly abandoned the situation, feeling a strong need to return to my residence. Little did I know that this would be only the first and the least horrific in a series of abuses.

Hastily, I left the plaza and ran three blocks to the Jesuit school and our newly built residence, located behind the cathedral and surrounded by rice paddies. Nearby, we were beginning construction of a new college building. We were a community of seven American and four Filipino Jesuits. As we talked, we agreed that the Japanese were crazy to attack the United States. Our mighty navy and superior air force would quickly make them a sorry lot.

The radio news puzzled us. The Japanese were claiming a great victory at Pearl Harbor, but the U.S. response was not clear. That day and the days following we listened for the good news. But the virtual silence about what U.S. forces were doing to retaliate against the Japanese attacks seemed ominous. Then we also noticed that our regular English-speaking stations from Hong Kong and Shanghai were broadcasting in Japanese.

On December 8, while out on the school basketball court, I saw a low-flying Japanese plane drop leaflets on the road and around the cathedral yard. I wondered how such a slow double-winged plane could elude our powerful air force. I picked up one of the leaflets and read: "Dear Filipino citizen, we are your friends. We are your brown brothers. We have come to liberate you from economic exploitation and racial disdain. We have come to establish the great Asian coprosperity sphere. We invite you to join us with our great plan. You have nothing to fear from us. But if you aid or assist our enemy, the Americans, you will be severely punished." The bottom was signed commander-in-chief of the Japanese landing forces.

I thought the propaganda was clever but foolish. Who did this commander think he was? How was he going to land? The rickety plane couldn't fly very far or very fast. It must have come off an aircraft carrier. But how could an aircraft carrier be so near without being sunk?

For several days rumors of war prompted the townspeople to leave, carrying all they could on their backs or in whatever wagon or wheelbarrow they could find. I saw a man carrying a mattress on his head. The local fire engine, loaded with bags of rice and household goods, joined the endless procession. With some students, I stood on the edge of our basketball court, next to the main road and asked some of the travelers where they were going. "North, a Japanese battleship has landed at Lagaspe," they answered. Lagaspe was about fifty miles south of us. Though the refugees were heading toward Manila, no road went through to the capital. The only transport to Manila, still under Filipino-American control, was a single track railroad. Ordinarily the train came south every morning and traveled back the same afternoon.

The next day, the street was crowded with people marching south, some of the same people I had seen the day before going north. "Why are you returning?" I asked. "What happened?"

"The Japanese never landed in Lagaspe. We made a mistake. It is an American battleship at Lagaspe."

"Where did you hear that?" This was big news.

"A major told us."

I walked with them until we reached the plaza where a crowd of about twenty people surrounded the major of the constabulary, the highest ranking official in town. With no military in Naga, he had taken over control from the mayor. The crowd was asking him questions, and he looked harassed and confused. His hat was off, his hair disheveled, a bandolier of bullets slung over one shoulder and across his chest. Over the other shoulder hung his rifle.

When I got a chance to speak to him, I asked about the news of the American battleship. When he knew no one else could hear, he said, "It's not American. It's Japanese."

"The people told me that you said it was American."

"I told them that to calm them down."

"What will happen when they find out the truth?"

"We've got to calm them down and get them off the roads."

"What will happen when they find out?" I thought, "Whom will they believe now?" As the old adage says: In war the first casualty is truth.

On the way back to the Jesuit residence I met one of a handful of Americans in town and told him what I had learned. He told me of a small house he had on top of Mt. Isarog where he and a few others planned to hole-up. They believed that the danger would blow over in a few months, that the Japanese would be too busy with the war to bother them. He invited me to join them and I was keen to do so, but first I had to get permission from the Jesuit superior.

Back at the house, I met Father Burns on the second floor porch. When I asked if I could accept the offer made by my American friend, he replied, "I will think it over and let you know." The next day I asked again, "Did you decide on it?"

"I still have to think about it," he said. With some impatience, I pushed him. He gave the same answer.

"You know the Japanese are getting closer every day. If you don't make up your mind before they arrive, there will be no use deciding at all." He gave me a reasoned reply. "If I don't decide by the time they arrive, then my decision will be "no." When the Japanese arrive, I hope the bishop will persuade them to let us stay here under his care. After all, as civilians we are not supposed to be harmed. And there's another consideration: There are seven of us Americans here, everyone in town knows. If the Japanese arrive to find only six of us, we may be punished because one is missing. I have to think of that." Satisfied, I accepted his answer. I hadn't thought that my absence might endanger the others.

Looking back on it now, I see God's Providence in Father Burns' refusal. As the war dragged on and without any clear hope of rescue, the Americans on the mountain began to think life in a concentration camp with other Americans would be better than theirs in fearful isolation. All but one finally agreed to accept the public Japanese offer to all American civilians: Turn yourselves in and you will be interned with other Americans in Manila. A Japanese patrol accepted their surrender and started walking them down the mountain. Halfway down, the Japanese shot them. They claimed the Americans tried to escape.

Everyday for the next week I went to the plaza to hear the local rumors. By this time everyone knew that the Japanese had landed in Lagaspe to the south and in Lingayen Gulf, north of Manila. They were on both ends of the island and coming toward us. A rumor floated around that the Japanese had captured the locomotive in Lagaspe and were using it to advance.

Because I am an American, many townspeople thought I might know more than they about troop movements and how long the Japanese could last. I sensed they felt loyal to America and worried what would happen to their American friends. I told them I knew only what I heard on the radio and, to me, it all seemed bad.

Some of the other Jesuits were more optimistic. I learned later that Fr. Burns had advised them not to talk about the war all the time, especially with me because I was so discouraged. I had less hope than did Fr. Burns that the bishop would see to our being treated like civilians. It didn't fit with what I had heard about the Japanese and how they treated prisoners. I wrote a letter to my mother and gave it to a student named Deo Gratias asking him to mail it to the United States once the post office reopened. I told mother that I loved her and detailed my experiences since the news of Pearl Harbor.

I put a few things together in a white cloth laundry bag in case we had to leave in a hurry. I felt like Robinson Crusoe, shipwrecked on the island, saving only a few things for the long haul. In the bag I put the New Testament in Latin and Greek, a Spanish dictionary and *Cortina's Spanish in Twenty Lessons*. I figured I could study these books for a long time without exhausting the challenge. I also packed a map of the island of Luzon, just in case we had a chance to escape. I took a mosquito net, the kind that we always hung over the bed at night. That's about all.

One morning as I stood on our second floor porch and looked across the rice paddies, I saw on the main road what looked like Boy Scouts wearing short khaki pants. "The Boy Scouts are out on the street," I said to one of the community.

"They aren't Boy Scouts. The Japanese came into the city during the night. We didn't want to tell you until you found out by yourself. It is not good news."

Fr. Burns then instructed us to stay together in the house. "Bishop Santos is going to see the Japanese commander and ask that we be put in the bishop's care. He'll come soon to let us know."

About noon, the bishop arrived in white soutane with a gold cross around his neck and a red skull cap covering his gray hair. We sat around him in our parlor. "The Japanese would not agree to anything. I told them you are my boys. I will be responsible for you. I need you for my work." He was in tears, tears that told us of his affection for us and his fear that we were in danger. He had been very good to us, even taking us into his home to live until we had built this new residence.

When the bishop left, Fr. Burns suggested that each of us go to our rooms to rest and pray as preparation for whatever might happen. My room faced the road that led to our new school. From my window I watched as two busloads of Japanese soldiers in full battle dress stopped at the empty school. They pulled up near our house, then ran toward it. Acting more calmly than I felt, I went down the hall to Fr. Burns' room and told him the Japanese soldiers had encircled the house.

"Tell everybody to stay in their rooms. I don't want the Japanese to think we are ganging up on them. I will go out the front door and wave a white flag." It was good advice. I didn't see how the Japanese would ever think we were ganging up on them, but they might have, considering the way they acted. I went back to my room and sat at my desk. "This is the moment I need God's direction," I thought. Since I already had put my New Testament in the laundry bag, I picked up *Imitation of Christ* by Thomas aKempis. I randomly put a pin between two pages to see how God would speak to me. On the first page I opened, my eyes fell to these words: "Your time here is at an end. See how it will be with you in a better world."

As I was reading those sentences, a Japanese soldier, holding a bayoneted rifle and a pistol burst into my room screaming, "Kurrah!" and a dozen other words. He rushed at me and shoved his pistol to my head. I didn't move or answer him. I could only guess at what he was saying. Still holding the pistol to my head, he looked at my desk, saw a drinking glass full of pencils and ball point pens. He laid the pistol down on the desk, grabbed a few of the pens and stuffed them into his pocket. I was more angry at him for taking my pens than for threatening my life. A thought passed through my head: "I could easily pick up his gun and shoot him." It passed.

A Japanese who spoke English came by the open door and said, "Everybody come into the parlor." The soldier backed away as I got up and walked down the hallway to the parlor where all of us assembled. Within minutes, the Japanese interpreter ordered us all into the buses. Fr. Burns asked if we could pick up some clothes. Japanese soldiers escorted us to our rooms for the last time to collect a few things. Relieved to have my bag ready, I picked it up and walked to the bus. The seven of us sat on the front benches of the bus, the soldiers behind us with guns pointed at our backs. Through the open-sided bus we were visible to all our friends and students who stared as we passed their homes. There was sorrow in their faces as they saw us being taken away. The date was December 13th, 1941.

2 ❖ *Off to Jail*

Our destination was soon apparent. From the plaza, we went along a narrow alley between the wall surrounding city hall and the high, white wall of the prison. At the prison, the bus stopped and we were ordered out into the prison yard: about thirty feet by fifty feet in area. The green wooden doors of the cells lined the yard. How quickly a scene can change. Just a week before, these same cells had held the Japanese; now Japanese guards led us down the yard and into a cell. A group of Americans in the next cell called out, "Welcome. Sorry to see you here. But glad to have some company."

When all seven of us were inside the cell, the guard stood on the threshold, motioned to the doorway, and said, "Please do not go past this line," as if we had a choice. After he closed the heavy double doors and before we were padlocked in: "What do we use for a toilet?" The guard pointed to the corner of the room. I asked if anybody brought a mosquito net. Before they could answer, the door opened and the guard handed in a five gallon gasoline can with the top cut off. "Toilet," he said. Before the guard could leave, Fr. Burns asked him about mosquito nets. When he indicated that he did not understand, I showed him mine. With signs we asked if they could send someone to our home to get them. Fr. Burns offered to go himself. "No go," the guard said. "Me go." Not sure he understood, we were pleasantly surprised a half-hour later when the door opened and the mosquito nets arrived. It's amazing how that little event cheered us up.

As we tied the nets to our beds, someone whistling our school song passed by. I rushed to the window. It was Deo Gratias, smiling and waving to us. Friends on the outside cared about us and knew we were here! Fr. Burns quickly added his order to instructions we had received from the Japanese: "It's dangerous to wave to passers-by from the window," he said. "The Japanese may think we're giving signals and punish us or the students. No one should go to the window except me." It was probably another wise decision.

When supper-time passed and the door remained closed, we wondered if we would get anything to eat that night. It was almost dark when the lock rattled and a guard pulled the door open. A Japanese woman brought a tray with rice and small canned sausages. Though her English was obviously limited, she said, "My son Appanao." Appanao Danada was a student in our high school. We sensed that Mrs. Danada, the jail cook, would be helpful to us if she could. We thanked her for the food, found seats at the table, as well as on the bench and the beds, then we thanked God for our long-awaited supper.

There was only one electric bulb hanging from the high ceiling of the cell, hardly enough to read by. And, to make life interesting, the switch was outside the door. One of us had brought along a deck of cards, and that first evening Fr. Burns insisted that we all play one hand of solitaire. I didn't care for the game, but Fr. Burns prevailed. "It will be good for morale, and it will give us something to talk about besides the Japanese and the war." I soon got into the spirit, offering a sausage saved from my supper as the prize for the winner.

The next morning it was easy to assess the bed bugs' damage head to toe. We could see them in the mosquito netting, so we spent hours picking them out. But it was impossible to see the ones hidden in the rattan matting. We never did get rid of them.

Late in the morning of the second day we were allowed out to walk in the yard, and there we met the Americans from the next cell. All strangers to us, some of them had run the city transportation company. Their wives and families had returned by ship to the States when the situation began to seem dangerous. The men had remained until the last minute to dispose of the buses and other property. They had readied a speed boat to escape to Singapore at a moment's notice, but had stayed too long. Like us, they believed they soon would be free.

We were there only a few days when a soldier came in to our cell with an interpreter. The word was ominous: A transmitter had been found in our house, and we would be shot as spies the next morning. Fr. Burns did not take kindly to this announcement. When he started to argue that we didn't have a transmitter and that we were not spies, the Japanese officer hit him in the face, punched him and knocked him down. When Fr. Burns was on the floor, the guard kicked him, screaming in Japanese all the while. Responding to the noise, other soldiers came to the door of the cell and dragged Fr. Burns out. He was thrown into a solitary confinement cell at the end of the yard. Since our imprisonment, I had wondered what my response would be if one of my religious superiors was attacked. The reality of Fr. Burns being so severely beaten only a few feet from me put that question to rest. It was a sight I never want to witness again.

Someone in our group had brought along a bottle of beer; so that night, when Mrs. Danada came with our supper, I spoke to her in my newly learned Spanish. I opened the beer bottle in her presence, handed it to her and then asked her to take it to the American prisoner "over there" as I pointed to Fr. Burns' cell.

"Tell her in English," said Fr. Joe Bitner. "She doesn't understand your Spanish." If only I had. . . . Joe kept the door open a bit to watch what she did with it. In a minute he screamed.

"What's the matter?" I asked.

"She poured the beer down the toilet. That's how good your Spanish is." Given our predicament, the comedy of this error escaped us.

That night we prayed and prepared to die. Morning came and nothing happened. Nothing. Not even breakfast. About noon the door was unlocked and we were allowed into the yard. That afternoon, Fr. Burns was returned to our cell.

"What happened?" we asked him. "The Japanese had seen our phonograph [on which you could stack several records] and some of them thought it was a transmitter. Higher officers knew what it was, so we're not going to be shot." How grateful we were.

Later, I worried about other evidence that might "prove" we were spies. I was especially concerned about the letter I had written my mother and given to Deo Gratias. It was obvious that no mail was going out to the United States.

For the Japanese, Naga was just a stopover on the road north to Manila. The guards changed continually. Newly arrived soldiers, who looked like high school students, came into the prison to get their first glimpse of Americans.

Two or three at a time would come to our open door and say something like this: "Me spleak melican," unable to get the "l"'s and "r"'s right. They would run their hands over our faces and hair — I suppose to convince themselves that what they were seeing was real. We would ask them, "What's the news?"

"Melicans belly bad. Nippon rand haholres Kentucky." Translated, that meant the Nipponese have landed on the shores of Kentucky. Upon hearing that, one of us replied, "You're full of bull, Tojo." That brought a laugh. It was one of those small victories in the war where you could laugh at your enemies without their knowing you were laughing at them.

With the constant change of troops, we were often forgotten in our cell. Eight or nine times the lock had to be broken; whoever had the key either had left and taken it with him or hadn't told anyone it's location. When this happened, one of us would look through the little hole in the door and hail a passer-by.

Everyone except me that is — I could hardly talk in the jail because just before we were arrested, I had strained my vocal cords while screaming at someone who was running across the field after stealing stuff from our new school. The strained vocal cords and my voice were only getting worse, so Fr. Burns asked the guards if I could see a doctor. They allowed a Filipino to come in. While looking straight into my throat, not turning his eyes away at all, he said very softly, "Good news, the Americans on Corregidor [the island at the entrance of Manila Bay] have a magnet that pulls the Japanese planes out of the air." No doubt he wanted to cheer us up, and he probably believed it himself. As for my throat, the doctor's diagnosis was torn vocal cords. He said I would need good protein food like milk, eggs, and meat before it would heal.

It was just as well that we were without any reliable source of news in the Naga jail. Only much later did we learn that the Japanese had advanced to the islands south of us, that they had captured Singapore and entered Burma and Korea. By our own propaganda, we had been so convinced of U.S. military superiority that the bad news of Japanese victories was hard to believe — even later when we heard it from American sources.

The days dragged into weeks, months. We never knew what would happen next. One day, as we were out in the yard, the guards brought a slightly-built Filipino in a white suit through the prison gates. We had heard rumors that some local civilian guards of Japanese descent, formerly bazaar workers who'd been rounded up by the police on Pearl Harbor Day, were using their new position of power to take out grudges they held against Filipino officials. This man might have been one of them. I reasoned that he had probably dressed in the white suit in order to make a good impression when called into court.

Right inside the gate the guards had a roofed shed in which they "questioned" the Filipino who responded with an ever-rising shrillness. The guard asking the questions held a baseball bat. Fr. Burns saw what was coming and told us to move into the cell. He may have been concerned that the guards would attack us if we watched. From our cell I heard the screams and the thuds of the baseball bat against flesh and bone. We didn't know why the Filipino was beat. It was bad enough to hear such savagery, so foreign to my experience, but to hear it when I was locked in the bat holder's prison made the horror even more acute. It was as though I felt the blows. I shared the same human vulnerability as the small man in the white suit. A few days later, we heard he was still alive, but suffering in the cell across the yard from us.

Months passed, and we learned how little one needs to survive: a little rice, a little water, a few vegetables. We learned about the jolting odor of stale urine and feces. For example, one day when I removed the newspaper lid that covered our gasoline-can latrine, Joe Bitner screamed, "Who let the cat out?" We laughed and nobody needed to ask what he meant.

As a child, I had imagined the "what if" of war. What if I were on the enemy's side of the fence and could find out what was really going on in their camp. I must have pictured the two sides as separated by a wall. Now I was on the opposite side of the wall, on the enemy's side, and I was learning practically nothing about what either side was doing.

I remember how amazed we felt to hear rumors that there was a battle going on at Midway Island or at Bougainville. Was it really possible that the Japanese were halfway across the Pacific and thousands of miles south of us near Australia? What was happening? Was this really the end of the world as we had known it? We talked about this in the prison yard with other Americans. We had no way of telling rumors from fact. What we did know was that time was passing, and we were still prisoners. One day a group of three Japanese officers came in to question us about our wives. Where were they? We explained that we were Catholic priests and had no wives.

"Ah - so - your wife she hide in woods."

"No, we have no wives."

"Ah - so - your wife - she San Francisco?"

"No. Tokyo. Catholic priest. No wife. Naga. Catholic priest. No wife."

"Ah - so - wife United States?"

We were surprised one day when two Japanese officers came into our cells and told us in Latin that they were Catholic priests. They said that they were attached to the propaganda section of the Japanese army. We told them about the questioning about our wives. They replied, "The Japanese have no way of understanding what a Catholic priest is. Their idea of a priest would be the Banzis of Japan."

We were intrigued by a proposal they brought to us. "We think we can get you moved from here to the Jesuits in Manila. You will be safer there. In a small place like this, nobody knows what will happen. In Manila, you will be listed with the Red Cross. Do you want to go?"

Without hesitation Fr. Burns thanked them and asked them to try to arrange it. One reason for the sudden decision to have us moved may have been recent rumors that local guerrillas might try to rescue us. Initially we were glad to hear the rumors, but after giving it some thought, joy turned to dread when we considered the myriad of things that could go wrong: Would we be killed as our rescuers attempted to blow up the wall or the door of the jail? . . . What if the rescue attempt failed . . . would we all be shot by our captors? . . . Maybe the rumor reached the Japanese and prompted them to send us to Manila.

The Japanese priests who visited us were part of a group brought into the country as part of a clever effort to propagandize the predominantly Catholic Filipinos. The invaders seemed to need help in that regard — we had heard of brutal measures taken by the Japanese to maintain order in Naga. Although the Japanese said they were trying to win over the public, when Filipino children were caught stealing rice, they shaved their heads and tied them to telegraph poles near the plaza where everyone would see them suffer in the sun. The Japanese thought this would teach them to not steal rice. Instead, the people learned to hate the Japanese. In another story we heard that on the road near Naga, snipers killed two or three Japanese from a bicycle battalion. In response, a Japanese armored car drove through town machine-gunning homes, leaving twenty or thirty dead bodies on the road behind them as an example.

One afternoon, a Japanese officer said, "Be ready to go tonight." After dark the Japanese ordered us out of the prison, onto a truck and then drove three or four miles to the China Sea coast. The truck pulled up to a wharf, we were ordered aboard a motorboat about twenty-feet long. Soon the boat, without lights, moved out onto the dark water on a cloudless night.

We had about sixty miles to go for Manila. Prisoners — either asleep or dead — were laid out on the ship's deck. We knew very little about what was going on and could talk with no one outside our group of seven. In the dark silence we realized that the Japanese in this small boat were afraid of being sunk by an American submarine. So were we. We didn't want to die, but there was some comfort in knowing that the Japanese were as vulnerable as us.

— ❖ ❖ ❖ —

3 ✣ House Arrest

Hours later, before dawn, we landed south of Manila and boarded a covered truck. Destination: Ateneo de Manila, the Jesuit University, where Jesuits and others were under house-arrest. About one-hundred fifty Jesuits, American and Filipino, welcomed us and eagerly shared news. It was March of 1943 and we learned that the American army was still fighting in Bataan just across the bay. At night we could see the gun flashes in the sky. During the day we could see Japanese planes bombing the island of Corregidor at the entrance to Manila Bay. Rumors abounded that help would soon arrive, that Japanese and American prisoners would be exchanged.

I picked up a bit of news that my brother Frank, an Oblate priest, was a prisoner in Santo Tomas, an internment camp in Manila. He had been pastor in a church in Cotabuto on the island of Mindanao. Together with other priests he had been rounded up and shipped to Manila. I wanted to contact him, but it was risky to send a note into the camp. Not long after my arrival in Manila a letter from Frank was smuggled out of the camp and delivered to me at the university. I was forbidden by superiors to try to send a note back to him. Their argument was reasonable: that all of us may suffer if my letter was discovered.

Life under house-arrest was much better than jail. We had room to walk, a gym for exercise, a library and a complete seminary faculty that taught courses in theology for the nearly fifty of us who were still not ordained. We also had more company, more food, more news — even if it was bad news. We learned about General MacArthur's departure from Bataan and the Japanese advance along the peninsula and the surrender of General Wainwright which opened the harbor to Japanese ships and chilled our hopes.

From a high window overlooking the harbor, we watched the Japanese who occupied some of the nice homes. If they tended their flowers and cut the grass, we took it as a bad omen: that they expected to stay a long time. At night they used flashing searchlight beams to communicate among ships — probably Morse code. None of us knew how to interpret it, but there was some satisfaction in knowing that they were worried about using their radios.

One day while we were in class, a group of Japanese soldiers came into the house. They marked the furniture with chalk as if they planned to take the furniture out later for their own use. As they marked tables and bookcases, a Jesuit or two followed with a rag and erased the marks — another small victory in the midst of ever broadening defeat. But not long after, the Japanese ordered us out and took both the house and the furniture.

Consequently, the theology students, both American and Filipino, were sent to San Marcellino, the unused seminary of the Vincentian Fathers. Because the Fathers were Spaniards and part of the Axis powers, the Japanese did not seize their building. The seminary had no grounds or outside space for exercise. In cramped quarters, four stayed in a small room. We were short on food and books, but over-staffed with professors — so we had empty stomachs and minds full of theology.

By now we received news via the Voice of America from San Francisco. The Japanese would severely punish, even kill a person who spread the news from the Voice of America. Filipino Jesuits, who could freely walk the streets, brought us the news they had heard from Americans in other parts of the city. Both Americans and Filipinos took the risk and listened. In retrospect, I question the wisdom of risking lives to deliver the news. The Japanese required all radio sets to be fixed so that they could not receive the Voice of America. Fr. Burns would read a tightly-folded onion skin carbon copy of the news to us as we sat around on the floor in the hallway of our residence. In accordance with instructions, the paper with the news was destroyed immediately after its reading.

Somehow the Japanese got the name of one of our Jesuit couriers, Horatio DeLa Costa, S.J. Horatio, being a Filipino, could freely walk the streets without the identifying armband that was required of all American prisoners. Japanese authorities came to San Marcellino where he was living with us and took him away for questioning. Other soldiers tore his belongings apart and searched his possessions. Apparently, they had intercepted a message from the southern Philippines saying that he was a courier of the news between Americans in Manila and the Jesuits in the south. After a few days he was released unharmed. However, if they had found a transcript of the Voice of America, he might have been killed.

Just after the news one afternoon, six of us sat discussing the American landing in North Africa. Someone said, "I have a cigar that I have been saving for a big occasion. I'll go get it so we can celebrate the good news." He lit the cigar, took a couple of puffs, and passed it around the circle to those of us sitting on the floor. I had not smoked since the war began. Thinking the victory a reason to celebrate, I took a long puff and passed the cigar to the person beside me. Almost immediately I felt sick and had to leave the "celebration." The stale cigar on an empty stomach was too much for me, and I have not smoked a cigar since.

I remember one hot day at San Marcellino; we were in class supposedly learning Hebrew taught by a Filipino who spoke Latin with a Spanish accent. About twenty feet away, outside the open window of our classroom, the Japanese hammered on a corrugated tin roof; they were taking the nails out of the roof to use for something else. The noise, the Hebrew with the Hispanized Latin, the lack of food, the crowded conditions all seemed absurd. Why were the Japanese so eager to get the nails? Why did we continue classes under such conditions?

Such conditions didn't last long. After a few months they moved us into the walled city, San Augustino, a residence attached to the ancient Spanish-style monastery of San Augustino. At night from the window we could see into a building across the narrow street. We got a glimpse of a long row of Japanese soldiers sleeping under a very large mosquito net. From San Augustino we could still see Manila Bay with ships flashing their signals through most of the night.

Here, Jesuits didn't have space for classes, and besides, we didn't expect to stay very long. Rumor had it that the Japanese needed more and more buildings for the increasing numbers of troops coming to Manila.

Rumors soon became reality. One morning in June of 1944, Japanese military trucks with brown canvas covers rolled into San Augustino yard. We were ordered into the back cargo area and soldiers pulled down the flaps. We rode off into the unknown.

We peered through the cracks in the canvas and after a few miles could see we were entering the gates of Santo Tomas University, an internment camp holding about five-thousand American and Allied prisoners. Ordered off the trucks, we sat on the ground of an indoor basketball court. As the hours passed, more prisoners were brought in: part of a roundup of five-hundred fifty religious of all denominations who had been allowed to live outside until now. On the stage at one end of the court, a group of Japanese officers talked to one another. Presently, one of them addressed us in Japanese, which was interpreted. The speech went something like this: "For your safety and security you are here for a short time. After we check all your names, you will travel to another location. When we call out your name, you will stand up and say 'here.' You will get nothing to eat until we get your name." This was bad news. It was early afternoon and we hadn't eaten since the day before. In long lines prisoners waited to get into restrooms at one end of the basketball court. After the speech the Japanese on stage had another conference and then someone began screaming out the names. About the fifth name called was John Littlewood. No answer.

"You are going to stay here without food until we find John Littlewood," threatened a Japanese officer. "John Littlewood." Still no answer.

The Japanese were fuming. Did he escape? Was their list any good? He repeated the threat: No food until we find John Littlewood. An American among us who spoke Japanese stood up and yelled, "Try John Smallwood."

There was a conference on stage and finally the interpreter yelled out, "John Smallwood." An American stood up and said, "Here."

"Why did you not stand up before?" screamed the Japanese.

"Because my name is John Smallwood, not John Littlewood."

The Japanese on stage had another long conference with lists in their hands. Apparently their lists were written in Japanese characters. Wasn't "little" the same as "small"? No. After a long discussion, the interpreter announced, "We will use another system. We will call out your name and you will reply by giving your age. Then we will check your age against our record." After successfully identifying a few people, the interpreter called the name, "Anna Jones." A middle-aged woman stood up and answered, "Here."

"Give your age," yelled the interpreter.

"I certainly will not," replied the woman. We burst into laughter. Here we were hungry and waiting for food and she refused to give her age. The Japanese screamed and threatened. They thought we were laughing at them.

Another conference. The Japanese-speaking American was called up from the basketball court. He explained that we were not laughing at them, but rather at the foolishness of the woman not willing to give her age. They devised yet another system which finally worked enough to satisfy them.

While I sat there, I wondered where the other American prisoners were. I knew my brother Frank was here somewhere. When the name calling ended, I saw him. He and some other Americans wearing signs with Japanese writing came through a door and across the floor at the front of the stage. Frank was pushing a wheelbarrow full of watery rice. How could I get to talk to him? Behind him walked a Japanese soldier carrying a bayoneted rifle. Clearly, Frank was unable to mingle with us. But when he reached the middle of the court, Frank set down the wheelbarrow, turned to the seated crowd and shouted out, "Dick! Where are you?" I jumped up and answered, "Here I am!" The soldier began beating him with the rifle butt. Frank paid no attention to him and yelled, "Don't bother about this monkey. I'll see you in a few minutes."

"But how?" I wondered as I quickly sat down. After a few minutes he came from behind and sat down beside me. As one of the food managers of the camp, he knew how to get around. Before he was arrested and brought to Manila from

Mindinao, he had been free for more than a year since the start of the war. Consequently, he had much more news from home than I did. One of our eight sisters was now married, another had entered the convent, one brother had joined the marines, another had joined the navy. "Life at Santo Tomas isn't so bad," he said. "The spirit is good." We talked for an hour or more. I hardly wanted to eat, but he had to return to the food serving so I finally got in line to get some rice.

Almost immediately after we ate we were ordered back into the trucks. A rumor circulated that we were going to another internment camp south of Manila.

4 ❖ *Concentration Camp*

Soldiers herded us from the trucks onto the train: regular passenger cars with every seat filled. Armed troops guarded each end of our car. Once the train started, after a long delay, it was great to get a glimpse of the outside world. Except for the soldiers on the train, we saw few signs of war. The train rolled south about twenty-five miles. We stopped near Los Banos and the Philippine Agricultural College, which was now Internment Camp #2. Nearly two hours passed while we waited in the train. No reason given. Even if our guards knew why we were waiting, the language barrier prevented them from telling us.

In the sweltering tropical summer heat I swore I'd never again complain about the small delays in "regular" life. It's funny how when one finds him or herself in such a situation – trapped, uncomfortable, powerless – that we do things like bargain with God (let me get through this and I promise I'll . . .) or swear an oath of greater patience and compassion.

Finally, the soldiers ordered us off the train and told us to sit on a nearby slope of land. There we waited for another hour before some buckets of rice and lentils were distributed. I still recall how much that little bit of food cheered me up. Again we waited while the guards divided us into groups of ninety-five and assigned us to long huts roofed with nipa grass. All eighty-eight Jesuits managed to get into one of the huts along with about ten other prisoners, including one Canadian. I think we were the only barracks of single men.

There was also a hut for Catholic sisters. The rest housed families including several hundred children.

In the huts bamboo compartments lined both sides of a center aisle. Each held six rattan-matted, wood-framed beds that rested on a bamboo platform about six inches above the ground. The windows, just holes in the outside wall with nipa awnings, could be closed during the frequent wet season rainstorms.

Although this camp had a water system with latrines and showers, it didn't work: there was no running water for either a shower or latrine.

The camp, which held about two-thousand five-hundred prisoners and two-hundred fifty Japanese guards, rested on the side of a hill and spread out over an area of about six city blocks. Inside the camp were some open fields with high grass. Outside, on the hills above us, we could see coconut palms. Around the camp ran a six-foot barbed-wire fence guarded by the soldiers in watchtowers, each within sight of the next.

The camp had a building for the guards and another which served as a small infirmary. Two other long huts served as chapels, one for Protestant and one for Catholic worship. The Catholic hut was partitioned into about sixteen sections for small altars along the walls. Each day, except when the Japanese set a curfew, all the priests offered Mass for the Scholastics and lay Catholics in the camp. We received wine for these Masses through the Apostolic Delegate to Japan. Each priest was allowed seven drops of wine for his Mass. A scholastic went around to each altar and delivered the seven drops with an eye-dropper.

Food and news became the big event of any day. Each morning at the camp gate the Japanese dropped a big bag containing our rations of rice. On a bad day, the ration was thirty-three grams, about one level teaspoon of dry rice per person per day. On a good day, we got two or three tablespoons each. Rarely did we get anything else. The Japanese expected us to manage cooking and food distribution ourselves. This meant some of us were allowed outside the camp in order to cut firewood to use as fuel for cooking fires. For this, the wood crew received a larger ration of food. Over these cooking fires, the kitchen crew boiled the rice in huge pots and delivered it to the barracks twice daily.

Along the aisle running through our barracks we waited in long lines to move up and get our food. Each person was checked as he or she received portions of smoky water with a few grains of swimming rice, usually in half a coconut shell. The process of waiting and eating took about two hours, most of it spent waiting. No one ever ate quickly lest they have to watch, still hungry, while others were eating.

We found that water would take away the pain of hunger, but it didn't give energy. We always had plenty of drinking water, although we had to stand in line for hours to get it because there were two trickling spigots for the whole camp. We also collected rain water in anything we could for drinking, showering, watering the garden and flushing the latrines.

Adjacent to our huts each group of six had a small piece of land. Although some of it was good for growing food, we had few shovels, few or no seeds, and we were all very weak. This meant that we split up the work between finding seeds in the Japanese garbage, digging, and ferrying water.

The day we set about this project a Jesuit friend came by and said it was unpatriotic to plant a garden.

"Why?"

"Because it shows that you don't expect the Americans to arrive anytime soon."

This was a sample of the great divide between optimists and pessimists. The optimists were a ten-day club (believing they'd be there only ten days). The pessimists said it might take twenty years and even then the liberators might bypass us. We answered our critics: "If the American troops come before harvest, we will be just as happy as you are. If they don't come, don't expect to get some of our squash."

When our first squash was about as big as a golf ball, we began to wonder whether it would be stolen. Would we stay up all night in shifts and watch it — or eat it? We finally decided to eat it.

In addition to the garden, we searched for other food, like slugs and fat worms that clung to the underside of many leaves. We removed their insides and boiled them; it added some calories. According to the expert biologists among us, ninety percent of all greens in the camp were edible. So we looked for greens to add to our rice.

Only a few care packages got into the camp although many were sent every month. When they did arrive, they were stretched out to last for a very long time. Ironically, some Americans, while saving food under their beds for a "rainy day," died of starvation before we were liberated.

As I said, aside from food, news was the big event of the day. "What's the news?" we would say to each other as we met. There was one underground radio in our camp. During our first days in Los Banos an illegal news sheet with recent news was spread around. One day the Japanese found a discarded copy and searched the camp while all of us stood four abreast on the road out in the hot sun. The few who used the radio had time to reflect on the foolishness of trusting the whole camp with the news.

The Japanese didn't find the radio; it was literally buried underground. But from then on the news transmitted orally became a mixture of truth and rumor. The false was intentionally added to hide the source of the news. Over a period of weeks one would hear the true news repeated constantly and the false news would fade out. So we never knew the truth until we had heard it for about three weeks.

To power the radio, a prisoner pedaled a bicycle inside the latrine. The bicycle generated electricity which was carried by wire buried beneath a garden to the radio. The operator, apparently weeding the garden, listened. A lookout was posted to warn of any approaching guards. One day, a guard walked into the latrine and found the bicyclist. The lookout gave a warning and someone pulled the wire away from the bicycle before it could be seen.

"What are you doing?" the guard asked.

"Getting exercise." The guard smelled a rat, but couldn't find the radio.

The American population included experts of all kinds, and each night someone gave a lecture. A popular speaker was a former chef of one of the President Lines. His ship had docked in Manila just minutes before the Japanese planes raided the docks. He and his men had run for the ship, revving up to go out into the harbor to avoid the bombing. Many of his companions jumped aboard at the last minute, but he was overweight. His friends yelled, "Don't jump. We'll be back in a couple of hours." They never came back. "I should have jumped," he would say as he told the story.

At first he was the chief camp cook, but soon the oversight committee heard complaints that the cook wasn't losing weight like everybody else. His answer was, "Just breathing in the smell of the food is all I have to do to keep my weight." But when he was fired from the kitchen, he soon lost weight. When critics said that proved their point — that he had been sneaking food, he said, "No, it proves that I need to breathe in the smell of food to keep the weight."

He punished his critics by giving lectures, lessons on how to make delicious cakes and pastries. The starving people would listen as he pretended to mix the batter and pour on the sugar and coconut to make devil's food cake or some other delicacy. He had nothing at all to show, but he went through the motions and told them how to do it. Strangely enough, they went back again and again to hear him talk about delicious food.

Each day that I was able, I sat on the ground at sunset and used the back of the barracks for a back rest. There I wrote a journal of the day. Mostly I wrote about what we ate that day, the rumors of the day, etc. I wrote these entries on student copy books. However, journals were on the list of forbidden activities.

Keeping them was dangerous; so as I finished a book, I stuffed it into a hollow part of a two foot bamboo pole. Then I drove the bamboo into the ground far enough from my barracks to make it impossible for the Japanese to trace it back to me.

Included in my journal entries was the story of Fr. Joe Mulry who had bleeding ulcers that threatened his life. Fortunately, the prison camp population included a few doctors. Unfortunately, especially for Fr. Mulry, they had no anesthesia. So when the doctors operated on Fr. Joe, he was tied to the table. He suffered the surgery in silence and died during the operation. He was not with us on January 6, 1945 when we awoke to find the Japanese gone.

Our guards had disappeared during the night! We acted quickly in raising an American flag above the Japanese barracks. The flag was hand-made over a long period of time by one of the prisoners using bits of cloth and threads from worn out or cut down clothing. We gathered around to listen to the radio. It was the very day of President Roosevelt's State of the Union address. After that we kept listening to hear why the Japanese had left. We expected to hear that there had been a landing right near us. No such news. We decided that we were obviously still well inside Japanese lines. Being surrounded, leaving proved too dangerous. We decided to stay put, but celebrate. The Japanese had left behind a big black bull which we butchered and cooked for supper with plenty of rice.

As we listened to more news, we learned that Lingayen Gulf, where the Japanese had landed in 1941, was crowded with American ships. Now all the news was as good for us as it once had been for the Japanese. Still, we didn't know what happened to our guards. The answer began as a rumor: The guards were going to return. At sunset the American flag was taken down. The guards, some, not all, returned just as they had left, in the middle of the night. Some were bandaged. When we asked why some of them were bandaged, they denied that there had been any fighting. They knew that what was bad news for them was good news for us. They wanted their bull; they wanted their radio. Again, they stood us in line four abreast while they searched the camp for weapons. Since we suspected their return, we had returned the casing of their radio with an unworkable interior. We had kept the insides of the good radio. First thing that morning our committee asked them to sign a receipt for the returned radio. When they discovered that they had been fooled, they didn't want to admit it. They didn't demand the radio, but they cut down our ration of rice to weaken us. At least we had gotten one day of good meals and had a taste of what lay ahead if we got through this alive.

Days dragged on as the food ration sank to starvation level. All through our time in Los Banos the Japanese removed the very sick from the camp. We heard that they were sent to Manila for medical care, but we never heard of them again.

5 ❖ *Liberation*

On the morning of February 23, 1945 I was still in bed just at sunrise when Bill Rively called to me, "Dick, get up. Come see these planes." Bill was outside our hut cleaning his teeth with coconut strands. "Nobody knows what the planes mean, Bill," I said, still lying in bed. "We have seen lots of planes."

"Get up! These are big planes and they're flying low."

I got up, went outside and looked up. Just then, the planes roared out of the dark section of the clouds and into the light. The lead plane had something hanging out of it that looked like a clothesline. Other planes followed. Someone screamed hysterically, "It's paratroopers! We're saved!" I had never seen paratroopers before, but I soon recognized them as the parachutes started to open and they began to land outside the fence. But just as they began their jump and before their parachutes opened, I heard shots and explosions all around the camp. Someone screamed, "Down on your faces! Hit the ground! The Japs are cutting loose on the camp!" Fr. Willman yelled out, "This is a battlefield and I am going to give general absolution, so make an act of contrition." And I heard him say the words, "I absolve you of your sins in the name of the Father, the Son, and the Holy Ghost."

Like most in the camp, I had planned on what I would do and where I would go when the expected emergency came. There was a ditch behind our barracks for water runoff, and I jumped into that ditch and lay on my back. But just as I lay down, I saw, towering above me, six Japanese guards with rifles in their hands. They took one look at me, then dove into the high grass to my left. As I turned my face back to the sky, I saw a pistol pointed right at my forehead. "Johnny, where are the Japs?" I wanted to get that pistol away from my head so I pointed to the bushes and said, "Right there." The Filipino who was holding the pistol jumped up and shouted "Pasuk" which means "Come on, let's go." A group of people with him headed toward the bushes and fired their automatic rifles as they ran.

While all this was happening, bullets tore through the camp about head or chest high. I later learned that they were tracer bullets; every fifth bullet had a light on it so you could tell where the shots went in the semi-dark camp. A few seconds after the gun was removed from my head, I heard a scream, "It's an American soldier!" I looked in the direction of the screaming and saw a very husky American G.I. running up the hill into the next barracks. This was the first American soldier I had seen since the war began. He looked like Superman compared to the skeletons I had been accustomed to seeing in the camp.

After a few minutes, the explosions and the shooting stopped, and I heard someone say, "I have some coffee. This is the last day we'll need it." Like most prisoners he had kept something for an emergency and this was it. So three or four of us began to boil water for the coffee on a little home-made stove we had outside the window of our barracks. We were sitting on the floor and thinking we were safe when an American soldier put his foot over our windowsill and looked at us. "Would you like some coffee?" someone asked. The soldier looked at us as though we were out of our minds and yelled, "The Japanese will be lobbing mortars into the camp any minute. Get the hell out of here!"

That was all we needed. We had waited for those words for almost four years. Without further thought for baggage or anything else, we started running down the hill. The soldier yelled at us to run to the tanks at the bottom of the hill. As I ran down the hill toward the tanks at a level spot, I saw an American soldier talking into a walkie-talkie. I was amazed! I had never seen one before. This was something that was developed during the war. I thought to myself, "It's no wonder we are winning the war when we can talk to the planes from the ground." As I passed a couple of water drainpipes that ran under the road, some American soldiers were pulling out Japanese by the legs and shooting at them. Of the 250 guards at the camp, all but one was killed on the spot. The one who escaped was later captured and hung. At the bottom of the hill, I found more than fifty amphibious tanks circled like covered wagons in the old Western movies.

Only later did I understand the liberation plans: The previous night the 511th Airborne Division was called to get ready to rescue the prisoners. They were to take off from Nichols Field, an airport near Manila, and prepare for the short flight to Los Banos camp, to arrive just at dawn. They knew that at 7 a.m. the Japanese day guards would be getting ready to take the place of the night shift in the pill boxes and doing group calisthenics outside the camp gate. The guards always stacked their rifles near the front gate as they did their calisthenics. The U.S. Army knew this routine because they had sent two American officers into the camp about ten days before. They had sneaked under the barbed wire to get the layout of the camp and the schedule the Japanese followed. Then they sneaked out the way they came and gave that information to the army and air force.

As the air force got their orders, fifty-seven amphibious tanks called "alligators" were ordered down the Pasig River from Manila toward Laguna Bay about three miles from our camp. It was going to be a miracle for the noisy alligators not to be detected. The Japanese controlled the Pasig River, south of Manila. Would they suspect the purpose of the tanks? The U.S. air force around Manila was told to protect the roads around Los Banos so no Japanese reinforcements could be brought in to save the camp.

The main line of the American forces, south of Manila, had plans to make a push, at least the appearance of forward motion, during the day to draw the Japanese troops away from the camp. That same night a group of about 150 guerrillas, led by American officers, were to approach the camp from all directions in small groups of four or five. This was done in small groups so that any discovery wouldn't give away the presence of the larger force. The guerrillas were to surround the camp, each group assigned to a specific pill box, having it in hand-grenade range. All of these groups — the amphibious tanks, the guerrillas, the paratroopers — were to converge just as the sun was coming up. The signal was a visible one: Lt. Ringler, who led the 511th Airborne, would lead the charge by jumping from the plane.

The amphibious tanks came ashore in a line a mile long. Everything went like clockwork. The American planes overhead patrolled the roads. Though the Japanese used 50 mm guns to shoot at the tanks on the road, there were no American casualties. As the tanks approached the camp by the road, they let soldiers out to defend the road so the tanks could retreat safely. So the tanks entered the camp empty except for the driver and the gunners, forming the wagon-train type circle in the level part of the camp to protect us prisoners. It wasn't long before the tanks started taking POWs to the safety of the American lines: "Women and children first into the tanks!" came the order. The back of the tanks opened like the back of a very large truck and about thirty people went into each tank.

To evacuate two-thousand five-hundred people, the rescue had to go in stages: out into the water, along the shore, and then twenty miles to the American lines, disembarking and returning for more. I went in the second or third wave. As we rode down toward the water, machine gun bullets struck the heavy steel sides of our convoy. We crouched low and our gunners fired back. When we got to the edge of the water, we were ordered by radio to wait under the palm trees until some of the gun positions on shore were knocked out. We could hear the officer in our tank calling to the planes. "Dumbo one, come in Dumbo one."

Then we would hear the answer, "Chris six, Chris six coming in to Dumbo one." They were taking out the pill boxes.

In a few minutes the tank rolled into the water. It amazed me how the tank floated like a boat, the treads becoming propellers. What a joy to see the world beyond the camp. Though the tank was eight or nine feet high, you could see out by sitting on the topside. I was sitting up at the top of the tank. I looked back; the camp on the side of the hill was on fire. Only then did I remember my journal. It was gone, left behind. I never did get back to Los Banos. Maybe it's still there where I buried it.

I was looking at the fire when I noticed rain approaching from the shore, at least the water was being stirred up as if it were raining. "Rain?" I asked a soldier. "Rain? That's not rain. It's machine gun fire aimed at our tanks. Everybody down!" We all quickly obeyed and a second later we heard bullets hitting the side of the tank. Nobody was hit.

After about an hour, we came ashore behind American lines. Soldiers were actually right there, firing cannons toward the Japanese. Being the middle of a hot day, the soldiers were stripped to the waist and sweating profusely. Surprised to see us, they asked, "Is there anything we can get you?"

"Food!" we answered hopefully. They had brought along some lunch and opened a large barrel of white sugar. Immediately the crowding ex-prisoners dug into the barrel with their hands. Some even filled their hats and mouths. Some got sick immediately. It's no way to come off a starvation diet. Then one of the soldiers took out and opened a long can of Spam and placed the meat on top of a wooden barrel. I was amazed! A two-foot long piece of Spam! Then he took out a big knife but with so many hands reaching for the Spam, the soldier couldn't slice it. One of our group who had been assigned to handle camp rations quickly said, "Let me have that knife. Nobody will stick their hands under it when I'm wielding it." He was right. He sliced that Spam and no one interfered. None of us had seen food like that for a long time.

After fifteen or twenty minutes some army trucks picked us up and took us down the road. We didn't know where we were going, but we were very happy and feeling the joy of freedom. As we passed, some Filipinos came to the side of the road and gave us the victory sign. "Victory, Joe!" We came up a hill to the old Filipino prison of Munting Lupa now being used as the U.S. 6th Army headquarters. When I saw an American flag flying above the building, I thought, "They had better take that flag down before the Japanese see it." Then it dawned on me, "'That flag is not going to be taken down by the Japanese. We are free. It's wonderful to be under that flag and I never want to be under any other flag."

As soon as we stepped off the trucks, American soldiers surrounded us. They wanted to hear the details of the rescue. We just sat down right there on the lawn and began to talk. As other groups arrived, they joined us. Some people met relatives, others heard stories from home. All of it was good news. Of course, what we were really interested in was food, and the American army immediately set up a soup kitchen. As we lined up for the soup, the soldiers continued the conversation and assured us of a more substantial meal that evening.

Some American soldiers combed the countryside, scrounging up eggs for us. Eventually we were told to form the line for the evening meal of eggs and rice. This was real rice, not the smoky water grain we had been fed for so long. This was going to be the best food we had ever tasted. But before the line was half finished, the eggs were all gone. "That can't be!" the soldiers said. "We had five-thousand eggs!"

The explanation was simple. We said, "You gave out eggs to whomever came to you. Some said they wanted eggs for three or four, and you obliged. They ate them. That's what happened."

The food distribution group from the camp said, "If we handled the rations, there wouldn't be any more cheating." So from then on food distribution was handled by the food manager from the camp. Meanwhile, we sat on the ground all day long, before and after eating and even into the night, entertaining the troops with the songs we had made up while in the camp.

After dark, the last of the eleven-hundred soldiers who had taken part in the rescue came back on the tanks. We met them and thanked them. They told us how happy they were to be doing rescue work instead of some of the other disagreeable jobs. We finally did get to sleep in the double bunks. They once held Filipino prisoners, now they held American ex-prisoners finding rest at the end of a happy day. The memory of it still remains strong, five decades later.

I had been at Munting Lupa Prison only a few days when I fell sick with chills and a fever. When an Army nurse was called and saw the number of blankets on top of me, she said, "This is ridiculous." She had me transferred to a hospital tent. Though the fever did not seem to be connected to my throat ailment, my vocal chords were never far from my mind. The doctor had said that I needed good food. But now I wondered if it had been too long. I prayed for a cure and put my trust in the Sacred Heart.

Now as I lay in the dark hospital tent, I felt nauseous. The food, though nourishing, was too rich for me. Not wanting to throw up inside, I left the tent and went outside to the adjoining field. As I retched, my throat went into spasms. Then, suddenly, the nerves and muscles near my vocal cords, on the very spot that had pained me for so long, began to jump and contract. I put my hands on my throat. I stood there about a half an hour just thanking God and relishing the feeling of the muscles jumping. When my throat quieted down, I went to the tent and slept, believing that my prayers had been answered: I was cured. In the morning when I tried to put some timbre into my voice, I could talk without pain. Again, the neck muscles near my vocal cords started jumping. I put more resonance into my voice, just to try it out, though I was afraid to speak too loudly, not wanting to strain my vocal cords. Yet again my muscles and nerves jumped as if they were knitting together. I even looked for a mirror to see what the muscles were doing.

I never learned what caused my fever; maybe the shock of good food! It soon disappeared. Both the cure and the rescue from Los Banos deepened my confidence in the Sacred Heart of Jesus to whom I had prayed daily during the last three years.

At Munting Lupa prison camp we were dressed in U.S. Army clothes and were often mistaken for soldiers. One day a young Filipino boy shouted to me, "Hey Joe, do you want a pom-pom girl?" I asked him if he thought he was helping Americans, or Filipinos, by offering pom-pom girls to Americans.

One evening at dusk as I was walking through the camp, two American soldiers came toward me holding a small Japanese who was stripped to the waist, arms tied behind his back. The arms of two Americans were locked with his at the elbow.

"Where are you taking him?" I asked.

"Outside the camp."

"Why?"

"We have orders to get rid of him."

It was clear they intended to shoot him. I suppose the Japanese did not understand English, but by the look on his face he certainly seemed to understand his fate. "What has he done?" I asked. "Is there anything I can do to help him?"

They just shook their heads and moved on.

I suddenly felt the horror that had disappeared when I left the prison camp, the horror of war. Actually I felt it more at this point than I had ever felt it as a prisoner. Here were two young Americans, on my side of the war, taking a prisoner out to kill him. I didn't want to think that "my side" would do this. The closeness of these three men, linked arm in arm, made the scene worse. The Americans carried rifles and wore uniforms; the Japanese was half-naked. For me the war was over with our rescue; for this Japanese the war would end today with death. For the two Americans the war continued. Maybe they would live through it, maybe not. I was better off than any of them. But that did not overcome my sadness and revulsion.

After we'd been at Munting Lupa about a week, I was eating pancakes for breakfast in a large army tent when I heard over the loudspeakers, "Is there anybody here named McSorley? A soldier is looking for you outside the door of the mess tent." I quickly left the pancakes and hurried to the front where I saw a soldier who embraced me and said, "Dick, I sure am glad you made it!" I recognized him as one of my younger brothers. But which one? Somewhat embarrassed, I had to ask his name; after all, I had been gone six years. It was my younger brother John who had been little more than a child when I left home. He joined me for breakfast and as we talked, he answered all my questions about family and gave me news from back home. I had heard nothing for three years.

John had joined the marines in 1942 and then, with the hope of rescuing Frank and me, volunteered for a marine air squadron that was going to the Pacific. He became a rear gunner in a Dauntless dive bomber. His squadron had helped in the aerial surveillance of the camps, both Los Banos and Santo Tomas. They flew low over the camps to take their photos. After the Manila camp had been rescued, he had borrowed a jeep from his base and had driven down to meet Frank. When he learned Los Banos had been rescued, he came further south to find me.

As I started to tell him part of my story, he interrupted and said, "Let's talk on the road. I have to take the jeep back as soon as possible, and I want you to go back with me. We can pick up Frank in Manila when we pass through there." The Jesuit superior at Munting Lupa approved my leave and we started out right away.

The war was not entirely over in the Philippines. There were military road blockades, and I had no papers or credentials. But I was in a military uniform and looked enough like John that they accepted me as his brother just released from prison camp. In about two hours we reached Manila, a bombed-out city. The city was so devastated that it was hard to tell where you were. Almost all the landmarks were gone including much of the heavy walls of the Old City. Most of the traffic was military.

Knowing Santo Tomas University held American prisoners, the American military had not bombed it. In January a quick tank blitz in advance of the main army line had broken through to free the prisoners before the Japanese killed them. Although some shells fell into the camp after the rescue, very few were killed. We found that Frank, one of the leaders in the camp kitchen, still was actively helping in the distribution of food. As soon as he saw us, he said, "Let's get to the newspapers and send the news home."

So in the jeep we roamed the streets of Manila looking for the offices of the American war correspondents. Nobody was very helpful, but finally someone directed us to the BBC which thought the story of three brothers, two of them ex-prisoners and one of them a marine, was worth writing up. An Australian newspaper printed the story with a picture of the three of us and gave our names and addresses. Back in the United States the *Philadelphia Inquirer* picked up the picture and put it on the front page. That very day my mother was in Misericordia Hospital as a patient with a minor ailment. When the nurse attending her saw the picture and the story, she walked into Mother's room and announced, "Mrs. McSorley, here I have the remedy for what ails you." The nurse was right. Mother was instantly cured. This was the first word she had that all three of us were alive, and the news was only one day old.

During the three years that we had been in prison, the family had kept a large map of the South Pacific on the wall in our dining room. They put pins to mark the advance of the American lines. Each evening after supper they gathered round the family table and said the rosary for our safe return.

The newspaper story gave the family the first reliable news of our whereabouts. Prior to that, John's letters home had been restricted. By the time any letter reached home, weeks had passed. When they read the letter, they could only guess if he was still alive.

The family also had received some confused news about Frank. A newspaper had carried a group picture of people rescued from Santo Tomas camp. The caption had given Frank's name under somebody else's picture. Mother and Dad thought they had picked out Frank, but weren't sure — he was so thin. In this picture with his two brothers, there was no doubt.

We were not long together: only three or four days. I had to return to Munting Lupa and ready myself for the trip home with the other American Jesuits. Frank was planning to remain in the Philippines and return to Mindanao with the U.S. Army when they reclaimed it.

I arrived back in Munting Lupa camp just in time to receive the news that our group was ready to leave. After that, there was a flurry of events in rapid succession: the Purple Heart conferred on us ex-prisoners by none other than General Douglas MacArthur himself; a hurried trip by truck to Manila; then on board a ship bound for San Francisco. Near the docks we saw acres of government supplies piled high: jeeps, tents — everything needed in war from trucks to toothbrushes. Later I learned that much of this was turned over to the Philippine government after the war.

As we passed close to Corregidor Island at the beginning of our voyage, we heard an ominous message over the loudspeaker: "Now hear this. All passengers go below. The smoking light is out. Crews man your battle stations." We needed no repeat order. We were too close to getting back home now to take any risks. On board the new Liberty Ship, we mingled with thousands of prisoners from Santo Tomas camp. We slept in four-tiered canvas bunks below deck, and we ate good food in clean navy mess halls. Although generally we had to stay below deck because of the danger of Japanese submarines, when we could go top-side, we sat on blankets spread on the steel decks. Everything about this ship was wonderful to me: the radar; mattresses high in the air; the speed of the ship; the convoy of protecting destroyers; the friendly, happy company; the American sailors. This was a part of our newly recovered freedom.

We made our longest stop at Ulithi Atoll. There we saw hundreds of ships, including two aircraft carriers. Ferrying between the ships were navy launches. At night we watched movies on deck, the first we had seen since the war began. It was an ideal place to watch a movie, with glittering stars above and the friendly lights of the ship all around, soft breezes and a very appreciative audience.

While we were docked in Ulithi on April 13, 1945, the loudspeakers announced that President Roosevelt had died. The ship's flag was lowered to half mast. I reflected on the meaning of this event for the country and realized even then that it was a time of profound historical significance.

Leaving Ulithi, we said goodbye to the protection of the destroyers. The Liberty ships were built to be faster than submarines, so subs could attack us only by laying in wait — which was next to impossible the way we constantly zig-zagged. Before long, we were in Hawaii. Although we could see the outline of the coast from where the ship was anchored, we were not allowed to go ashore. We stayed only a few hours, long enough to take on some returning soldiers and whatever supplies we needed.

Days later, seagulls flying around our ship gave us the first clear signal that we were near the United States. Six years before I had sailed out under the Golden Gate Bridge, ready to spend my life in the Philippines. (There was a possibility of staying on after my four years of theology studies.) But the war changed all that. Now I envisioned passing under that same famous bridge on my way home.

As we neared land, we discovered that we were docking at San Diego rather than at San Francisco. We had been detoured because a United Nations meeting in San Francisco made for heavy traffic. A brass band at the docks blared out a welcome. Thousands of people cheered as we pulled in beside the pier. When we got off, we found in the crowd a welcoming group of California Jesuits. The Red Cross was there offering free telephone calls to our families, money to buy new clothes, and railroad tickets home. I phoned home and talked to Mother and Dad. "I'm in San Diego, and I'll be leaving here at noon tomorrow. With the troop trains disrupting regular schedules, I don't know just when I'll arrive in Philadelphia. I'll phone along the way as soon as I find out."

That night the Jesuit university in San Diego housed all forty-five of us scholastics in one huge room, the first time we'd all been in one room together. Lying in bed in the dark we talked and laughed about the trip and compared our life here to life in Los Banos. The war had matured us, but in one sense we were still boys and this was our last night together, the talk continued for hours. The next morning we had a group photo taken before we went out to buy clothes. Each of us was returning to his home province and eventual assignments. Most of us got on the same train heading east, five going to Philadelphia. I don't remember stopping overnight anywhere, but we did have delays in the stations along the way.

When I arrived at the North Philadelphia Station, there was a big crowd on the train platform. Families of all of us Jesuits were there as well as newspaper reporters and photographers. Mother was in tears. Dad was there and six of my brothers and sisters. Soon we were in the family car and on the last stage of the journey home.

Six years had surely changed the size of the eleven brothers and sisters still at home. I had to relearn their names, and I'm sure I was a stranger to the youngest ones. It took some time to exchange stories, filling in details of the intervening years. I had used some of my Red Cross money to buy a white satin bathrobe for mother. As a souvenir from the camp, I had brought the half coconut shell I had used as a bowl and some of the used 50mm casing I had collected from the guns of our rescue tanks.

A newspaper photographer came to the house to take pictures and interview me. Surrounded by family pictures, I sat in the family parlor as my mother and some of the children listened in. I was surprised to learn that I was considered a hero for having been a prisoner of war. I didn't choose to be a prisoner; I was so by force. After all, I'd have been shot if I hadn't stayed in prison. What kind of a hero is that?

I was invited to talk at a couple of war bond rallies and at a communion breakfast of the Knights of Columbus. I told war stories. I don't remember asking anyone to buy war bonds. I have since changed my attitude about war and now would not be willing to take part in any kind of rally like that.

Years later, one of my younger sisters told me that she had been afraid to go near me on that visit. She'd heard me say we had eaten slugs. She did not want to get near the worms. My week at home, at my mother's table, refreshed me. The family routine that had so strongly influenced me and my vocation had changed little in my absence. Dad still ruled the roost and his faith still inspired all who entered the house. And Dad still drove off early every morning to go to Mass, just as he had when I was a child.

II

The Early Years

— ❖ ❖ ❖ —

6 ✤ *Once I Was a Child*

My path to peace and justice began early in life. I was the second oldest of fifteen children in a staunchly Catholic family in Philadelphia. Mother was a homemaker and Dad was a lawyer.

Each day my Dad drove to the 6:30 a.m. Mass at our parish church. He asked all of us children over the age of ten to go with him. We joined him if we were successful in catching the old Ford and jumping on the running boards as he backed out of the alley the length of a city block. Dad maintained that he didn't force us to go to Mass. True. But when we would ask permission to go to a movie, he might say, "Maybe you don't have the grace to avoid temptations you might find at the movies. Did you miss Mass last Tuesday morning? Maybe you better stay home." After one or two refusals like that, we rarely missed Mass even though we sometimes missed the running board of the Ford as it backed down the alley. There was always that last desperate jump aboard when Dad had to back out on Chester Avenue and then turn before going forward. The Ford was an open touring car, so you could climb in once you made the running board. Many times, from inside the car, I saw a younger brother or sister left behind to walk the five blocks to church — often on a cold winter morning.

Mother couldn't go to Mass because she always had small children to care for and had to get breakfast for us. But she showed us very clearly that she agreed with Dad. (We children never saw any sign of disagreement between Dad and Mother while we were young.) Even during the summer months when we stayed on the shore at Sea Isle, New Jersey with Mother while Dad remained working in Philadelphia, she always insisted on our attending Mass.

During Lent and Advent, Dad read to all the children, even the very young and inattentive, at breakfast after morning Mass. We all sat at a long kitchen table as Dad stood at one end and read the *Imitation of Christ* by Thomas aKempis and selections from the scriptures. He didn't read very long, only a paragraph or two, with stops to tell the younger ones to be quiet and listen. Then he ate breakfast with us. Every night after supper, we knelt at our chairs to pray the rosary. No one left the supper table until the rosary was over. Dinner guests were invited to join us. If they didn't, we said it anyway. It was clear that Dad deeply believed in the values of prayer and the Mass, both for himself and for us.

The influence of our daily practice of faith was scarcely perceptible to us. I remember one morning I was in the dark dining room looking for my high school books when Dad came in to put his breakfast reading book on top of the china closet. When he saw me, he asked, "Is it all wasted on you? Do you remember anything at all of what I read to you?" Quickly I mumbled, "I remember 'Vanity of vanities and all is vanity, except loving God and doing His will.'"

"Well, if you remember that," Dad replied, "I guess it is not all useless." I was surprised at his response. What did I say that pleased him? What did it mean? At the time I had little or no understanding, but I remember it now because of his unexpected satisfaction at my answer.

Besides teaching us the importance of prayer, Dad taught us to desire to serve God rather than desire wealth. At lunch one day, near his downtown office, he told me, "It's pitiful to hear these business people talking about money. They never seem to get to the end of it." I'm sure he meant to impress me about how money can entrap you. Dad had never encouraged any of us, as teens, to work for a salary. He said, "You'll be long enough in the army of workers. You don't need to start while you're a child."

Dad claimed that he never had a hundred dollars in the bank. He trusted that God would provide, and God did provide. Dad, generous with whatever money came in, always gave to people in need. He believed, "Whatever I give out comes back like bread upon the water." He offered the example of his donation of four-hundred dollars to a poor widow in great need, and the next morning a check for four-hundred dollars came in the mail to him from an old debt.

I remember his comment on a depression era March for Jobs in Washington, D.C., "That is the way poor people have to act to have their voices heard." I recall that and other efforts he made to teach us about the poor. For instance, once he brought Dorothy Day and Peter Maurin of the Catholic Worker to our home to visit. At fifteen years of age, I hardly knew who they were, so they didn't impress me very much. Later in life when I developed a great appreciation for their work, I remembered that first meeting.

On one occasion, Dad took several us children to the New York Catholic Worker. Afterward he asked me what I thought of it. I said something about it being very poor and dirty. Dad was clearly disappointed in my reaction. However, Dad's efforts and contact with the Catholic Worker did make an impression on me: Years later I started the first Catholic Worker House in Washington, D.C.

By the time I started that Catholic Worker, I was opposed to war. Looking back, I see that in all my years of Catholic education I never had any sign that my faith taught that killing was wrong. And yet, because of the Incarnation, because Christ was God on earth and taught a gospel of love, because He was a model for all of us, I would have to face the question of Christ and violence.

Three of my brothers were in the military. Two others were assistants to military chaplains, although they were not in the military themselves. But neither they nor anyone else in the family praised or extolled the military life as great or something to be followed. Though Mother and Dad never precisely taught us nonviolence, I do remember a comment by Dad as we watched a military parade, "If they would require the military to wear bloody aprons with a bloody knife stuck in their belt, then they wouldn't deceive people so much about what they are doing." Though I was very young and knew nothing about war, that statement impressed me.

One very unsettling incident brought up the issue of Christians and war: I was visiting home from seminary and sitting at a local deli when a stranger said something like, "Well, you're a Catholic. How can you believe in war?" I said, "Well, I don't believe in war, but it's not the same — killing somebody when you're wearing a uniform and acting on your own. [I had learned this in the seminary.] When you do it by yourself, you act privately and don't have any authority to act. But when you wear a uniform, you don't act in your own name, but rather in the name of the government, and then it's all right." I remember the strangers response: "Aren't you twisting things around a little bit?" Of course I defended my position, but later in life I changed significantly.

While my parents said little about the military, it was clear that the greatest thing a boy or girl could do with his or her life was to serve God, to be a priest or a nun. Out of fifteen children, eight would join religious orders: four priests and four nuns. One time at dinner, with the family all present, a friend of Dad's said, "Well, Dick, I suppose you hope that out of this large family you'll get doctors and lawyers, professional people?" Speaking to all of us as though he were speaking to a jury, but directing his attention to our guest, Dad responded, "Not at all Bill. If they don't realize that the only thing worthwhile is to serve God, then they might as well go out to the garage now, turn on the motor and stay there until it's all over."

My parents' actions showed great respect for priests or sisters. They refused to allow any criticism of them. Mother often had nuns visit our home, and she always had them eat in the dining room. (We always ate in the kitchen.) She put out the family silver, the best dishes from the china closet; they got the best food. I remember the smell of lamb chops for the sisters. I don't remember that we ever got lamb chops! Mother would say, "I think every young Catholic girl dreams at some time of becoming a nun. I know I did."

One summer, Fr. Nieuland came from Notre Dame University to visit us at our summer home on the shore. Mother and Dad moved out of their bedroom (with an adjoining private bath) and gave it to him. During breakfast, one of my younger brothers wryly asked, "Did you know that Fr. Nieuland has silk underwear?" (He must have gone into the room to snoop around.) My father looked directly at him and said, "Now mind your p's and q's. When you're dying and looking for a priest, you won't be wondering what kind of underwear he has!" That reprimand was for all of us; no criticism was permitted, nor did Dad ever criticize the Church, though he was aware of some of its shortcomings.

The religious influence of my parents' lives was strengthened by that of the Sisters of the Immaculate Heart of Mary who taught me at St. Francis de Sales parish school. I clearly remember one sister talking to us about becoming priests. "If God knocks at the door of your heart and asks you to be a priest and you do not open the door, God may not return to ask you again. Some people turn to God in old age, they offer God the shell of their lives. When you offer your life to God when you are young, you offer the kernel of life to God."

These two simple comments stayed in my mind as I thought about what to do with my life. They kept me from delaying my decision. When I told Dad I was planning to be a priest, he said, "That is a long way off for you. You don't have to decide today." I repeated the sister's remark of giving your youth to God. I knew he would be happy to see me enter the seminary, but he wouldn't say it plainly. His objection was just his way of pushing me to overcome the objection. But he made no effort to refute the sister's argument.

I believe I never thought of being anything but a priest. I did dimly see some of the difficulties of the life. When I was fifteen, a sophomore in high school, I told Mother I planned to be a priest. She asked, "What kind of a priest?" She never said, "That's good" or "Congratulations." She didn't need to because I knew she would approve. "I'm thinking of being a Franciscan," I answered.

"Why a Franciscan?"

"They wear sandals and a white rope belt."

"Why not a Jesuit?" she asked. She was a member of a teacher's sodality run by Jesuits.

"I don't know anything about them."

"Well, find out," she said.

I went up to our family bookcase in the second floor sitting room and looked up Jesuits in the Catholic encyclopedia. Within the first few lines I read that the Jesuits were a religious order, and I closed the book. That, plus my Mother's preference, was enough for me. I didn't want to be a secular priest because a secular priest could own property and that seemed to me as not giving yourself completely to God.

Mother's sodality met at St. Joseph's Prep School run by the Jesuits, and at the time the sodality was offering a half scholarship for anyone planning to be a priest. Mother applied for the scholarship for me, so I transferred to St. Joseph's where I met my first Jesuits and liked them. Many were young seminarians doing three years of teaching as part of their training. The idea of the fourteen-year training of a Jesuit did not phase me. I thought that if I was going to give my life to God, it didn't make any difference how long the training would take.

In my teenage years I continued to join the rest of my family at our summer home on the shore. There I played tennis and swam in the ocean every day and danced every night at the free outdoor platform set up by the city on the ocean side of the boardwalk. After the boardwalk dancing, we usually went to a soda-bar where you could dance some more if you ordered something to eat.

My strong interest in girls never did deflect from my plan to become a priest. Girls were nothing new to me; I had seven sisters living with me every day. I liked girls and I liked dancing with them, but I wanted to give my life to God as a priest. The girls I met were aware of that. So they never got very interested in me, nor I in them, thus making the relationships much less complicated or uncomfortable.

My brother Frank entered the diocesan seminary in Philadelphia when I was a senior in high school. His story of life in the secular seminary convinced me more that I wanted to be a religious priest rather than a secular one. "It's just like college. You can't whistle in the hallways. If you do, you get punished," he told me. He got me, and sometimes even his old girlfriend, to bring ice cream out to him at midnight. "If you don't like the rules, why don't you quit?" I asked him. He did quit after the first year and joined the Oblates of Mary Immaculate. That further confirmed my plans to be a religious.

The summer after high school graduation, 1932, I was out in the ocean at Sea Isle in a canoe when someone swam out to give me a telegram saying I had been accepted into the Jesuits and was to report to Poughkeepsie, New York on August 14. I never expected to be refused, so acceptance didn't much please or surprise me. But I didn't want to leave Sea Isle in mid-August, nor did I want to go to New York because there was two good weeks of summer left. I telegrammed for a delay in entering and received a refusal. I didn't like it, but decided that two weeks shouldn't change my life-long plans.

My last night in Sea Isle Frank and I danced at the boardwalk as usual. After that closed, we borrowed Dad's eight passenger Pierce Arrow and took a crowd of girls and fellows to the nearby beach resort of Avalon. There we danced on until they closed. Then we drove the twelve miles to Ocean City to look for another dance floor. It was closed, so we drove back to Sea Isle and circled around until 5 a.m., then we took the two McPhillips sisters to their home. We were on their porch talking when Mother drove up in the family's second car, the old Ford.

"What do you think you are doing?" she asked from the street.

"Just talking," I said.

"Well, come home with me right away."

When we arrived at our house, Mother and I walked along the boardwalk. "What were you doing all night?"

"Just riding around after the dancing closed. We wanted to celebrate my last night."

"Well, don't you think that after seventeen years of caring for you, I would want to be with you the last night? Don't you think your departure means anything to me?"

I didn't answer. I felt so stupid. Here was the one who loved me, whom I had thoughtlessly neglected. "Come, sit in the pagoda," Mother said. "I couldn't sleep all night worrying about you and Frank and wondering what I would do if the car was still gone in the morning."

As Mother talked with her back to the ocean, I saw what looked to me like a ship on fire on the horizon. "Mother, look, there is a ship on fire."

She didn't even turn to look and said, "That's no ship on fire. It's the sun, a symbol of your new life rising."

By the time we returned to the house, the Pierce Arrow was at the curb and Frank was in bed. When we started for New York, Dad noticed the empty gas tank. "Where's all the gas?"

"We looked for a station to get some gas, but they were all closed."

"Where did you go?"

"Not very far, just Ocean City and Avalon."

"According to the odometer, you must have gone a couple hundred miles."

We admitted that we had driven all night. Dad didn't like it, but dropped the topic, much to Mother's relief.

That evening in New York we went to the top of the Empire State Building just as the sun was setting. Mother stood beside me at the rail looking at the sunset and said, "Dick, the setting sun symbolizes your old life ending."

The next morning we drove seventy-five miles north of the city to Poughkeepsie. There on the banks of the Hudson River I entered the novitiate of St. Andrew-on-the-Hudson. Dad and Mother met Fr. Webber, the novice master, and after a short visit, departed and left me to begin my life as a Jesuit on August 14, 1932.

My family life prepared me for the new community into which I had entered. I was used to getting up early each morning and going to Mass. I was used to living with many people around me. Fourteen other young men entered the novitiate with me. Getting to know them and the ninety or so other novices kept me busy, so I didn't long too much for Sea Isle.

We were created to praise, love, and serve God and our neighbor and in this way to save our souls. This I had been taught at home. Now I had the belief expressed, developed, and exemplified by the lives of all around me. I felt I had been given a good bargain. The purpose of life was the same as the purpose of Jesuit life.

By the time I was there a year, I felt it suited me perfectly and exceeded my fondest dreams. I appreciated my family all the more for having helped me decide to join a religious order. I wanted to be as generous as I could in serving God. At the time, the Jesuit province of Maryland-New York was sending men to do God's work in the Philippine Islands. This seemed to me a most generous way of serving God, so I wrote the provincial superior and volunteered to go to the Philippines.

Seven years later my offer was accepted after I'd completed two years of learning the life of faith and five years of college, including a licentiate in philosophy. In July 1939 I sailed under the Golden Gate Bridge aboard the President Pierce toward the Philippines. I didn't know then if I would ever return to the United States. The offer was undertaken for life. But God had other plans.

III

Ridge, Maryland

—❖ ❖ ❖—

7 ✣ *From Seminary to Pastor in the Woods*

After my return from the Philippines, I was allowed only a week with my family before I had to report to Woodstock College, located northwest of Baltimore, to continue my theological studies. Woodstock College was not new to me. Before going to the Philippines in 1939, I had spent three years there studying philosophy. To welcome us (students imprisoned during the war), the students and faculty put on a show that included a song, "You're back at Woodstock, Mr. Jones." The point of it all was that we'd find Woodstock much like a prison camp, with one big difference: there was no hope of being rescued by the marines. Many old friends and former classmates at Woodstock told me that they had felt isolated from the war. Studying theology, they missed the "excitement and adventure" of the war years. I told them I gladly would have let them take my place.

I soon learned the extent of my own ignorance of the war when I heard of the invasion of the island of Okinawa. I had to get a map to find where it was. I was amazed to learn of the near total destruction of the navy at Pearl Harbor. The stories of the German invasion of France, the Battle of the Bulge, etc., were all new to me.

On August 6, 1945, while still at Woodstock, I heard the news of the atomic bombing of Hiroshima. At the time it didn't make a deep impression on me. It would be much later before I realized the change the splitting of the atom would make in my life and in the history of the world.

A particularly persistent case of amoebic dysentery returned home with me from the Philippines. On several occasions during two years at Woodstock I would ask to see physicians only to be sent to doctors who were inexperienced in tropical diseases and who would find nothing wrong with me. My superiors were prone to believe the doctors' diagnoses. Having heard reports of my inability to speak during the war, they judged me to be a hypochondriac.

As a result, just before ordination I was called in to see the rector of the seminary, Fr. Wheeler, who told me that there was some question as to whether I was healthy enough to be ordained. I was so angry when I heard this that I didn't care what they decided. I was prepared to do God's will, even if they didn't ordain me, even if that decision was based on error. Fr. Wheeler then asked the opinion of Fr. John Hurley, our superior during the war years who turned out to be an advocate for my ordination.

After the controversy regarding ordination, I decided that enough was enough. I finally insisted that the house doctor, who was unable to find anything wrong with me, send me to someone who specialized in tropical diseases. He referred me to the Federal Marine Hospital in Baltimore. A specialist there immediately diagnosed a very specific type of amoebic dysentery, so developed that Johns Hopkins Medical Center asked for a sample to study. The doctor at the Marine Hospital gave me a pill that cured me almost instantly. I was tested, then re-tested and finally came out with a clean bill of health. Cured! But by then the damage to my reputation had been done. The Jesuit bureaucracy could not believe that I was anything but a hypochondriac.

Instead of relief at the decision that I would be ordained, I continued to feel annoyed that my ordination had been questioned on a health basis. Additionally, I struggled with several internal questions: Does God want me ordained? Was I pressured at the age of seventeen to join the seminary? If so, now, fourteen years later, do I want to take this step of my own free will?

Those nagging questions not withstanding, I was ordained on March 24, 1946. All my family except my brother Frank, still in the Philippines, came to Woodstock for the joyous day. Following ordination I spent another year studying theology at Woodstock and then moved to Auriesville, New York for the final year in the Jesuit course: a year of prayer and study of the life of faith. At the end of that year I was ready for my first assignment as a priest. The night before the new assignments were to be posted, I talked with Clarence Martin, who had been in Los Banos with me. We went over the list of possible assignments, choosing what we considered the best and the worst. In those days there was no consultation beforehand, so I didn't know what to expect. My "worst" choice was a little rural parish in Ridge, Maryland. I didn't want to be in a parish or in the country. The majority of the assignments were in the city, teaching high school or college, and that's where I wanted to be. Next morning Clarence and I went to the bulletin board to see our assignments. He had been reassigned to the Philippines, as he expected. My assignment was, yes, Ridge. I could hardly believe it. It was bad enough that I was losing my friends — many were returning to the Philippines — it was worse that my assignment was so disagreeable. After three years in an isolated prison camp, two years in Woodstock, and one year in Auriesville, I was going to rural Ridge!

Ridge was so rural that you couldn't even reach it by bus. It was on a narrow strip of land between the Potomac River and the Chesapeake Bay, seventy-five miles south of Washington, D.C. As you go south, the bay and the river come closer together until at Ridge they are about one mile apart. I was to live at St. Michael's rectory with Fr. Merle Baldwin, pastor of St. Michael's and the Jesuit superior, and with Fr. Horace McKenna, pastor of nearby St. Peter's Church. I was assigned as pastor of St. James, just six miles north of Ridge and as associate pastor of St. Michael's.

So I went to Ridge. The rectory was an old rambling house with five bedrooms, a library, two dining rooms, a kitchen, a parlor and a chapel. It had a second floor porch that would have overlooked Chesapeake Bay except that a line of evergreens blocked the view. It was located on the only north-south road, which ran right "on the ridge." Of the rectory's three empty bedrooms, I could take whichever I wanted. They were all about the same: a bed, a bureau, a chair, and a wood stove that took up much of the room. I picked the one facing south.

In retrospect I see that my arrival was a great disappointment for the two priests already there. It had to be obvious that I didn't like being there, and surely they must have asked for an assistant who was interested in parish work. Instead they got a young priest with a reputation for being sick and disinterested in parish life.

It was very unusual for a newly-ordained Jesuit to be sent to the "counties," as we called them. This was part of the reason I didn't like Ridge. It meant that I was looked on by other Jesuits as sick or on the shelf.

The day after I arrived, I drove up the road to get my first look at my church. As I neared the church, I saw an old man sitting on the porch of a house. Thinking he might be one of my parishioners, I called out, "Nice day."

He curtly replied, "Are you the weather man?"

Still trying to find a friendly response, I asked, "How are you?"

"Are you a doctor," he asked. Unfortunately, I later discovered, this was typical treatment for "outsiders."

I moved on to the church: a small wooden structure entered by five concrete steps. The front door was locked, but I had a key to the sacristy on the side of the church toward the back. Passing a window, I looked in to see a very small sanctuary with space to seat about sixty people.

Once inside I saw a simple altar raised up on a platform two steps high with a wooden rail separating it from the rest of the church. A middle aisle divided the rows, six benches on each side. At the back of the church a small choir loft could hold about ten people alongside the small foot-pumped organ. Behind the main body of the church there was a vestment room. A narrow stairway led to a room where a former pastor, Father John LaFarge, had lived. A hundred yards away from the church, at the edge of a woods, I found St. James Hall.

It was so depressing. Had I trained for fourteen years for such work? I thought of my companions heading back to the Philippines and all the different things they might do there. I would be ashamed even to tell them what I was doing. Strangely, it never occurred to me that I would be here only a couple of years. I say strangely because I should have had the maturity to realize that my assignment was only temporary. But in my despair at that moment, it seemed that I would be there forever: I had allowed the devil to deceive me with future burdens that would never exist.

8 ❖ *The Racist Within*

Despite my bad attitude, I carried out my duties as a pastor, and a routine soon developed. Each weekday morning at St. Michael's rectory, Mrs. Smith along with her two sons arrived for Mass in the little chapel on the first floor. Some few others might also attend, but usually not. It was summertime; the schools were closed, yet other than the two Smith boys, there were hardly any young people around. Life seemed very dull.

On Sundays I borrowed a car and drove up to my church for the two Masses. I was surprised to find that the Negro people (only later did they use the term "Black") sat together in the rear of the church while the whites sat in front. The Negroes always received Holy Communion after the whites. I had never seen this before, but I thought of it as a mutually satisfactory arrangement — more civil than elbowing one another out of the way at the communion rail. By the time a year had passed, I reversed my opinion on this and started to think it might be better if they did fight one another at the communion rail rather than use the Mass and communion as a ratification of their racial attitudes.

Soon after my arrival at Ridge, I wrote a letter to Fr. David Nugent, the Jesuit provincial, stating that I found life at Ridge very difficult. I had no experience dealing with racist white people and had no idea what to do about it. (Later I realized that this amounted to a self-recommendation to stay there because Father Nugent didn't want anybody doing anything on the racial question.) I didn't actually ask him for a change, so he replied with only a friendly letter reminding me that difficulties borne often bring us closer to God. With that, I resolved to give the new assignment another try.

At least my living arrangement was agreeable. Fr. Baldwin, both pastor and Jesuit superior, while easy to live with, was quiet and reserved. He never asserted his authority in any disagreeable way, and I believe he had a great deal of patience with me. Fr. McKenna, a small wiry man with gray hair, a little over fifty, was full of energy and kindness. He was so anxious to do things for me, like lending me his car, that I couldn't help but like him. He invited me to see his all-Negro church facilities: a grade school, vocational school, and a credit union. I felt deflated and apathetic in comparison to him, so enthusiastic. I couldn't understand why he was so happy about his work. Evidently, he liked being at Ridge and with the poor Negro people. I admired Fr. McKenna and found his company a great blessing, even though he was always belittling himself, saying something like, "I am in a fog about economics. I don't know what I'm doing." He just laughed when I warned him that such comments would only encourage those opposed to his ministry.

Though I didn't realize it at the time, Fr. McKenna's example and company began to open my eyes to the evil of racism. He was so devoted to his parish and so kind to everybody that even the whites who thought he was wasting his time with "those Negroes" would say, "He's a saint."

The revelation of my own racist tendencies came on a cold Sunday morning, early in my first winter at Ridge. I arrived at the church about 7 a.m., an hour before Mass, to light the stove and to hear confessions. Well, with no success at all in starting a fire, I had quite an audience. Whites were lined up on one side of the confessional box and Negroes on the other. Very frustrated, I wondered why no one would come over to help me. A moment later a strong-looking Negro man came up and asked, "Can I make that fire for you, Father?" He made the fire, and I heard confession — whites first.

After Mass I asked about the man who made the fire. I found out he was Aloysius Butler, the husband of Bea Butler who used to clean the church and take care of the altar. Was I ever embarrassed — one of the first things I had done when I arrived was to fire Bea. After all, why pay someone to clean the church and put flowers on the altar when it could be done by volunteers? I gave no thought to the fact that she might need the money and that volunteers might not appear. Now here was her husband volunteering to help me. After Mass I thanked him for starting the fire. I remember using the title "Mister" when I talked to him and feeling very fair and American because it wasn't a title given to Black people at Ridge. I asked him if he would be willing to make the fire every Sunday. "Sure, Father, I'll do it."

"It's a service necessary for the church, so I'd like to pay you for it."

"You don't need to pay me for it, Father. I'se glad to do it."

"How much do you make at your regular job?"

"I makes ninety-five cents an hour driving a truck for the naval station."

"Suppose I pay you a dollar an hour?" I said, thinking how generous I was.

"You can't do that, Father, I'se doin' this for Gawd."

I felt as if I had been hit on the head. I turned away from him so he wouldn't see the consternation in my face. "What is happening," I asked myself. "How come he has to tell me that he is doing this for God. He's a Catholic. He's in a Catholic church. There is no one else here but the two of us, so he's not saying this to impress anybody else." Slowly the answer came, "Because you are treating him differently than you treat white people. You are racist!"

He probably noticed my confusion, though I was not even looking at him. Finally I turned to him and said, "Thank you Mr. Butler. I'll be glad to have you do it for God." After he departed, I thought, "There is a man of faith. I fired his wife and yet he volunteers to help me and wants no payment." This incident opened my eyes to my own racism, but not to all the racism around me.

The faith of that one man opened new doors to me. I gradually saw that something here was very wrong. Mr. Butler's faith came to mind later when I was visiting a white family of the parish. I was sitting in the parlor with the husband and wife, chatting about a celebration honoring an Indian tribe that used to live in St. Mary's City. In the course of our conversation I remarked that the Indians had been treated worse than the Negroes. "If you talk like that down here, Father, you'll get the reputation of being a nigger lover," said the lady of the house. As she finished the last sentence, she held the back of her hand up to her lips to kind of hide the fact that she was using the word "nigger." I was annoyed, both at the gesture and at her effort to instruct me. "I will be careful," I said. "I don't deserve the reputation of being a 'nigger lover'." As I said the words, I held the back of my hand in front of my lips in imitation of her gesture. I continued, "I don't deserve that reputation because that is the reputation that Jesus had." She looked over at her husband. He looked back at her. Neither of them said anything. After a moment I said, "It seems as though we have run out of conversation. I suppose it's time for me to leave."

In silence they accompanied me down the front steps of the house. With typical southern hospitality, they walked me to my car. After I got in and was ready to drive off, the husband walked up to the open window and said, "Well, Father, why don't you just put it down to the fact that we are ignorant southerners and don't know no better?" This was his way of saying, "Let's forget it all and start over." But I had the memory of Aloysius Butler in my mind, so I just looked at him and said, "OK, you are just ignorant southerners and don't know no better. Goodnight." I drove away knowing that I was going to get the reputation of being pro-Negro.

As I look back on those days, I see that the whites at Ridge were good people who wanted to help me avoid trouble in the parish. They did this by coaching me in the "customs" of white southerners. Unfortunately, this included segregation. But because of my experience with Aloysius Butler and his faith, I rejected their instructions However, I did not yet see that the whole business of segregation was wrong — that would take awhile. But I was now sensitized to the issue, and new shocking experiences were not long in coming.

An elderly Negro woman who cooked for us in the rectory lived in a little shack across the field from the church. One day one of her grandchildren came running across the fields with a message, "Grandma is sick, and the ambulance says it won't come for her. Will you call the ambulance?"

I had heard reports that the Leonardtown Hospital ambulance, twenty-five miles away, sometimes refused to take Negroes to the hospital, but it never seemed of any importance to me or any concern of mine. Now here it was right on my doorstep. Fr. Baldwin was out, so I phoned the hospital and asked them to send an ambulance to the rectory immediately. About half-an-hour later, the ambulance rushed up to the rectory door. I met the doctor (not a medic) and said, "Right across the field there. I'll go with you."

"I thought this was an emergency at the rectory."

"It is an emergency. The lady who works for the rectory is sick."

I could see he didn't like it at all. When we arrived at the woman's house, he went in to see her. He soon came out and told me, "She has an obstructed intestine. She needs to go to the hospital, but we can't take her. You can go examine her yourself."

I sternly replied, "I'm not a doctor, I can't tell anything from examining her, but I can tell you this: If she dies, I will spread the news all over the county that you were here and refused to take her to the hospital. Besides, if you don't take her to the hospital, I'll take her myself and still publicize your refusal all over the place!" He yielded and told the stretcher bearers to go get her.

Another compelling incident occurred at roughly the same time: The chaplain at Pautuxent Naval Station, located just a few miles from Ridge, asked me to substitute for him while he was away. One of my jobs was to continue the religious instruction for sailors preparing to join the Catholic Church. Among them was a young Negro — the first Negro to whom I had given religious instruction. When I asked him why he wanted to become a Catholic, he answered articulately, "It seems to be the only religion that speaks with clear authority and is fair to Negroes. Catholics believe that we are all equal before God and in the eyes of the Church."

"That's all true. That is our belief."

"How are the Negroes treated in your parish, Father?"

Before he asked that question, I thought I had an acceptable answer. But the answer didn't fit very well in the present circumstances. It wouldn't do much good to say, "The white Catholics in my church don't follow what the Church teaches. They follow their own southern custom of segregation." So I muted my answer and replied, "The Catholics in my church don't obey me. They don't obey the pope. They don't obey the gospel that teaches us that we are all children of God. They follow their own customs." As I spoke, I could see the disappointment register on his face. He never came back to instruction while I was there, and I found out later that he did not return for any further instruction.

When I told this story to the white people of St. Michael's parish, I pointed out the fact that at the naval base Negro sailors ate, slept, swam with the white people. I added that sailors did this for national defense, but we were not willing to do it for the love of God. I was astonished at their reply, "That Negro sailor must be a communist." Nonsense. Maybe segregation was not his reason for discontinuing instruction, but he didn't have to be a communist to be opposed to segregation. It amazed me that they would ignore such a story.

I soon noticed some strange patterns of life at Ridge. For instance, the children at St. Michael's (at the time it didn't strike me that they were all white) kept the priests at arm's length. They resisted invitations to come to the rectory for a cookie or a soda. This was not like ordinary Catholic children. When I played baseball with the high school students, they didn't choose me as one of the captains of the team. They put me in the worst place, right field. Out on the school grounds I built a basketball standard. I went up the road, chopped down a tree, brought it back to the grounds and helped them put it up. But when we got the game started, they didn't even pass the ball to me. I put up with it, but I wondered why this pattern was so different from that of children in Philadelphia and other places I had been.

A further puzzle was the parish boundary lines. Although I had received a letter from Archbishop O'Boyle naming me pastor of St. James, I had no idea where the parish boundaries were. In my last year of Jesuit studies I had resolved not to work at any assignment until I had sized it up and knew all the implications of the job. So I wrote to the archbishop explaining that there were no parish lines; under canon law a pastor has to have a specific territory. I finally got an answer saying that, until parish lines were drawn, my territory would be confined to within the church building. Considering that the Catholic Church had been in the area since the landing of the "The Ark of the Dove" (1634), it seemed strange that no parish boundaries had been drawn for any of the churches in the vicinity.

The bishop's letter didn't fully satisfy me. I kept writing him every time a problem would arise due to ambiguous parish lines. Here is a typical letter:

> Dear Archbishop,
>
> At two o'clock this morning Fr. Baldwin came into my room and awakened me to say that I had a phone call from a parishioner who was dying and needed a priest. "Where does she live?" I asked. When he gave me the information, I said, "I don't know if that is my parish." But I did get up and give her the last sacrament. I bring this to your attention, Archbishop, because nobody had any responsibility to visit her for the months she was sick and close to death as there were no parish lines. And a doubtful responsibility is nobody's responsibility. . . .

Gradually the pieces, like a jigsaw puzzle, began to fit into place. Why were there no parish lines? Because the churches were segregated, but neighborhoods were not. Parish lines would necessarily put white and Negro people in the same parish. Why did the white children stay at arm's length from the priests? Because their parents were afraid that someday some priest would tell them that segregation was wrong.

And I knew that other elements were at work. For instance, the Jesuit provincial preferred to have one Jesuit superior in charge of an area instead of three independent pastors. But the archdiocese wanted each pastor to report to the diocese for each church. Even this division of opinion seemed to have a relation to racial segregation as there were no official parish lines, yet parish "boundaries" *did* exist — based on the color bar.

As the truth of the wide-ranging effects of racial segregation dawned on me, I resisted being part of it. Why were almost all the Jesuits in nearly twenty-five Maryland parishes saying nothing about racial segregation? When I brought up the matter at a Jesuit meeting, I was told, "You'd better not talk about it. You won't find a single white person who will support you. They'll run you out of town on a rail, and you'll lose money in the collection."

Following one poorly attended meeting called to discuss moral issues — the topic was marriage in the Byzantine rite — I told the priest in charge that

I could suggest a topic that would bring full attendance. "Don't tell me you're thinking of racial segregation?" he said. "They wouldn't discuss it. Nobody would agree with you. We won't even bring it up as a topic." But I felt a responsibility as a pastor. Luckily, or more accurately, in God's providence, I was in a job I didn't like. I had no fear of being relocated because, in my mind, any move would be a promotion. It was true that I had my own church; I was pastor, I had my own small bank account, my own car. This was new to me, but I didn't really like any of it nor was I eager to hold on to it.

As I consulted brother Jesuits, this was the advice I received: If you speak out about segregation, you will never be appointed to any position of honor in the Jesuit order. I knew of no one else in the province who spoke out against segregation. I would be alone. Yet I felt obliged as a pastor, as a man, to do something. I decided I would do the very minimum required: I would in no way approve of segregation even by my silence. I made a simple resolution in my own heart and told no one but God: If anyone used the word "nigger" in my presence, I would not be silent. At least I would do that.

The first test of this resolution came quickly and unexpectedly. I had been writing some local news for the county newspaper, *The St. Mary's Beacon.* I wrote my column under the pen name JB, the initials of Jasper Blankensop, a name I had come across in St. Mary's County history. It struck me as unusual and funny. I assumed the pen name partly because I was including news about Negro and white people in the same column. Only the editor knew my true identity.

In one printed edition of my column I found a sub-heading "Negro News." I phoned the editor, Mrs. Sterling, to complain that the newspaper had separated my column into Negro news and other news. Some white people were named under the "Negro News" caption, and I didn't think that would be appreciated by the whites.

"Will you make the separation yourself so there won't be any future mistakes?" she asked.

"No! I don't think the news should be separated. If you don't want to print my column, you don't have to. But if you are going to print it, leave out the sub-heading 'Negro News'." *The Beacon* continued my column all in one piece.

Since my working relationship with Mrs. Sterling was so amiable, I arranged to visit her on my next trip to Leonardtown. The visit began quite peacefully, almost idyllic: As I chatted with Mrs. Sterling and several of her children in the parlor, I could hear other children playing violin and piano.

However, peace turned to tension when, in the course of our conversation, one of her adult sons said, "Well, one thing for sure Father, once we get that new church built there won't be any damn 'niggers' sitting in the front pew."

As I heard the words, I realized that the moment had come to act on my resolution. Few families in the county had more prominence, and even before I spoke, I realized that this was a watershed. Once I took my stand, I could never go back. The vulgarity of the remark and my confused silence suddenly brought everything to a halt — the piano, the violin stopped. I could hear my heart beating faster making speech more difficult. Everyone was looking at me. Finally I said, "I don't want to be ungrateful to your kind hospitality, but I think that as a pastor I should not be silent on this matter, and by my silence seem to approve when an epithet is used about a large number of Catholic people. That's all I want to say. I don't want to talk about it anymore."

As soon as I finished, the son who had made the remark said, "Oh Father, we don't mind talking about it. We like to talk about it."

By now my heart was back to normal, so I composed myself and began to question the son: "I often hear people down here say, 'The Negro is all right in his place.' What is the Negro's place?"

"I'll tell you, Father. A Negro knows his place, and we know our place."

"That may be true, but I'm not from here. I'm from the North, and I don't know what you mean by that. You haven't answered my question."

"Their place is on Park Avenue," he answered laughing.

His sister cut in, "He's laughing because Park Avenue is an unpaved street."

At this point Mrs. Sterling came into the conversation as a mediator: "Father, we want you to understand that we love the Negro. I had a Negro living on our property who was sick. Every day I went to help her, sometimes even in the middle of the night."

I told Mrs. Sterling that whether or not she loved Negroes was not at question, only the definition of their "place," and that her family still had not provided me with an answer.

Still no reply. After an awkward silence, I continued, "As a Catholic, the Negro's place is right beside you at the altar rail, and as an American citizen, his place is right beside you in the voting booth."

At this point the oldest boy, who had made the initial comment, spoke up, "I'll tell you something. Father, I was in the navy. We had Negroes in our company who weren't human. We had to chain them under the house." His brother came in right away with, "Aw, why don't you quit that stuff. I was in the army, and we had white soldiers that we had to chain under the house."

They began arguing among themselves. I stayed out of it and soon departed.

The next day I wrote a letter to Fr. John LaFarge, S.J., editor of *America* magazine, and told him that I realized that segregation was wrong, and I wanted his advice. LaFarge, a former Ridge pastor, wrote *The Negro and the Race Question*, one of the first books by a Catholic priest on this moral issue. He founded the Catholic Interracial Council of New York which had been imitated in many dioceses throughout the country.

He replied that I should first form separate study groups of white and Negro Catholic leaders from all over the county to study church teaching on social and racial justice. Then, I should eventually have one of the leaders of the Negro group exchange places with one of the leaders of the white group. He also advised that I avoid trying to "reform" programs and activities that were segregated before I got there.

Following his advice, I began the Robert Bellarmine study group for white people and the St. Augustine study group for blacks. Opposition to segregation was not a requirement, only interest in Catholic thought on the issues. I picked out leaders from across the county and asked them to join. Soon each group had eight to ten members, and we began to meet separately once a week in the St. James Church sacristy. We wanted no publicity about our meetings, but it was not easy to keep things secret. People driving by could tell who was at a meeting by the cars parked outside. The lady at the post office would see my notices going out for the meetings. She would even hold the letters up to the light and read the names inside.

9 ❖ *Turning Up the Heat*

A few marines from Pautuxent Naval Air Station were interested in racial justice and volunteered to come to the study group meetings or at least be nearby to act as security guards. While I was grateful for their attendance, I let them know that a "security detail" would be unnecessary. At the meetings we discussed Fr. LaFarge's book *The Negro and the Race Question*; the working of the Catholic Interracial Councils; the Papal encyclical on African slavery; the sermon on Christian cannibalism by Fr. Heithouse (of St. Louis University); and the pamphlets of the Markoe Brothers (Jesuits from St. Louis). All these resources were new even to me.

With the study groups going, I began to explore the possibility of desegregating parish programs that had been established since my arrival at Ridge (per Fr. LaFarge's advice). I settled on the roller skating activity at St. James Parish Hall which I called the Woodland Roller Skating Rink. Months before, I had hauled in a truck-load of hardwood flooring, bought at a bargain, from Washington, D.C. Several parish members and I nailed it down over the old floor. I then purchased roller skates to rent out with the hope of recovering the purchase cost. Previously, there had been no local option for young people who wanted to get together for recreation. Before I understood the evils of segregation, the rink was open on Sunday afternoon for the whites and Tuesday evening for the Blacks.

So the decision was made: The skating rink would become the venue for our parish's first steps toward integration. From the pulpit I announced that skating would now be held only on Sunday afternoons. I kept this proclamation sufficiently vague so that those in attendance could interpret it any way they wanted. Privately, I did tell some of the Negro children that they were welcome and should come on Sunday afternoon. Our marine friends also heard about what was happening, and some of them came to help in case there was trouble. I didn't expect any serious unrest, but I was glad they were there.

On Sunday afternoon skating began as usual with only white skaters on the floor — though three or four Black children were putting on their skates in the back room. I just kept skating around the rink. Wilfred Owen, the area electrician, skated up to me and said in a friendly voice, "Father, it seems there are some Negro children putting on their skates. What are you going to do about it?"

"I'll see if they can skate."

"You're not going to stop them?"

When it became clear that I was in fact sanctioning integrated skating, Wilfred quickly departed. After a few minutes a series of cars driven by anxious parents pulled up to the church, and most of children were hurried home. Some of the marines, three or four Negro children — so small that they could hardly stand up on skates — and a few other white people remained to skate.

As I drove back to St. Michael's that evening, I knew that integrated skating would not continue. (After a couple more tries we did close down.) Cynically, I felt that if we closed down the rink, I would consider myself fortunate to have Sunday afternoons free. After all, that would be preferable to overseeing segregated activities. However, the youth were penalized with the loss of their only recreational outlet.

There was one place within the parish that was fully integrated: the cemetery. Located just behind the church building, the cemetery was laid out with the graves of Black and white parishioners placed side by side. Many graves were unmarked because the family of the deceased was too poor to afford a gravestone. When a new grave was needed, an old Negro man had to be consulted on where to dig. He was the only one who knew exactly which spots were empty and which were occupied.

One of the most moving scenes I have ever witnessed took place in that cemetery. While preparing for the funeral of a young Black man, I watched from the sacristy as his father dug the grave. It was hard enough for a father to grieve over his son, but much more painful when he had to dig the grave. Or was there some comfort, some sense of closure in the act?

Because the church choir was composed of whites only, there was never singing at Negro funerals even though the Negro parishioners sang well. Many of them had learned as children to sing the Mass and other hymns at Fr. McKenna's church and school. The all-white choir at St. James sang only at white funerals. I was usually the only white person present at a Negro funeral and burial.

I decided to speak to Mrs. Dunbar, the leader of the choir, about training some Negro parishioners to sing at Negro funerals. However, I didn't want to start a Negro choir — that would only reinforce segregation. Her response fascinated me, "Father, I don't think the choir members would agree to welcome Negro members into the choir. I have no objection myself, but I don't think the others will agree." I pressed her further to make the request and she agreed. A couple weeks later I asked Mrs. Dunbar if she had any answer about the choir. As I expected, Mrs. Dunbar explained that, like herself, the other choir members had no personal objection to Blacks joining them for practice, but all were sure the other choir members would object. No one wanted to take responsibility for it, but the decision was made: No Negroes would rehearse with the choir.

Once again, the direct approach seemed to fail and a more subtle tactic seemed in order. At Mass the following Sunday, I announced that on the coming Wednesday evening we would have practice for congregational singing to which all were invited. I sold the idea on the basis that congregational singing was recommended to increase lay involvement in worship. When Wednesday night arrived, the choir went up to the loft and about a dozen Negroes sat in the main body of the church downstairs. To speak to them both at the same time, I stood on the altar platform and led the singing just as though all were together.

The Negro people sang well; they knew the hymns and they outnumbered the choir. These "rehearsals," though not entirely successful in integrating the choir, did result in a fine group available to sing at the funerals of Black parishioners.

Emboldened by this minor success, I decided to take on another issue. Although many Negro children had served as altar boys for Fr. McKenna, none were serving at St. James. They simply did not feel welcome. To make them welcome I arranged a training for new altar boys and made a point of inviting several young Blacks. Two or three of them showed up, and they already knew how to serve. When the parents of the white children who showed found out, only two white boys continued to serve with their parents' blessing. In time, on many Sundays we had both Negro and white altar boys serving at the same Mass. Ironically, with a decreased number of servers I had money to buy the boys new cassocks and collars so they looked better than ever.

Nearly fifty years later, looking back at the situation, I see that some of the people at St. James had a very strong faith. They put up with me and my views even if they didn't agree with me. However, I did not stand utterly alone at Ridge.

Each of the parishes had a festival and a dinner that generally brought in twice as much income as the entire yearly offerings of the parish. This was because the festivals were attended by people from around the region. The St. James weekly collection averaged seventeen dollars and fifty cents, a yearly total of about eight-hundred and ninety dollars. In contrast, the annual turkey dinner ordinarily would bring in about two-thousand dollars, all of which went to the church. Parishioners donated everything that was sold, including the food. But, like everything else, the dinners were segregated.

I was expected to attend the planning meeting for the "white" turkey dinner. The meeting was set to take place at the farmhouse of Pete Carroll. I told Fr. McKenna that I wanted to skip the meeting for fear of an open confrontation about segregation. "Go — let them dump on you if they want to," he wisely advised. He was right; I was making an issue of segregation, and I couldn't hide now from the consequences.

Because the annual dinner was an event that pre-dated my arrival at Ridge, I had no intention of trying to integrate it. Yet, because of my recent efforts at integration, I thought the white parishioners would cancel the dinner and blame me for creating dissension. Blaming me for cancellation of such a large church fund-raiser could be very effective in eliminating the little support that did exist for integration.

At Pete Carroll's home, we gathered around a table in a large room. The thirty or so people in attendance were the workers who made the turkey dinner go. They knew each other well. Many were related. We were just getting started when one of the Carroll men cried out loud enough for everyone to hear, "Before we start the meetin', I'd like to know who let the niggers in the roller skating rink?"

Because the question was vulgar, the crowd became silent. I answered, not looking at the speaker, "When a question asked of me contains an unkind epithet about a large group of Catholic people, I have no intention of answering it. If you want me to answer, you'll have to repeat your question and omit the epithet." He rephrased the question, "Who let the Negroes into the roller skating rink last Sunday?"

"I did," I replied. In the most matter-of-fact tone I could muster, I gave my rationale for the integrated skating and stated my wish that it should continue.

"We'll burn the church down," he threatened.

"It's your church; if you burn it down, it won't hurt me. I don't depend on that church for my living."

A young woman sitting to my left stood up and spoke in a loud voice: "Why don't we admit that Father is right? We have known all along in our hearts that segregation is wrong. Why don't we admit it?"

There was dead silence. The speaker, Marguerite Dalton, one of the Carroll family, was respected by all in attendance. I was stunned and surprised. I had been told that I would be alone if I opposed segregation, and I had believed it. Now here was a white woman standing up to defend me in public. She continued for a short time to chastise her friends and family for engaging in such hateful behavior. When she sat down, no one wanted to say anything more about the matter.

My repugnance for the meeting ended. I was full of joy. I thought to myself, "This meeting is already a success beyond my dreams. Let's get it over with and get out of here while it's going so well." The meeting moved on; we settled all the details about the turkey dinner; and I left as quickly as I could. Still, I was emboldened by the knowledge that I was not alone in opposing segregation. The young woman who defended me was the mother of children involved in the skating rink controversy. Her husband disagreed with her. The problem she had taken on was gigantic compared to what I was doing. When I got back to the rectory, I phoned to thank her. She said, "You don't need to thank me. We want to do what's right."

For a few months Marguerite was able to serve as an important member of the white study club — until her husband ordered her to stop attending my church. When she broke the news to me, I was disappointed though I understood her need to honor her husband's wishes.

Other members of the white study group were under the same pressure from friends and loved ones. We agreed to help one another by formulating a set of responses to the most common questions and objections. Equipped with these "talking points," members of the study group became articulate spokespeople for the group and our work.

Many members wanted to take action, at least symbolically, that would make our work together more visible to the wider parish community. I suggested that they could wait until some of the Negro parishioners approached the alter for communion and then come up with them. When they did this, I would make it clear that I approved: After I said the Latin prayer required at the distribution of Holy Communion, I added, to the white people and to the Negroes who received together, a hearty "God Bless you."

At St. Michael's Church I was confronted by the racial issue in a different way. For this all-white congregation I was expected to hear confessions of the school children and occasionally to give benediction. I wondered how I could do either without giving my blessing to segregation. I found a way in both cases.

The confessional box had a slot in the screen between the priest and the penitent through which a printed prayer card could be slipped. I did not use the slot until I bought several hundred holy cards with the image of St. Martin de Porres (a Black man) and a prayer to him. After each child's confession, I pushed a holy card through the slot and said, "For your penance say the prayer that is on this holy card." I figured the children would carry the cards home in their pockets. My hope was that knowledge of a Black saint would begin to challenge the racism learned at home and in community life.

Some of the children must have told their parents about the holy cards, because one night Fr. Baldwin walked into my office, right up to my desk, and spoke in a mild, but serious tone: "Dick, are you telling the people that segregation is a sin?" Because he used the word "sin," I backed off a bit. Perhaps he was trying to trap me, to find that I was not orthodox in my theology. A few months later I would have quickly answered, "Yes!" But I wasn't ready for that. He was the Jesuit superior, and he might have some special meaning to "sin." So I replied, "I am teaching them that it is wrong."

"You don't understand life down here. It's not wrong; it's just a way of life."

"So is prostitution a way of life," I replied.

Merle didn't answer. He just walked out of the room without saying another word.

The next morning Fr. McKenna told me, "Dick, I was awake last night in my room, in bed above your office when you were talking to Fr. Baldwin. I could hear every word you said. Short as it was, that was the greatest discussion that has ever gone on in this house." I felt greatly encouraged because I knew Horace was a holy man. I didn't realize until much later what a blessing it was for me to spend those years in his company.

My dad also struck-up a lasting friendship with Horace McKenna. It began when my father and mother came to Ridge during my first year there. In the course of their visit I introduced my dad to Fr. McKenna. Dad asked, "What do you do here, Father?" Horace rummaged around in his pocket, pulled out some brown paper with some numbers on it, and said, "This is what I do, Mr. McSorley. Here's a bill for a well that was dug for a poor woman who can't pay. The woman can't live without water, so I'm trying to find the money to pay this off."

My father took the paper from Fr. McKenna and said, "I'll take care of that." Later I said, "Dad, that was very quick. You didn't take long in agreeing to help him." My father said, "He's a man of God. I could tell that the minute I saw him. I want to have a share in his work." My father sized him up much more quickly than I had.

Years later when my dad was sick in Philadelphia, Fr. McKenna wrote him a letter. When I visited my dad, he said, "Dick, I've received many letters since I've been sick, but the one that impressed me the most deeply was a short note from your friend Fr. McKenna." He wrote, "Mr. McSorley, you have been a one-man St. Vincent De Paul Society for the poor people of my parish. When you go to the poor house because you are out of money, I will come and bring you a basket of strawberries."

One day , while I was reading the paper in the second floor sitting room of St. Michael's rectory, Fr. McKenna came in with a desperate look on his face. "Dick, can you spare five minutes for me? I want to get your advice." Indeed, Horace was very discouraged. He had just returned from the bishop's office where his request for another Black nun to help with his ministry was turned down. There was simply too much to do and he was doing none of it well. Horace was sure that some of his ministry would have to be cut back unless he got more help.

This was my chance to offer a criticism that I had before now kept to myself. " Horace, you are bearing the burden of segregation for all of the parishes. They send you their Negro children, and then they don't have to bother about getting them into the white schools. You get all the poor and you can't pay for them. The little money the parishes are sending you doesn't cover your costs. You shouldn't have to kill yourself trying to pay for it. In the long run it's not helping your people or the church."

"Give me two minutes to think it over," Horace said and he left. In a few minutes he came back and sat down beside me. He blessed himself with the sign of the cross and said, "In the name of the Father, and the Son, and the Holy Ghost, I am through with segregation. I will no longer be a band-aid on the mystical body of Christ."

I was surprised at the solemnity of his statement. I realized he spoke out of deep faith.

The very next day he returned to the bishop's office. At first they didn't want to see him; the chancellor said that there was no use asking again. They couldn't get him another sister. Then Horace surprised them. He hadn't come to beg for an assistant, but to announce that he was going to close the school. Suddenly there was time to see the bishop, and soon they were begging Horace to keep the school open.

On his return home Fr. McKenna joyfully related the story to me and concluded that their reaction only confirmed that segregation is wrong and that they knew it. Additionally, he was even more convinced that closing the Negro school in favor of working to de-segregate all Catholic schools was the right thing to do.

In another Maryland town, Morganza, Fr. Michael Cavanaugh, a Jesuit and a friend to both Horace and me, was trying to integrate two grammar schools, one Black and one white. He wanted to talk to us about it, so we agreed to meet him at the Officer's Club at Pautuxent Naval Air Station. I had an officer's card that would get us in for a cheap dinner, and there we could talk freely. We enjoyed each other's stories and company so much that we laughed all through the dinner.

In a serious vein, I told them that I had been invited to preach a novena of grace in honor of St. Francis Xavier at St. Michael's, the all-white church, and that I planned to speak about segregation. Some of the people, like Marguerite Dalton, were bearing too much of the attack for their stand against segregation. I said it was time to publicly denounce it.

They both thought it was a good idea. Since they were both preaching the same novena at their churches, we agreed that on the third day of the novena all of us would preach on the evil of segregation. In this way we could support each other and our parishioners who were in favor of ending segregation. We hoped a united front of opposition would strengthen our position.

In Fr. Cavanaugh's words, "The people running up the road with the news of the sermon would meet the people coming down the road with the news about the same sermon." It seemed to be a great plan.

I wrote out my sermon carefully, weighing each word, and I made a tape recording of it. I expected to be misquoted by some unhappy listener so I wanted to have a ready refutation.

A novena service consists of prayers followed by benediction of the Blessed Sacrament. The church was crowded by 8 p.m. We had selected the third day of the nine-day novena in order to reach the maximum number of parishioners. I walked out to the altar led by the two altar boys, genuflected, and then went to the top step of the altar to speak. I paused and looked around. I knew that this was a big moment in my life. My heart raced and I could hardly catch my breath. After I had looked around, I started with this sentence, "If St. Francis Xavier were here tonight, he might look around the church as I do now and ask, 'Where are the dear, good colored people?'" There was an intense silence. Fr. LaFarge had given me this opening sentence. During an earlier visit with LaFarge, he had remarked to me, "I often thought that I would like to ask that question from the altar."

I continued, "If St. Francis Xavier were here tonight and asked that question of you good people of Southern Maryland, one of you might answer him, 'They are at St. Peter's church, not far away. They don't come here. They have their own church.' If St. Francis, who was used to Indians and Portuguese attending the same church, continued to ask you, 'Why do you have two churches? Are you not all members of the one Catholic faith?' One of you might answer, 'Yes, we are all of the same faith, but we have a custom here of being separated.'"

I continued the sermon as a dialogue between St. Francis Xavier and a voice representing Southern Maryland. I had St. Francis Xavier ask the questions that my study club members had asked, and I had the representative of Southern Maryland give the typical answers. I talked about the unity and the universality of the church, about our obligation to love one another. Toward the end I said, "There are at least fifty-seven canonized Negro saints, including St. Martin of Tours, Martin de Porres, Pope Innocent III, and the martyrs of Uganda. They are in heaven with God and there is only one heaven. That makes it necessary for us to choose. You can either choose to go to heaven and share the beatitudes with God and his fifty-seven Negro saints or you can go [I paused] some place else!"

After the benediction a crowd of people surrounded the sacristy. Marguerite Dalton said, "I looked around the church, and everyone was there who needed to hear it. It was wonderful." Though an opposition parishioner said, "I should have walked out right away. I don't know why I stayed. I stayed because I wanted to hear what you would say next." Colonel Cobb, a member of the study club said, "It was well done. We needed it."

Like Colonel Cobb, most of the people who talked to me were study club members. Fr. Cavanaugh and Fr. McKenna preached on the same night. Of course, the Negro people at St. Peter's gave Horace no opposition. But his talk did help to make it clear that this was not the opinion of just one person.

Soon afterward, I took up the invitation to speak with Cardinal Patrick O'Boyle. I went to Washington to tell him about the integration of the roller skating. He said, "That's unusual. Recreation usually is the last thing to be integrated, yet you began with it. Do what you can, but don't expect any help from me. I'm up to here [he put his hand to the top of his head] with segregation in the District. Just last Tuesday I called in a Monsignor who refused to give Holy Communion to a Black man, who turned out to be an ambassador from an African country."

Later the Jesuit provincial, David Nugent, told me, "I would have moved you in a minute [he snapped his fingers] as soon as I heard you were talking about segregation, but the archbishop asked me not to. The archbishop did not want to appear to be yielding to racism."

10 ✣ A Hot Time in the Old Town

It may have been the sermon that roused the white opposition that turned into action a few weeks later. One morning the Negro children of St. Peter's parish came to join the white school children of St. Michael's for Mass. This was not unusual. Whenever Fr. McKenna was away, the two groups came together, though usually under the direction of Fr. Baldwin. But he was also away, so I was the celebrant of the Mass. Maybe this, plus my reputation, set off a rumor among the white people that the two schools were going to be integrated. That afternoon Fr. McKenna told me that some of the white people were planning to meet at St. Michael's school hall. He explained, "They didn't ask my permission, they just said they were coming. I didn't say anything except that I would be there."

Some study club members came by the rectory to tell me the same story. They agreed to attend the meeting and to bring along all the other study club members they could find. Since Fr. Baldwin was away, I was in charge of St. Michael's property. I asked Fr. McKenna if he thought we should let them in. "Sure," he answered. "Let them talk. There is nothing to the rumor of integrating the schools." I went over to the school to prepare for their arrival. To discourage them from staying too long, I turned up the heating system. I also set up a tape machine to record the meeting. While preparing for the meeting, we got bad news: A crowd was at the firehouse getting warmed up for the meeting with a few drinks. The good news: Colonel Cobb got himself selected to chair the meeting.

When the crowd started to come in, I was trying to start the tape recorder. Suddenly, Fr. Morgan Downey, S.J., from a nearby parish, walked in the door. He stopped about twenty feet away from me and then called out in a military style voice, "Father McSorley, I have orders from the Jesuit provincial for you. You are to go to the nearest closed-circuit phone and call the provincial immediately." He then turned about-face and departed.

I asked Horace what I should do. We both knew that any private phone was miles away. I would miss the meeting. "Go," he said. "I will be here to represent you." I left it all in Horace's hands.

As I turned to leave, Leo Weiland, a good friend and the director of an interracial choir at a local parish, asked if he could go with me. "Sure, you could be a big help. This may be the end of my time at Ridge. I may be ordered to leave immediately. That kind of thing has happened before." I had heard of Fr. George H. Dunne, and Fr. Claude Heithouse, ordered out of the Jesuit residence at St. Louis University without a moment's advance notice. Both had called for racial integration of the university.

Wanting to take all my files and other belongings with me, I headed for the rectory. But on the school playground Leo fainted and fell unconscious. With the help of one of the men going into the meeting, I carried him into the rectory and laid him on the sofa. The phone call would have to wait; Leo might be dying, so I would stay with him. Suddenly he opened his eyes and said, "Sorry, Father. This always happens when I come out of a warm building and suddenly hit the cold air. I'll be all right in a minute."

"Maybe you should stay and rest. I can manage alone."

"No, no, I want to go with you."

"All right, stay here. I'll go get my car and bring it around to the rectory." By now there were dozens of cars alongside mine in the dark school yard. My car was a 1948 Chevrolet. I put the key in and drove around to the back of the rectory.

Leo and I began packing my files and a few other items into cardboard boxes when five or six men came up on the back porch and knocked on the door. Leo opened it and they said, "We want to see Fr. McSorley." I came to the door.

"What do you want?"

"You took my car," one of them said in a hostile tone.

"When?" I asked.

"Now. This car right here is mine." He pointed to the car I had driven out of the school yard.

"In the dark the car looked like mine. The key fit, but if it's yours, take it. I'll get mine from the lot."

"We'll carry you over to the meeting." The words sounded ominous, but they weren't. In Southern Maryland dialect, "carry" means "give a ride to." I didn't accept their offer, but they didn't leave right away. So I motioned Leo to go back into my office. When he did, I stepped into the middle of the back room which was cluttered with unused furniture. I intentionally stood right under the naked bulb that had a string hanging from it. "Good night," I said and I pulled the overhead string. We were in total darkness. To get to that string they would have to know the layout of the rectory better than I. Many a time I had hunted for it unsuccessfully in the dark. Leaving them, I went out the front door, found the car that actually was mine and loaded my belongings.

Leo and I were soon on our way. When we reached a pay phone in Lexington Park, I called the provincial's office, Fr. John Long answered.

"I was told to call you," I said.

"Yes, I have information that you will be shot if you stay in the rectory tonight. So I wanted to advise you to stay away."

"I don't think that I'm in danger. The people going to this meeting are not dangerous. They're cowards."

"The person who informed me of this says he's a friend of yours. He thinks you are in danger, but if you think you're safe, I'll leave it up to your judgment."

I gave the report to Leo and told him I would return to the rectory that night. Since it was too late to make the meeting, we decided to stop at his home for a beer and to unwind.

When we got back to St. Michael's, we learned about the meeting: After the call to order, Colonel Cobb, asked Fr. McKenna to begin with a prayer. Horace blessed himself and began, "Our Father. . . ." At the conclusion people started to sit down, but he continued with the Hail Mary. Again they started to sit down, but Fr. McKenna continued with the Glory Be to the Father and then recited the Creed. Their patience was wearing thin when he blessed himself and concluded. They didn't want to appear rude to Fr. McKenna or seem opposed to prayer, but they wanted to get the meeting started.

Colonel Cobb announced, "We are here to discuss Negro children attending Mass at St. Michael's school this morning." He asked Fr. McKenna to comment. He said that it was the ordinary practice when only one priest was present for all to attend the Mass together at St. Michael's.

He was interrupted by someone who shouted, "We want to know about the integration of the schools!"

Fr. McKenna responded with a soliloquy about how the model for integration and for all unity in the body of Christ is the Holy Family of Jesus, Mary and Joseph and how they lived together in perfect harmony; apparently, he continued on along that vein for five or ten minutes. When he finished, Colonel Cobb asked if there were any more questions.

"Do the priests think that we will accept putting our children together with the Negroes?"

Fr. McKenna answered with a sermon on the unity the faithful paralleling the Holy Trinity — a monologue that went on longer than the first two. This was not what the people wanted to hear. They wanted to question me. One observer noted that Fr. McKenna was as elusive as a ghost. They couldn't grab hold of him. They wanted Fr. McSorley. They were completely frustrated by Horace's prayers and sermons. Some of the crowd began to leave to continue the discussion elsewhere — at the local bars. The next day I heard that at Raley's bar at about 4 a.m. one of the men, who by that time had drunk more than he needed, got up and said in a slurred voice, "Do you know what Jesus said just before he died?" There was a chorus of "No."

"It says right here in the Bible that Jesus said, 'I'm sorry I ever made niggers.'"

There were other examples of liquor-induced theology expressed that night. I slept soundly in my own bed without any fear; although if I had known they were drinking, I wouldn't have slept so well.

Shortly after this meeting, a petition was circulated to have me removed from the parish. The study club members started a counter-petition to have me stay — a move not expected by those who started the first petition nor by me I was told later by the Jesuit provincial that the petition to have me removed never reached him, but the petition to have me stay did.

By now I no longer found my assignment at Ridge so difficult. It's paradoxical: Working for racial justice was no easy job, but the very difficulty gave me assurance that I was doing something important, something God wanted me to do, something needed for the Church and for the country.

The year was 1950. Martin Luther King, Jr. had not yet arrived on the scene. I didn't have any broad knowledge of racism in America, but I was learning. All along I knew I had the support of many Black people, and I began to develop friendships in the Black community including Aloysius and Bea Butler. I always felt welcome in their home and humbled by their faith and lifestyle. Every time I went to Aloysius' yard, I saw two or three children there, but they weren't always the same children. I finally asked him how many children he had. "We haven't got any children of our own so we take care of our neighbors' children." Over a period of years Aloysius and Bea raised fourteen children. They were adoptive parents without any legal arrangement.

The Butlers lived in a small home they had built a few hundred feet off of Three Notch Road, not far from St. James church. The house had a small porch, two small bedrooms, a parlor full of holy pictures, a kitchen with a wood stove but no running water. There was no bathroom, but an outhouse located some distance from the house. Aloysius built other people's homes and piped water into their kitchens; but when I asked him why he had no indoor plumbing or water in his own house, he said, "We don't need it. We have a well with a water pipe attached in the backyard. We have our own outhouse in the backyard."

"What do you do for hot water to wash the dishes and to take a bath?"

"We heat water on the stove."

"Are you planning to put running water in someday?"

"Maybe someday I'll get around to it."

But he never did.

Like most Black men at Ridge, he held many part-time jobs: oystering during the season, building and drilling wells at other times. He took me out on his oyster boat several times. Sometimes he used the long wooden-handled tongs that would scoop up oysters from a depth of twenty feet. Other times he would hand pick the oysters from shallow water.

Once we went to a picnic on the edge of the water. Some of the leaders of the Negro study group were there, and I felt most welcome and at home, sharing their joy in each other's company. I laughed at the funny stories they'd tell about efforts at desegregation that hadn't worked.

I needed times like this because after my sermon on the evil of segregation, everything I said and did was interpreted by the whites as an attack on segregation. If I talked about baptism making us all children of God, this was anti-segregation. If I ate supper with a Negro family in the parish or even went to a Negro wedding party, I was breaking the color bar. Everyday living in this culture afforded me new experiences that confirmed my growing conviction that segregation was sin: A Negro father of six children from another parish asked me for instruction in the faith. He asked me the inevitable question: "How are Negroes treated in your church?" I answered, "The people in my church don't follow the gospel, the pope, the bishop, or me. They follow their custom of segregation. I suppose, if you can't suffer that, you can't be a Catholic down in this area."

"Don't worry about me, Father. I figure that if some people think they are better than others and sit on one side to show it, I just ask myself, 'Which side would Christ sit on?' That's the side I want to sit on."

Then there were the Knights of Columbus. I had accepted the invitation to be their chaplain before establishing my conviction about the evils of segregation. With this new conviction I asked about the admittance of Negro members. I learned that a new member's acceptance could be blocked, using secret ballots, by the "no" vote of only two members. I knew we'd never get anywhere by that direct route, so I initiated a public discussion about it at the council meeting. I argued that the Knights could be a great help to the church if they led the way in the difficult struggle for integration. The discussion soon became so heated that Leo Weiland asked me to lead the council in the peace prayer of St. Francis of Assisi. It was clear that no Negro would be admitted. One of the arguments was that the Knights of St. Peter Claver, an All-Negro Catholic fraternity active in the area, would be adversely affected. To that, I replied that this council of St. Peter Claver was formed because of the Knights' refusal to admit Negro members. If this group wanted to join with the Knights of St. Peter Claver, I suggested it would be worth trying.

As a follow-up to this discussion, I asked the Knights to invite Fr. LaFarge (who was coming down to Ridge for one of his regular visits) to speak with them. They agreed. At the meeting one Knight said, "I'd rather sail off to convert the heathens in China than invite Negroes to come into my bar."

Fr. LaFarge agreed that it might be easier to go off to China. Another Knight asked Fr. LaFarge, "Why should we be burdened with integration when all the Catholic churches and schools around are segregated?"

"Suppose," said Fr. LaFarge, "that you were sitting around at a meeting four hundred years ago in Paris to discuss how you should lead a holy life. Suppose the argument was as follows: Why should we lead a holy life when the pope is away from Rome in Avignon, the local bishops are off hunting, the nearby pastors have concubines, and the mother superior in the convent is a drunk? What would you answer?"

They offered no answer so he continued, "I think if all the leaders in the Church fail to do their job, fail to be holy, it's even more important that lay people be holy. If we really believe that the Holy Spirit is guiding the Church, then all of us have an obligation to obey the Holy Spirit no matter what others do. The same thing applies to segregation. If all the church leaders were doing their job of opposing segregation, it wouldn't be as important for lay people to do anything. But since, as you say, they are not doing their job, then it's more important than ever that you do yours."

No one at the meeting was converted, but no doubt what these men heard weakened their resistance to ending segregation. Fr. LaFarge told me that the Knights of Columbus in Cleveland were struggling with the same problem. I think that is where the first Negroes were admitted to the Knights.

At the time, I wrote to the bishop who was the supreme chaplain to the Knights and asked him to advocate for a change in the admission procedure that would allow Negroes to join. I also told the St. Michael's council that if Negroes were barred, I would not be able to continue as chaplain. I resigned and they chose Fr. Baldwin.

I also wrote a letter to *America* magazine congratulating Fr. Joseph Ficther, S.J. on his biography of Bishop Healy, entitled, *Holy Outcast*. Bishop Healy was the son of a Negro woman and a white man from Georgia. The father brought the family north so the children could get an education. One of the sons became the first bishop of Maine, another, a Jesuit, became president of Georgetown University. In my letter, which was printed, I said that parish priests like myself were aided by biographers like this. My letter read, "We try to chip away at the mountain of segregation: Your writings dynamite the mountain." A short time later I was summoned by the Jesuit provincial to come to Baltimore. When I arrived, he said, "Who censors the letters you send out?"

"Fr. McKenna is the house censor."

He restrained a laugh and said, "From now on anything you write about segregation is to be sent to this office for censorship."

"But *America* is a Jesuit magazine," I insisted. "The editor of a Jesuit magazine is generally approved as a censor."

"Not for you. What might be read and found acceptable in New York would be quite objectionable down here. For instance, in New York you could have colored and white boys serving Mass together, but you couldn't have it down here."

"I'm glad you bring that up, because I've had colored and white boys serving Mass together in my church for over a year now." He did not comment, but his prohibition remained. It was very clear to me that nothing opposed to segregation would be approved for publication.

As a parish priest, I was fortunate that my archbishop, Patrick O'Boyle, was one of the national leaders opposing segregation. I never expected to be in a situation with two superiors holding contradictory views on a moral issue. I knew they both couldn't be right.

My relationship to Jesuit authority was illustrated in a dialogue with Fr. Baldwin. One afternoon he asked me, "Can I see your parish books?" meaning the financial records.

"Merle, if you are asking as a friend the answer is 'Yes, you can see the books.' But if you are demanding to see the books as Jesuit superior of the house, the answer is 'No.'"

"Why are you making a distinction between my asking as a friend or as a superior?"

"Because as a friend, you are requesting. As a superior, you are ordering. As a pastor, I take no orders regarding the parish from the order, only from the diocese."

"Who says so?"

"Canon law says that a religious who is pastor is exempt from all his obligations to his religious order that interfere with his duties as a pastor."

"You are cutting my authority very thin, aren't you?"

"It is not I who am doing the cutting. I never wanted to be a pastor, but now I am. I will act like one. Besides, you know very well everything that's in the books. You know how much comes in each week, how much is recorded in a year. You managed the books before I arrived."

"As Jesuit superior in this house, is there anything over which I have authority in regards to you."

"Yes," I said, pausing to think of something. "If I were to going away on vacation, you would have authority to give me money for the vacation." Merle just walked away. Looking back, I thank God that Merle was so patient. He never said a harsh or unkind word to me. A man of few words, he never appeared angry.

11 ❖ *Called Up and Out*

After I'd been at Ridge about three years, I received a phone call from the Jesuit provincial. I was over at St. Michael's convent across the road from our rectory talking to one of the sisters. We were all on the same party line, and I heard the rectory phone code ring, the ring for St. Peter's, and then finally the code for the convent. It was for me.

When I got on the line, I was greeted by Fr. Nugent who asked, "What are you doing over there?"

"Talking to one of the sisters." From the silent pause I could tell he was annoyed by the simplicity of the answer.

"My desk is littered with reports about you."

I answered, "Remember you are talking on a party line."

We agreed to meet in Baltimore that afternoon When I told Horace about the phone call, he immediately offered to go along in support It was clear that segregation was the topic of our meeting and that my future at Ridge was on the line. I felt at ease about whatever might come. I still felt that any change for me would be a promotion, although by now I was no longer eager to leave Ridge.

When he was president of Woodstock College, Fr. Nugent had been nicknamed "Nifty Nugent" as he was always nattily dressed even though he wore clericals. He was about sixty years old, bald, round-faced, and rotund of build. As I sat down, I asked, "What is it you've heard about me?"

"Suppose you let me ask the questions?" His desk was not littered with anything. It was swept bare.

"If the Jesuit superior wanted to officiate at a marriage in your church, would he have to ask your permission?"

"Yes."

"Where did you get that authority?" he asked.

"From the bishop."

"When?"

"In the letter the bishop sent me when I arrived at Ridge." He seemed annoyed, yet with his doctorate in canon law, he should have known that pastoral appointments are made by the bishop.

"Suppose you wanted to celebrate a wedding at the Jesuit superior's church, would you have to get his permission?"

"No."

"You can officiate at his church without his permission, but he can't officiate at your church without your permission?"

"Yes."

"Why?"

"Because I am appointed as associate pastor at his church." He seemed miffed and frustrated.

"Let me pose another question. You will admit that Fr. McKenna's church is a colored church?"

"Well, I'll admit it's a red brick church."

His face flushed, "You're making distinctions that I didn't put in."

"You're making distinctions by calling it a colored church. It's a Catholic church."

His voice rose, "Well, rightly or wrongly, it's a colored church."

"Yes, wrongly, it's a colored church."

"It was set up to be a colored church."

"I'm glad you bring up its history. In 1915 Fr. Tynan, pastor of St. Michael's, brought a colored choir in to sing for Christmas. After Mass the white people stormed into the sacristy to demand that the choir never return. Fr. Tynan got so angry that he said he would never celebrate Mass again at St. Michael's. He built a chapel, St. Peter's, in the woods to celebrate Mass with the colored people."

I could see that this point did not impress Fr. Nugent, so I asked him again to enumerate the complaints about me.

"I was told you were organizing in Washington to get Negroes to refuse to work for whites. Is that true?"

I could scarcely believe the question. "I can't imagine where that complaint came from. Washington is seventy-five miles away, and I rarely get there."

"Have you had anything to do with the restaurants in Washington?"

I could only think of one possible incident: a trip Fr. McKenna, Fr. Cavanaugh and I made. Fr. Cavanaugh brought along with him his aged janitor and his wife. We went to see the musical *Madame Butterfly*. During the performance our guests napped. Later, the janitor remarked, "It was gran' sleepin' music." After the play, hungry and seventy-five miles from home, we headed for a restaurant. Five establishments refused to serve us because our guests were Black. Although we confronted the managers, we still didn't get service. On our fifth try, a Negro waiter told us that he would serve us if we moved into a corner and sat behind a screen. So after a two-hour try, we finally got served.

Fr. Nugent did not have any response or any further questions. On the way back to Ridge Fr. McKenna and I decided that I should write him an answer to what we thought was his hidden question: "Are parish lines a way to control the situation at Ridge."

What was behind Fr. Nugent's questions? He was looking for some reason to put the priests at Ridge in at least two parishes, not three. Then he could have more control. Yet he knew that the diocese wanted three parishes and three priests. Meanwhile, Horace and I had an agenda of our own: By combining the three parishes into one, the people would be integrated. I wrote to him as follows:

> Reflection on our conversation has led me to suggest that St. Peter's, St. Michael's, and St. James be unified into one. That would lessen the number of priests that the Jesuits have to supply, and it would lessen the economic expense. It might please the archbishop because he is interested in bringing the people together.

He promptly answered that it was very helpful to get on-the- spot suggestions from someone actively engaged in the area. He didn't indicate any understanding that unifying parishes would mean racial integration.

The response of Fr. Nugent reflected the prevalent attitude among the Jesuits in Southern Maryland. For example, one day while attending a funeral, I rode with Fr. Bill Kelly, a much older man and a former pastor at Leonardtown. He asked, "Does your opposition to segregation mean you condemn all the Jesuits like me who preceded you?"

I answered, "Quite the contrary. Your work prepared the way. In earlier times the opportunity to oppose segregation was not as great as it is now."

On a visit to the Jesuit seminary at Woodstock, I ran into a similar question from Fr. Harding Fisher, former master of novices and much respected spiritual director to the seminarians. At lunch he asked me if I thought the Jesuits should admit Negroes. When I advocated for admission of Negroes, he asked, "What could they do in the Society? Certainly the Jesuits would accept them, but the people would not."

"Well, as long as they were accepted by other Jesuits, they could be spiritual fathers like you or they could be provincials who deal only with other Jesuits. Neither position requires acceptance by the laity."

"You are very serious about this, aren't you?"

"Yes, I think this is a matter of faith."

I did make a favorable impression on Fr. Nugent by helping to renovate the old chapel at St. Indigo's, the site of the first Catholic church in Maryland. About three miles from the rectory at St. Michael's, it was right next to Pautuxent River Naval Air Station. Volunteers from Pautuxent and Ridge assisted in the renovation: clearing trees, repairing the roof, installing electricity, and piecing together broken gravestones and statues. I put together a little historical booklet, *Maryland's First Chapel.*

In studying the history of the old chapel, I learned that early Jesuits in Maryland kept slaves, though some objected and refused to participate. Finally the provincial ordered the Jesuits to get rid of the slaves in such a way that the families be kept together and have a chance to practice their faith. Because freed slaves were usually recaptured and enslaved again, the Jesuits sold entire families to owners in the deep South — a decision that met the provincial's orders, but was hardly just.

In June 1952 the annual list of province appointments arrived in the mail. I was surprised to see that I was appointed to teach philosophy at Scranton University. I did not expect this after the provincial had told me that the archbishop didn't want me moved. But I suppose he thought that four years had been a respectable tenure; in moving me now, he wouldn't appear to be surrendering to segregationists. The respectable position of philosophy professor would silence any rumor that I was being punished for my views. It looked like a promotion.

Before I departed, Horace McKenna organized a farewell party for me in the former skating rink at St. James hall. We had a dinner and dance, completely integrated, even the band. Even a year before I wouldn't have dreamed that this could happen. Fr. McKenna presented me with a book, *The Bishops Speak,* containing many social encyclicals. He had inscribed the flyleaf with this message: "To the Rev. Richard T. McSorley, S.J., of the Society of Jesus, 1948-52, Devoted Father of all, Teacher of Justice and Charity, Shepherd of inside and outside sheep, serviceman and civilian, Minister of that special love which His Holiness, Pope Pius XII himself feels for the Negro people of America, who need and deserve aid in religion and education, Pastor of St. James Church, Park

Hall, St. Mary's County, Maryland, Uniting all people in the chanted offering of the Holy Sacrifice of the Mass and in the brotherly participation of all people, this feast of St. Lawrence, 1952 from his people and his associates in the Sacred Heart of Jesus and the Immaculate Heart of Mary." He also wrote on the flap, a poem by one of the Negro women, Mrs. Andy Carroll:

> Just about four years ago
> A pastor came we did not know
> To our church he was a sign
> He'll make this parish rise and shine.
> An unusual man he seemed to me
> Faith, Hope, and Charity
> He had all three.
> His work made us understand
> He was a God-chosen man.
> He gave us privileges we never had.
> To leave us now it makes us sad
> To lose a friend so kind and true
> No one knows but God and you.
> Now comes that time when he must part.
> Gee, it really breaks our heart.
> We hope he'll always keep in mind
> Good old St. James he left behind.

And parishioners signed their names on several pages in the front and back of the book.

Before closing this chapter on Ridge I want to add two postscripts. First, ten years later on a trip to Ridge I had Easter breakfast in the home of Pete Carroll. Pete had been the leader of the petition to get me removed. In his home I was verbally attacked at the turkey festival meeting. This Easter Sunday morning he asked me to step outside to talk with him. Out in the sunlight on his farm he said, "Father, I just want to tell you that I know you were right ten years ago. You were right to get us to oppose segregation. All of the other churches have had their difficulties with it like we did. We were ahead of all of them thanks to you."

The other note: In 1972, I returned to stay overnight with Aloysius and Bea Butler. To a friend I introduced him as "the man who by his faith first opened my eyes to the evils of segregation." He had changed my life, and it seems I had changed his. Aloysius told my friend, "Before Father McSorley came here, if I was in a room and a white man came in, I would just move into a corner and be quiet. After Father McSorley left, I wasn't in the corner anymore. I just talk to a white man like I talk to anybody else."

I can now thank God for sending me to Ridge.

IV

From Parish to Classroom

— ✤ ✤ ✤ —

12 ✢ *Scranton*

My new assignment contrasted starkly to my previous life. I came from Ridge, the oldest Jesuit foundation in the U.S. to one of the newest: Scranton University, taken over from the Christian Brothers around 1948. They had moved me to the northern-most corner of the Maryland province, the furthest they could get me from Ridge and still keep me within the province. Scranton, Pennsylvania was a very "white" city, and I'm sure my superiors thought that with very few Black people around, my enthusiasm for breaking the color bar would wane.

However, distance did not deter me. I kept up correspondence with the study club in Ridge. Soon I got a letter from the provincial: "Some of the priests in the county complain that you are interfering with their work by writing to your friends in the county. Consequently, I order you to stop any such correspondence." I replied that my letters were encouraging and promoting racial justice. I could be interfering only with those who were trying to block racial justice. The provincial never answered, and his order to stop the correspondence remained in force.

My day-to-day life at Scranton was worlds away from life at Ridge. I remember making friends with only one Negro, Mr. Johnson. Because he was blind, he had a seeing-eye dog. One evening I took him to the university library to use a tape recorder. As we walked to the building, I said, "The steps up to the library are on your right."

"Tell the dog," Mr. Johnson replied.

I felt foolish trying to talk to the dog. What was I going to say? "You talk to the dog. I don't know what to say to him."

"Right," he said, and the dog turned right. "Up," he said, and the dog started up the steps.

I was impressed by his control of the dog. Although I got a good laugh when Mr. Johnson explained how the dog would get back at him when punished by leading him into a wall or a puddle.

From him I learned a bit about what it is to be blind. He lived alone in a world of darkness. His segregation from sighted people was so profound that he hardly noticed racial segregation. I told him about Aloysius Butler and my experiences at Ridge. Though he was interested, his sightlessness was a greater social obstacle than race.

I remember a day of great joy in 1954. I picked up the newspaper and read the headlines: "Supreme Court Outlaws Racial Segregation in Schools." I read all I could about that court decision. Remembering all our struggles at Ridge, I thanked God the tide had turned.

In that next year, 1955, I read about Martin Luther King and the Alabama bus boycott. From that day on I followed everything he did. My experiences at Ridge gave me great insight into his leadership, the danger he faced, and his faith in God. When the boycott ended a year later with a victorious Supreme Court decision outlawing segregated public transportation, I rejoiced and thanked God. During these years I thought that segregation was on its way out. Decades later I realize that it is still going strong, though it no longer has the institutional support of legal structures.

My first classes at Scranton were epistemology and metaphysics, which I had not studied since 1939. Before I could teach it, I had to learn it all over again, which gave me little time for anything else. I also taught Spanish, which I had learned on my own in the prisoner-of-war camp.

Scranton was a union town. The United Mine Workers of America had given the university a subsidy to send lecturers to nearby towns to teach the miners about their rights and social justice. Intrigued with this, I volunteered to go once a week with Fr. Frank Wallner to Hazelton and to some other towns.

I in turn invited Joe Walsh, union supporter and journalist, to come to my classes to explain the meaning and functioning of unions. Joe, a Catholic devoted to the teachings contained in the social encyclicals, had found that some Catholic priests were not at all interested in social justice. He quoted one priest as saying, "When I was in the seminary, I asked God to deliver me from the devil and from union organizers." At Joe's invitation, my philosophy class and I attended some of the union meetings of his Newspaper's Guild in Wilkes-Barre.

As I continued to teach philosophy, I requested time off to get a Ph.D. When that request was denied, I then enrolled in Ottawa University in Canada, one of the few places where a Ph.D. could be obtained in the summer. For my thesis I wrote on prejudice, using my experience at Ridge as the main topic. One week from taking the final exam, I was notified by mail that two of my three readers had not approved my thesis. My exams were indefinitely postponed and the degree denied. But like the disappointment of my assignment to Ridge, this eventually proved to be a blessing. Had I obtained the degree, I might have remained lost in philosophy for the rest of my life. As it was, I think I learned as much as if the degree had been granted. Perhaps it is lingering sour grapes, but my respect for the doctoral degree has declined as the years have passed.

In 1954, all Jesuits received a letter from the general superior, Fr. Jansen, asking for volunteers to go to Japan to be part of the international apostolate to promote the faith there. Since it seemed that desegregation was on its way and I would no longer be needed in the racial struggle, I volunteered to go to Japan. A few months later the Maryland provincial, Fr. Maloney, wrote saying that he was appointing me to be part of the Maryland mission in India. Years before I had volunteered to go to India and now an assignment was open. I wrote to Fr. Maloney to explain that I was waiting to hear about an assignment in Japan. He agreed to wait until I had heard from Rome. After several months I received a letter from Fr. Jansen, "In the opinion of some grave and pious fathers of the Maryland province, you would do better to use your talents in the U.S. rather than go to Japan."

I replied, "In the opinion of some of the grave and pious fathers of the Maryland province, anyone who spoke against racial injustice was imprudent and untrustworthy for any important assignment, and since I have spoken publicly about racial justice, the opinion you get from these 'grave and pious' fathers may be based on racial prejudice." He never replied. I never went to Japan or India. I got another contract at Scranton University. They were stuck with me.

As a general rule, the provincial made a yearly visit to each priest. When the new provincial, Fr. Daley, came to visit me in Scranton, he told a story he thought would please me: "You'll be happy to learn how we solved a racial problem in my sister's family. When a neighbor moved out, the community feared that real estate values would drop if the house were sold to a Negro family. So the neighbors solved the problem by collecting money among themselves and bought the house. Then they could decide who would come in." Unfortunately, this was not an uncommon approach to dealing with the "race problem." He, like others, seemed unaware of the destructive nature of this outlook.

In 1961 I wrote to the provincial reminding him that the Jesuit Constitution required the superior be changed every six years and that the time had already expired for replacement of the rector. I let the provincial know that if he were not going to remove the rector (who made it difficult for me to do social justice work), perhaps he should move me to a place where I could better serve the people of God.

Little did I expect that my request would be granted. I liked Scranton and its people, but the institutional impediments to work for social justice had become unbearable. So I was pleasantly surprised when, in June 1961, I found my name on the list to teach philosophy at Georgetown University in Washington, D.C.

13 ❖ *Georgetown and the Kennedys*

My first evening at Georgetown, the director of athletics, Fr. Hoggson, asked me to be freshman tennis coach and acting varsity coach. We met on the first day I entered the novitiate back in 1932, and he knew that I had been captain of the tennis team at St. Joseph's Prep School and had won tennis tournaments at the seminary. This would hardly qualify me to be a college coach, but I knew the game, enjoyed it, and was glad to accept the offer — an offer that would alter my life in a most dramatic way.

About a week later I got a phone call from a woman who introduced herself as Mrs. Robert Kennedy's secretary. "I would like to know if you can provide tennis instruction for Mrs. Kennedy's children?" I was incredulous and then suspected a prank by a fellow Jesuit — certainly she had been put up to this. I insisted she give me her phone number so I could call back. Stifling her laughter, she complied. I thought I was pretty smart until I called the operator and discovered the number supplied by the secretary was unlisted. Sheepishly, I dialed back and the same woman, still laughing, answered. I arranged to have our best varsity player instruct the Kennedy children. This seemed to work well for everyone.

It was through this simple introduction that I came to know the Kennedy family. I made a visit to Robert and Ethel's home in Virginia in order to check on how the tennis lessons were progressing and to invite them to visit Georgetown and meet the Jesuit community. We hit it off, and by that afternoon I was playing tennis with Robert and Ethel Kennedy. (I will not recount the results of our matches.)

Soon after our first meeting, Ethel asked me to tutor the oldest boys, Joe and Bobby, Jr.: "I would like you to help them with their homework, which they should begin about 4 p.m., and if you don't get it finished before supper, maybe you'd be able to stay and help them. You eat supper here when that happens." I agreed. Generally we didn't finish the lessons until late evening. I remember one evening Bobby, Jr. had to write the names of the U.S. cabinet members. Having finished all the list except the name of the attorney-general, he said,. "I think I just might write my name there."

Each evening I had supper with Ethel Kennedy and the children over five. Younger children ate a little earlier. During supper the children talked about all that had happened during the day. All of the children were precocious, distinct, and a joy to be around.

In 1963, a defiant Governor George Wallace refused to let Blacks into the University of Alabama. Robert Kennedy's job was to enforce federal law prohibiting such segregation. Tensions ran high. Through all of this, life at the Kennedy household remained calm and gracious, with Ethel and the older children giving Robert full and unconditional support. Along with the family, I watched the television reports with great interest.

A day after the Black students entered the University of Alabama, President Kennedy condemned segregation as immoral, illegal, and contrary to American ideals. I was delighted to hear his talk. He was the first president to use the full power of his office to condemn segregation.

In addition to weekdays, I was often at the Kennedy's on Saturdays and Sundays for tennis. One day Ethel said:

> "Last night we had Bishop Vagnozzi here for supper. We also had a Protestant guest, who didn't seem to know what to say to the bishop, so she said, 'What a beautiful crucifix. Where did you get it?' to which the Bishop replied, 'Oh, I have another more beautiful than this at home.'

> "It was disgusting. A bishop talking about jewelry. Bobby changed the subject: 'Bishop, what can you do about segregation in the south?' 'I am only the eyes and ears of the Pope. I don't touch ground,' he said. [Bishop Vagnozzi was the apostolic delegate at the time.]

> "Bobby said, 'Well, you know it's pretty discouraging as a Catholic to go down to Alabama and ask the governor and businessmen to end segregation for patriotic reasons and find that my own Church is one of the most segregated institutions in the South.' Bobby kept the topic on segregation throughout the meal, and the bishop didn't like it at all."

A few days after this conversation, I was on the Kennedy back lawn having a lunch of hot dogs and cokes with Ethel and the children when Robert, pulling a sweater over his head, came out of the house. When he got near the table, Ethel said in a loud voice, "Father, what can be done about Catholic schools that are segregated?" Robert paid no attention to the question.

"Well," I answered, "they should go to the bishop about it."

Ethel continued casting her eyes back and forth between Robert and me. "But suppose the bishop won't do anything about it? Then what can you do?" Robert still said nothing but by now was seated at the end of the table opposite her.

"You can go to the apostolic delegate," I said.

"Well, if the apostolic delegate won't do anything about it, what do you do?"

At this point Robert stood up and walked along the table saying, "Dear John, . . ."

Ethel exclaimed, "Oh Bobby, let me write that letter!"

At that moment a branch cracked in the tree above our lunch table. We looked up and one of the children was dangerously perched on that limb. A quick rescue forced a change in topics. But some time later John Kennedy met Pope John XXIII and talked about segregation. Not long afterward Bishop Toolan of Mobile, Alabama integrated the Catholic schools in his diocese.

Despite the hectic schedule kept by Robert, he always made time to be at home. Typically, he arrived from the Justice Department for a late supper and often brought guests with whom he discussed business. Ethel, having sat through supper with the children, dined with Robert. In the evening Robert would spend time reading and playing with the children, then return to work at home or back at his office.

Though I saw him less frequently, Robert and I developed a warm relationship; often he would express gratitude for my assistance on the home-front. In turn, I would express to him my gratitude for the efforts of his brother's administration, especially as it concerned civil rights and desegregation.

Meanwhile, back on the Georgetown campus, all was not roses. Not long after my arrival at Georgetown, I was refused permission to attend The National Catholic Interracial Council meeting in Chicago. While in Scranton, I had attended some local Catholic Interracial meetings in New York where I had always been welcomed by Fr. LaFarge. Though my expenses were to be paid by Crossroads Africa (because they invited me to lead of a group of white students who spent the summer working on housing and agriculture projects in Africa), Fr. Bunn, president of Georgetown and Jesuit superior, turned down my request.

Also, there was growing racial tension on campus. After the all-white G.U. basketball team was beaten by Fordham, whose best player was a young Black man from D.C., students began to complain. But even those who supported the idea of Black players were reluctant to recruit any, citing that with only one scholarship to give, the lone Black player would be isolated. There were other more practical problems: If a Black student at Georgetown needed dental work and went to the campus dental clinic, he would be told, "You go to Howard University [an all Black school at that time] to get your teeth fixed." The Georgetown dental school did not accept Blacks because "they have their own school." Memories of Ridge! Georgetown Hospital accepted Black patients, but in segregated wards.

Yet I saw at Georgetown and in D.C. many great opportunities to work for social justice. After a year or so of teaching philosophy, I volunteered to teach a theology course called "Catholic Social Teaching." (I was accepted to teach the course when no one else could be found.) That gave me a wide opportunity to teach social justice and introduced me to the theology of peace. I was soon teaching two sections of the course and, at my request, was moved into the theology department.

I discovered the weekly meetings of the Leadership Conference for Civil Rights and was accepted as a member even though most members were representatives of established organizations. The meetings, designed to organize a lobby for racial justice, were alive and practical. I rejoiced to be part of it and began walking the halls of Congress trying to get civil rights bills passed. Dr. Martin Luther King, Jr. met with the Leadership Conference on several occasions. That's where I first met Dr. King; his friendliness, intelligence, sense of humanity, and passion for justice were evident as I watched him talk informally with a few members following the meeting.

During the early days of the civil rights struggle, I was impressed by the faith of Fr. Dan and Phil Berrigan. Dan, a fellow seminarian, introduced me to his younger brother, Phil, who had come to visit. Phil was planning to enter the Josephite Congregation, a community dedicated to serving the Negro people. Having no special interest in civil rights at that time, I never talked to Dan or Phil about the race question. By the 60s they were in the news as the most public Catholic clergy active for racial justice. They faced arrest and even risked their lives on the "freedom rides": buses filled with Blacks and whites together from New York to Mississippi. As the buses reached the South, the riders were beaten and the buses burned. The Berrigans rode on!

One Southern bishop convinced their religious superiors to order them off the bus so they wouldn't ride through the bishop's diocese. But they were soon back, helping the Congress of Racial Equality groups desegregate lunch counters and public accommodations. Dan and Phil were the first Catholic priests I knew personally who risked their lives for the faith. In my estimation they, joined with Martin Luther King, Jr., have been Christ figures for our times.

My own experience at Ridge helped me appreciate their faith and the price of their leadership in the cause for racial justice.

My relationship with the Kennedy's continued to grow. One evening at supper, Ethel invited me to join her and the children for a movie.

"Which theater are we going to," I asked.

"I thought you knew. We're going to the White House."

Ethel drove the car with the roof down, and the children sang as we sped along the George Washington Parkway. We arrived at the south gate of the White House where the guard counted off the names of the children on his list. "And you can add on Fr. McSorley and these two children, friends of the family."

The guards seemed perturbed. "If you're going to add on more names, Mrs. Kennedy, the list is useless. But go right in." I got the idea that the guards had a hard time keeping track of the Kennedys, but wanted to take no chance on refusing them.

As we drove in toward the front door, one of the children yelled, "There's Uncle Jack on the porch talking to someone." The porch projects out over the front door on the river side of the White House and is called the South Portico.

"Quiet everybody!" ordered Ethel. "Uncle Jack has a visitor." As we pulled to a stop at the steps just under the porch, one of the older children yelled, "All right everybody. All together." They replied with a loud "Here we are!" President Kennedy leaned over the rail and waved, then returned his attention to his guest.

We went in and were led to the movie room. Everything was set up. Forty or fifty Kennedy children and relatives were already there. Ethel told me to sit in the front in a chair near some empty seats. "You will have a better view, and the children will not get in your way," she said. Soon after the movie started, I noticed that eight-year-old Michael Kennedy was poking someone in the chair next to me, then hid behind the chair, out of sight. The chair had been empty when the film began, but in the dark President Kennedy and the First Lady had taken the seats next to me. Michael was poking his Uncle Jack, who turned looking for the perpetrator only to find me. "I didn't see you there in the dark Father," he said, reaching out to shake hands with me.

"How do you like the film? " I asked.

"I've seen it before," he replied. It was *PT 109*, his biographical war story.

This film party was obviously an informal family gathering. Though they left before the film ended, I could see that the President and Mrs. Kennedy wore bathrobes. I seemed to be the only adult non-family participant. Apparently they came to see the children and to be sure that the program was running smoothly.

Some months later, I was invited to the White House by Ms. Mary Boylan, the social secretary to the president. "Come at about 10 a.m.," she said.

At the side gate the guard refused to let me in. "Your name isn't on the visitor's list," he said.

"Will you phone Ms. Boylan?"

"We are not allowed to phone."

I went across the street to the treasury office. I headed for the first-floor office of Jim Rowley, head of the Secret Service and brother of my friend Pat Rowley, S.J. I asked the secretary to phone Ms. Boylan and tell her I could not get in.

"Come right over to the guardhouse, and I will be there to meet you," she said.

Waiting when I arrived, she introduced me to the guard, "Major, this is Fr. McSorley. I hope you will recognize him and admit him the next time I invite him?"

"But the rules say no telephone calls for visitors."

"Major, if you can't bend the rules when necessary, you don't belong as a part of the "New Frontier" (Kennedy's name for his administration). The visit was basically a private tour of the White House, rooms not open to the public: the Lincoln Room, East Room, Oval Office, the press room. During the tour, the president's helicopter had landed on the lawn. We watched as he strode rapidly from the helicopter toward the house. From the first floor full of visitors came screams of delight as they saw the president. He waved and smiled at them as he passed. "He brings a great spirit to the place," Mary said. "We are all very happy to be here with him."

One day at the Robert Kennedy home, Ethel stopped swimming and from the pool asked me if I was interested in going to Hyannis Port during the summer? I expressed to her that I was beginning to worry that my close relationship with the family might prompt the then Republican university president to move me from Georgetown.

"Oh, I get the idea," replied Ethel. "You're just helping us until you get caught."

"It's not exactly that, but something like it."

She said no more, but the next afternoon I received a call from Bishop Hannan (the auxiliary bishop of Washington) who offered to smooth the way. By the end of our conversation, it was clear that the Kennedys had pulled some strings, and my concerns about being moved were allayed.

It should be made clear that my support for the Kennedy administration was based on its policies for racial justice and my personal relationship with the family. At the time I was not concerned about his war and peace policies.

When President Kennedy made his announcement of the blockade of Cuba, I was watching it on TV with a group of Jesuits. As Kennedy spoke, a Jesuit behind me said, "That is an act of war." But I was not disturbed because I trusted Kennedy. Later that morning a student asked if I would go to the chapel to hear confessions. "There are so many students waiting, but not enough priests," he said. At the chapel I found six or seven priests, but the lines were still long. I asked the first student who came to me in the confessional, "Why are so many students here for confession?"

"They are worried about nuclear weapons in Cuba."

"Are they afraid they will all be killed because of the blockade of Soviet ships?"

"Yes."

I began to think maybe I should be afraid.

Soon after hearing confessions, I got a phone call from a friend, Marie Carroll, asking me to join a picket line of the White House in protest of the blockade.

"Give Kennedy a chance to work it out," I said. "I trust Kennedy. There won't be any war."

It took thirteen days to end the danger, and Robert Kennedy was the major influence in what I saw as a peaceful solution of the crisis. Years later my opinion on the crisis changed. I now see the Cuban blockade as bringing the world to the brink of a nuclear disaster that could never have been morally justified.

Then came that fateful day, November 22, 1963. I was in the office of Professor Jesse Mann talking philosophy when someone came to the door and announced, "The president has been shot." As we hurried to a nearby TV, I thought, "This will be a warning that will make him more careful in the future." I prayed for his recovery; but slowly the news got worse. I was deeply saddened at the announcement of his death.

Not long after, I received a phone call from a Kennedy family friend suggesting that I go over to McLean to be with Robert's children. When I arrived, police were guarding the place to keep the scores of photographers and curious public outside the fences. After I was admitted by the police, I took off my clerical collar and black jacket; I figured a white shirt would attract less attention. On the lawn Robert Kennedy and Allen Dulles, director of the CIA, walked back and forth between two telephones that occasionally rang for them. Robert introduced me to Mr. Dulles, but under the circumstances, there wasn't much time for small talk. Over several days I was in and out, offering daily Mass in the family parlor.

On television I watched as President Kennedy's coffin was brought into the Rotunda of the Capitol. I had a hard time recognizing the man leading the procession. It was Lyndon Johnson; it was even more difficult for me to think of him as president. That evening I joined the huge crowd who visited Kennedy's mortal remains under the Rotunda of the Capitol.

On the morning of the funeral procession, I got a phone call from Jackie Kennedy asking me to her home in Georgetown. She wanted to talk with me. From there I went by Secret Service car to the cathedral, well ahead of the funeral procession. In the silence of the cathedral I could hear the klop, klop of the horses as they neared the church door. After the Mass I accompanied the body to the cemetery. As the cortege passed over the Memorial Bridge, I saw a Green Beret soldier walking in the opposite direction. He stopped, faced the passing casket and saluted. I remember thinking, "It is wonderful to have such a great president." Then in another moment I realized again that he wasn't with us any longer. At the grave-site, Air Force One flew overhead and dipped its wings in a last salute.

After the president's assassination, many people asked me if I believed he was killed by the CIA. I generally replied, "No, because Robert Kennedy remained attorney general. If he had any suspicions at all about the CIA or FBI, he would have pursued it, even if it cost him his job. He would have done anything in his power to reveal a plot."

A few weeks after the assassination I got a message to phone Mrs. Kennedy. I returned the call expecting to get Ethel and was momentarily confused and surprised to find I had instead reached Jackie. Ethel had recommended me as a tennis instructor. Jackie and I agreed to meet at Robert's house for instruction over the noon hour each week-day.

When I arrived for the first lesson, Jackie was already there with four-year-old John, Jr. Caroline was in school. It didn't take me long to realize that she had some experience with the game. We spent the first hour just volleying. Meanwhile, about once a minute John would run onto the court to ask, "Mommy, when are we going swimming?" He was keen to get in to the nearby pool.

We kept no score and talked as we played. She had a lot of incisive questions about the resurrection, eternal life, glorified bodies, God's knowledge of the future. I did what I could to supply answers. When I got back to Georgetown, I looked for better answers in books and consulted theologians. The next day during our conversation I told her what I had learned.

One day Ethel told me she and Robert had suggested to Jackie that she leave Washington where everything reminded her of Jack. I thought it was a good idea and seconded it.

As she departed for New York, Jackie wrote me a kind personal note of thanks and extended an invitation: "Whenever you are in New York, stop in and visit the children and me. . . ."

I did visit her many times in New York and usually took John, Jr. out for a walk in Central Park accompanied by at least one Secret Service agent. Jackie lived on the fifteenth floor of a high-rise, and the first time I came in, the elevator operator said, "Good afternoon. What floor please?"

"Fifteenth," I replied.

"You want the fifteenth floor?"

By the time he asked this second question, another man stepped into the elevator. I didn't know it then but he was a Secret Service agent. When the elevator arrived at the fifteenth floor, the door opened immediately into the parlor of Mrs. Kennedy's suite. She and John, Jr. were there waiting for me. I learned later that I would not have reached the fifteenth floor if Mrs. Kennedy had not given advance approval. The next time, I looked for the Secret Service agents on the first floor before I went to the elevator. I got to know one of them, Mugsey O'Leary, who sometimes walked in the park with John and me.

One morning after saying Mass at St. Ignatius Church on Park Avenue, I walked over to visit Jackie, who asked if I would like to take John to the World's Fair. Soon John and I were riding along FDR Drive in a Secret Service car with Mugsey O'Leary and a second agent. They asked John puzzles like, "Who is buried in Grant's tomb?" John, Jr. knew the answer, "Grant."

On the way to the fair we stopped at a military airport so John could visit the air traffic controllers. Our car was escorted right up to the base of the tower. While we were watching the planes landing and taking off, a plane caught fire so we saw the fire engines in action. No one was hurt but it was a great show for the small boy.

When we arrived at the World's Fair, the director, Mr. Moses, welcomed us and took us to the main office where we signed the guest list to the delight of the staff. He escorted us to an official white station-wagon tended by two uniformed fair policemen. Now we were five men and a small boy in an official car, two in police uniforms, one in clerical black and two Secret Service officers in mufti.

When we stopped at the steeple chase ride, the man in charge met us and took us to the front of the line. I rode with John, who loved every dive and turn. By the time we started for the next exhibit, we were trailed by photographers and reporters; soon we led a convoy of reporters on scooters. At one exhibit where we had lunch, the manager sat at the table with us. She asked John to sing a song. John began "America the Beautiful." He knew the words and gathered an admiring audience.

In the space of about four hours we visited seventeen exhibits, most of them entertainment for children. When we returned to Park Avenue, Jackie asked, "Did you attract much publicity?"

"I don't see how we could have had more," I replied, telling her about the convoy of reporters.

"I expected there would be publicity. You can't be escorted," she said, "and go through lines to exhibits without attracting attention. It was the only way John could see it. I phoned Mr. Moses before you arrived to tell him you were on your way."

One evening following supper together, I visited with Jackie and the children. As it grew late, Jackie told John, "You get ready for bed, and maybe Father will come in to say good-night." When John was in bed, I went in as Jackie stood in the doorway. She said softly, "Do you know 'Danny Boy'? His father used to sing it to him just before he went to sleep. He used Johnny instead of Danny."

"I can try it."

John stared at me with fixed attention all the way through the song: "Oh Johnny Boy the pipes, the pipes are playing. . ." Jackie stood silently in the doorway looking at us. The heavy burden of their loss pressed in on me at that moment as never before. I was either in tears or close to it as I left the room. Jackie went over to say a prayer with her son and kiss him good-night.

Not that it even slightly compared to their loss, but I missed John Kennedy. He was not the only president I had ever known personally, but I thought he was the best we'd had.

14 ❖ *Martin Luther King, Jr. and the Civil Rights Struggle*

In 1963 Martin Luther King, Jr. called for a "Mississippi Summer" and asked white students to go south and help with voter registration drives. Because many Georgetown students accepted his invitation, their involvement made it easy for me to join them. I spent the summer visiting with them and marching with them at the courthouses and federal buildings in Georgia, Alabama and Mississippi. We accompanied local Blacks as they registered to vote, and thus placed ourselves in danger from the Ku Klux Klan and from white police.

At Crawford, Georgia, people advocating Black voter registration marched every Sunday afternoon to city hall where they would pray, listen to a speech about the right to vote, sing "God Bless America" and march away. When I was there, the group received a threat from the Ku Klux Klan that said if we marched the next Sunday, we would be attacked. When I heard about the threat, I was relieved that I had plans to be in Chicago that weekend to attend a Catholic Interracial Council meeting. (The new Jesuit superior did not object to my attendance.) However, I received a phone call from Father Bob Begin, a Dominican priest from the Cleveland diocese. He asked me to return for the march. I argued that it would be better to cancel the march for one Sunday than to risk being shot. "But if they can stop us one Sunday, they can stop us permanently," he said. "I'm going to march." Despite my misgivings, because of Bob's urging, I agreed to return.

That Sunday afternoon at 2 p.m. we assembled in a Protestant church — one-hundred fifty people, all Black except for Bob and me. Friends guarded our cars parked a good distance from the church. A speaker opened the event: "Y'all know why we are here. The Ku Klux Klan is waiting just over the hill. They've been riding through town in caravans all morning. We're going to walk down to the city hall as usual, two by two along the sidewalk, and witness to our right to vote. Before we leave, we will have a moment of silence." From the front of the church a woman broke the silence in a sorrowful voice, "Lord Jesus, save us."

In prayerful silence and terrified, we began to leave. As we walked down the steps of the church, I fell in line with a middle-aged, nicely-dressed woman. All the people were in their Sunday best. "Are you afraid?" I asked her.

"I used to be afraid, but no more."

I thought about how she would feel the next day — and that I (if I lived through the day) would be leaving that night, back to my secure environment. She had to put up with the threat of the Ku Klux Klan all her life; she truly had faith that God would lead her. Why couldn't I do that? Suddenly my fear vanished. I was glad to be there. This was the best possible place I could die, walking with the poor, witnessing to their claim to justice. I looked around me. No one looked afraid.

The Klan cars drove slowly by us as we walked along the pavement. Television crews surrounded us. The Klan passed without incident and then waited for us at city hall. There we listened to a speech on the importance of civil rights legislation. "We will continue to march 'til we're allowed to register to vote, until Congress passes the voting rights bill." After the speech, a minister led us in prayer; we sang, "God Bless America" and marched back to the church. No one was attacked. Because the Klan had spread so much publicity about their threats, television crews from all over the country had rushed to the scene. The Klan did not want to carry out their threats when the whole world was watching.

Like the woman with whom I walked, the people I met on the various marches were wonderful company. I remember marching in another Southern town with a Georgetown student. He said, "You know we are the first whites ever to walk with Negroes in a public demonstration in this town." How fortunate we were to be part of that history.

It seemed evident that President Johnson envied the Kennedy popularity, but could not win it for himself. To hold on to some of it, he kept all the Kennedy cabinet in office; he also pushed for passage of the Comprehensive Civil Rights Bill of 1964. I lobbied almost daily in Congress in support of that bill. The day it finally passed, I was in Mississippi working for the Voting Rights Act. So I was unable to accept the invitation from Larry O'Brien, National Chairman of the Democratic Party, to be in the White House for the signing. But he did send a note thanking me for my efforts in support of this historic legislation. Enclosed with the note was one of the pens Johnson used to sign the civil rights bill into law.

Johnson's support of the civil rights bill and other key Kennedy policies helped him in the 1964 campaign. However, he still faced obstacles. He feared that Robert Kennedy would run against him or that convention delegates would nominate Robert as vice president, even if Johnson chose someone else. Heading into the convention, Johnson still refused to announce his choice for vice president.

I was in Atlantic City before Johnson arrived. I was with the Mississippi Freedom Democrats as they sat on the boardwalk to block the entrance to the convention until their delegates were admitted. I listened to Martin Luther King, Jr. as he tried to persuade them to allow the convention to settle on who should be credentialed as delegates from Mississippi.

Though I was not in the convention hall, on television it was obvious that as soon as Robert Kennedy appeared, the resounding applause lasted so long that it was an embarrassment to Johnson. Robert could have asked the delegates to nominate him for the vice presidency. As it was, the president got his way and Humphrey was nominated. Johnson even arranged for the film tribute to President Kennedy to be shown after the nomination for vice president. He was afraid the tribute would crystallize sentiment in favor of Robert.

After the convention, Jackie Kennedy invited all the delegates to a nearby hotel for a reception. A campaign front man for Kennedy, Marty McNamara, had organized the reception, and he invited me. Jackie was welcoming each guest personally; when I came through the line, she asked me, half-jokingly, "Are you a delegate?" I think she knew I wasn't.

The reception was a mix of joy and sorrow — joy to see so many Kennedy friends together; sadness that President Kennedy was no longer with us.

In 1965 participants in the first civil rights march from Selma to Montgomery were attacked by Alabama state troopers, some on horseback, who, without warning, charged the crowd and began to beat the marchers. I watched the brutal attack on television. I could not believe that the state police were viciously attacking civilians. When Martin Luther King, Jr. called on the nation to come to Selma to join in the second march, a group of Georgetown students and myself were among those who answered the call.

We traveled by chartered train from Washington to Selma. We were stopped at the station in Atlanta by the locomotive crew who claimed to be sick and wouldn't continue on. The truth was they didn't want to help a trainload of people opposed to segregation.

At the Atlanta station a group of hostile white people surrounded us. They yelled at us to go home, get out of the South. Since we had plenty of experienced song leaders, we started up the song, "We Shall Overcome." We sang, "We shall not be moved from Selma." Using our voices, we told them, "We will go to Selma; We are not afraid; No more segregation; We will live in peace." Soon we drowned out the complaints and overwhelmed the opposition.

Officials in Washington arranged for replacement engineers, and we made it to Selma. We joined the several thousand people already marching. Because we could not count on hospitality, we carried supplies with us in trucks.

I recall one hot summer night when we stopped in a large Catholic school yard. Before we went to sleep in the auditorium, we were entertained in a large field. Celebrities from Hollywood performed on a small platform, ten by ten feet. Among them were Harry Belafonte; Dick Gregory; Odetta; and Peter, Paul, and Mary.

Dick Gregory faced an audience that was tired and oppressed by the heat of the night. He began by saying:

> "As soon as I got here, I called George. You all know who George is. [They knew George Wallace, chief segregationist and Governor of Alabama., but their response was faint.] Well, I called the operator and asked to speak with George. 'George who?' asked the operator. The people here are pretty ignorant. They don't even know who George is. [The crowd laughed a bit.]
>
> "When George answered, I said, 'George, why don't you take a Greyhound and leave the driving to us?' George didn't know what I meant. [More laughter.] He never rode a Greyhound.
>
> "George, there's gonna be a 'nigger' in the statehouse. [The word "nigger" caused an uncertain silence.] Ain't you people ever heard the word 'nigger?' [Dick knew they had heard it too many times, but he repeated the word three times, getting louder each time. By this time the field was howling with laughter. Everyone was following Dick now.]
>
> "George didn't like it when I said there was gonna be a 'nigger' in the statehouse, but I said, 'It's too late George. I already wrapped up a 'nigger' and sent him to you by U.S. mail. Cost me $1.98. You'll be gettin' a 'nigger' in the morning. [Laugher.]
>
> "Well, you know, George doesn't read very much. He didn't know that I was talking about my book, *Nigger.* [Waves of laughter.]

The tired, sleepy crowd was now fully awake and enjoying every quip. Dick continued for half-an-hour, helping them to laugh at the very things that had hurt them: their sore feet, the cat-calls of the white Southerners, the unfriendly attitude of the National Guard.

At Montgormery we stood in the streets outside the statehouse and listened to Martin Luther King, Jr. speak at the very headquarters of the Confederacy. "How long must we wait until we can vote? Not long. How long will the bars of segregation last? Not long."

On the train returning to Washington, our joy dimmed at the radio news that Viola Liuzzo, a civil rights worker, was shot and killed as she drove from Montgomery to Selma, ferrying marchers back to their cars.

Only minutes after James Meredith began his planned walk across Mississippi, he was shot and seriously wounded. In response, civil rights leaders, including King, again appealed to a national television audience for those believing in civil rights to continue Meredith's march. Once more a group of students and I headed for the South.

This time we drove to Mississippi to join Stokely Carmichael, other civil rights leaders, and over eight-hundred people, Martin Luther King, Jr. at the lead. Generally, as we passed through towns, we detoured off the main road and went through the Black part of town. That way we could pick up hundreds, sometimes thousands, of people who would join us for a few miles. We walked twenty miles a day and then slept overnight in two large tents, one for men and one for women. Each night we had a meeting in which we caught up on news and discussed plans for the next day. As we came to populated areas, we found telephones and drinking fountains cut off. The gasoline stations were closed. It was like marching through enemy territory.

As we neared the city of Canton, we were told that the police had seized the tents that were being set up on the grounds of a Black school. King announced that we would continue into Canton. As planned, we gathered at the courthouse to pray and sing. There, Dr. King told us that additional tents had been secured and that we had a right to set up our tents. (City officials had granted permission before our arrival, but they were away at a convention.). So we marched to the school yard. There the tents lay on the ground.

I remember what a strong leader King made as he stood on the roof of one of the vans. A crowd of several thousand surrounded him. At the end of the yard, one-hundred police waited. King addressed the police, "I wish that you would join us. We are not just here for Black people. We are here for all Americans. We are all God's children, all of us, black and white together. We can show this by praying, so let us all pray together." He led us in the Lord's Prayer.

Then he said, "Remember, we are all in this together. If they are going to arrest any of us, they will have to arrest all of us. . . . All we need to do is pull the ropes and the tent will go up. And when we do, . . . the police are threatening to arrest us. So all of you who are willing to be arrested, join in the circle around the tents and hold hands together. In case the police attack, you may be knocked to the ground; so let us sit down without letting go of the hand of the person next to you." After we had practiced this maneuver, King gave the signal to raise the tents.

As the tents went up, police shot canisters of tear gas at us. Nobody expected this. The crowd was bewildered by the gas attack. I could hear King's voice above the crowd. It was a clarion call, "Follow me." He moved the crowd into the wind. Typical of King's leadership, he was ready with an alternate plan. He led us to a Catholic church compound which had a large auditorium, a school yard, a church building, and a rectory. He had already contacted the pastor, Father Mischell, and received permission to use the church property in case of emergency. The volunteer medical corps from Howard University came with an ambulance and took care of the people that had been hurt in the incident. One student in our group told us afterward that she had been instructed to avoid tear gas by putting her face to the ground. She put her face right in the mud.

At the church I met the priest. He gave me a warm welcome and seemed unphased by the number of people setting up for the night — wherever they could find room. I slept on the rectory floor.

The next day we met in the auditorium. King said it would take another day to get the tents up; city officials were returning from their convention. He invited those willing to go with him on a nonviolent journey sixty miles to Philadelphia, where only months before, three civil rights workers were murdered. We would witness at the courthouse and honor the slain civil rights workers. We would demonstrate by our presence that we were not afraid.

Following Dr. King, Stokely Carmichael asked for volunteers to go immediately to the school yard to set up the tents regardless of the police response.

I offered to go in the caravan to Philadelphia. About a hundred people convoyed in twenty cars. We were told to stay together; if one car stopped, all would stop. We arrived in Philadelphia without a mishap and parked a mile from the courthouse. We then marched together along the dusty road to the courthouse. The Nisyoba County Sheriff, with much macho, met us. At this site, where civil rights marchers had been stoned and heckled just days before, King spoke to the crowd of marchers; his back to the courthouse. Behind him, the sheriff and those responsible for the murders stood waiting. King's voice rang out, ":We are here . . . where three civil rights leaders were murdered and probably some of the murderers are here listening to what we are saying." Later in an interview King said he heard one of the sheriffs behind him say, "You're damned right we're here." He said he thought he would be killed at that moment. He showed no sign of fear.

After his speech, we sang "God Bless America," said a prayer, and headed back to our cars. King, dressed in a white shirt and tie, led the procession. He walked in the center of a line of twenty abreast. State police lined the sides. I saw a policeman take his club and jam it endwise into the ribs of the Black man walking next to me. The man swung his arm around at the policeman. I put my hand on his arm and said, "Remember what King asked of us, nonviolent response." It was hard, but he didn't repeat his swing at the policeman.

We were marching up the hill with police all around. A red convertible sedan started down the hill toward us. As the car approached, King yelled, "Open up. Let the car through." As he did, the police turned their guns on us. King shouted, "Why are you turning your guns toward us? We are not endangering anyone." The car passed through the crowd — all unharmed.

Back at our cars, my driver decided not to follow the convoy; it would be too slow. One of the people riding in our car needed to catch a plane. So we started without the convoy and were soon chased by a Klan-like group in another car. There was no point in seeking out police assistance, so the chase went on. Soon we were going eighty miles per hour. The car tried to pass us, but our driver blocked his way. We sped through an intersection, just barely avoiding a collision with cross-traffic. Soon after that the car behind us gave up the chase. We made it back to the camp safely.

The civil rights struggle was at its zenith. No doubt I would have to take these visceral experiences and translate them for application in the classroom. In that way, students could move from an academic, theoretical view of racial and social justice to concrete faithful action.

Opportunities to do just that were ahead for me. As the civil rights movement began to link with the anti-war movement — identifying racism and war as twin evils — so did I. The Vietnam War would escalate, the threat of nuclear war would increase, and, even with civil rights victories, the path was still rocky and long.

15 ✢ Teaching Peace in a Time of War

Dinner at the Naval Station on 8th Street: I sat around the table with the Admiral, most of his six beautiful daughters and their mother, a woman from Brittany, France who, being very devoted to the faith, seemed happy to have a priest as her guest. "Most of my daughters are against the war," the Admiral told me. "They keep asking me why I don't quit the Navy. I tell them I am doing more to slow up expenditures for Navy warships where I am than I could out of the Navy."

"Father, tell daddy where you are going after supper," said daughter Barbara.

"I'm going to a G.I. coffee bar to hear what military dissenters say about Vietnam."

"Daddy, will you go with him?"

"You see how they push me to do things, Father. Where is the meeting?"

He drove me to the coffee house not far away. He came dressed in civilian clothes and didn't say a word as he heard army, navy and marine officers and enlisted men give details of how they were punished for even speaking against the war. Lawyers present took records of their statements and told them that military law gave them the right to discuss the war. After the meeting my friend, Admiral Weymouth, told me, "Every high ranking officer ought to hear a session like that."

Throughout the 60s and 70s I became friends with a number of high-ranking military personnel who, ironically, were invaluable assets in my courses on war and peace issues. Included among my military friends is a man I met at a benefit movie for Vietnam War victims. Before the film started, he turned and asked me if I was a Catholic priest. I was in clerical dress.

"Yes."

"What is a catholic priest doing at a movie like this?"

"Supporting the victims of war. What are you doing here?"

"I'm in the Navy."

"I suppose you're an admiral," I said facetiously. In fact he was.

After the film I talked some more with Admiral Gene La Roque and invited him to speak to my War-Peace class. These days he is director of the Center for Defense Information (CDI), a Washington, D.C. group staffed by retired military officers who look over the shoulder of the Pentagon. They believe in a reasonable national defense, but criticize Pentagon spending as ninety-five percent protection of our power abroad and five percent national defense. They believe our defense depends not just on weapons but also on our economy, our social structure, and the loyalty of the public. As a retired admiral, Gene LaRoque is listened to. He says we don't need as large an army or navy, and we don't need twenty-thousand nuclear weapons. CDI officers don't see themselves as a peace group, but I see them that way.

Over the years I had many CDI staff members as presenters in my classes. As the students learned, so did I. Here were experienced military men giving plentiful details on the overkill capacity of our weapons and vast overspending by the Pentagon. CDI's reliable and detailed information on military technology, strategy and spending was an effective complement to my evolving theology of peace.

Eventually, I developed a course called "War and Peace." It started as a seminar in 1964 and made front page news in the student newspaper. This seminar, in the midst of the war, was labeled "the most controversial course" offered at Georgetown." The editor, who I knew was a supporter of the war, probably figured that by criticizing the course, he would discourage students from taking it. Just the opposite happened. It became wildly popular. By the end of the first semester I had learned what issues students were most interested in and scheduled the topics according to student priorities.

The students were primarily interested in nuclear technology, so the first two weeks of the course focused on what nuclear weapons are and what they can do. American scientists and the military were my main sources. That was followed by a week on U.S. chemical and biological weapons, what we have and what we can do with them. This approach demonstrated how weapons of mass destruction pose a threat to human and environmental health and safety, even if they are never used. Usually, this exposure allowed students to get past their psychological resistance based on the rationalization that the threat posed by the enemy outweighed any hazard endemic to the development, production and deployment of weapons of mass destruction.

By the end of the third week, students were wondering when they would hear about peace. As one student put it, "I came into this class to study peace, but all I've heard so far is about weapons for war." They were ready now to hear about theorists of peace: Gandhi, Leo Tolstoy, Martin Luther King, Jr. All three theorists presented a view of peacemaking similar to the gospel of peace. But it was phrased in the words of their culture, their faith. For instance, King's life showed how Gandhi's teaching could apply to the U.S.

These three leaders disposed the students to see with new eyes the life and teaching of Jesus as a peacemaker. The love command of Jesus was what Gandhi had expressed in his nonviolent pursuit of truth. Tolstoy and King taught and lived the same message directly from the gospel. With this introduction, the "love your enemies" command of Jesus appeared in a new light.

The course proceeded with A.H. MacGregor's *New Testament Basis of Pacifism.* When, after a few years, I found the book was no longer in print, I used the MacGregor's main themes and wrote my own book: *The New Testament Basis of Peacemaking,* including additional topics dealing with the Just War Theory and Old Testament wars. After presenting the biblical basis of peacemaking, I demonstrated that military conscription is antithetical to this faith imperative and that conscientious objection to war a natural consequence of Christian faith. Since the Vietnam War was raging as I taught, I was able to bring conscientious objectors into my class to tell their experiences with draft boards. These young men, almost the same age as the students, were listened to with great interest.

Following the gospel message, I presented the economics of death: the cost of war nationally and world-wide. Then I used the story of colonial and post-colonial Vietnam as a case study, applying all the preceding components of the course. Finally, I ended the semester with the process of peace — what can be done for peace by the individual and by groups, nationally and internationally.

Invariably, we would run out of time in the semester, and I found that the last section, "Process of Peace," was rushed. So I developed a new, separate course to cover that; I called it "The Nonviolent Revolution of Peace." On the first day of class I would tell students, "For two weeks we will study 'power,' what it is, its variety, its sources. After that the course will be entirely devoted to answering the question you have most often asked, 'What can I do for peace?' The answer will be given by guest speakers who are living what they talk about." I invited conscientious objectors, war-tax resisters, draft counselors, Catholic Workers, peace church leaders, people from Congress, Pentagon officers, and many others. Both courses were filled to capacity. In addition, two or three times more than the number allowed by the theology department tried to get in.

From my teaching notes, I developed a second book, *Kill for Peace?,* with a theme that in the nuclear age killing will not bring peace. It incorporated my teaching on nuclear technology, the Vietnam War, and the process of peace.

In addition to discussing the academic points of peace, I joined others, including students, in more active forms of peacemaking. I remember one student who came to me with the question, "How can we get ROTC [Reserve Officer Training Corps] off campus?" She had been in ROTC, but got out. After some deliberation, we came up with several options that included: picketing; distribution of flyers outlining the moral and academic reasons for the removal of ROTC from campus; and circulating a "pledge" to be signed by students stating that, after graduation, they will not donate to Georgetown while the military is on campus.

She started giving out flyers two or three times a week in front of the library during lunch hour. I joined the picket in support of her effort. Students and faculty would often stop to argue with us. At least it was a good way to bring up discussion on the topic. I usually answered questions on why I opposed ROTC on moral and academic grounds: From a moral point of view ROTC has no place on campus because the gospel asks us to love our enemies, but ROTC teaches us how to kill them. Academically it is an intruder, a counterfeit education.

One faculty member, Carroll Quigley of the government department, told me, "I disagree with you about getting ROTC off campus, but you are right that it is a poor education. If the university was interested in the good of the students, it would select the best teachers it could find, not whomever the Pentagon sends. I could give a better course in military history than the man teaching it here. ROTC here is a straight buy-in. At Harvard we never accepted the people who wanted to teach without charging a salary."

In fact, during the Vietnam War, Harvard had banished ROTC from campus. They lost $1,000,000 in grants as a consequence. The House Armed Services Committee Chairman was quoted in the congressional record as saying that "if our money has blood on it, Harvard will get no more of it." I found this quote and put it in a letter to all the members of the Georgetown Board of Directors with the comment, "This is evidence that universities profit for having ROTC." Several days later, while I was eating lunch in the busy Jesuit dining room at Georgetown, the President of the university, Robert Henle, S.J. strode in. He was about twenty-five feet away from me when he yelled, "If you ever say again that I acted immorally for the sake of money, I will knock your head off." I heard the words, then looked behind me to see to whom he was directing this verbal blast. I would never have dreamed that he was talking to me, but he certainly was.

One afternoon, a concerned student came to me with questions about my opposition to ROTC. She seemed very earnest and sincere. "Why do you oppose ROTC? No one is required to take it. It is voluntary."

"It is only voluntary after the university decides to have it here," I replied.

"What do you mean?"

"The number of options for courses is limited. The university must first select within those limits. It is only after that selection is made that students can freely choose. I will tell you why we include ROTC in that limited number of options by an analogy: What would you think of me as a sixty-three-year-old educator if among the courses I selected, I chose prostitution because a group of pimps offered me five-hundred-thousand dollars a year to select them? Suppose they told me they wanted to teach prostitution as an optional course. They would have Ph.D. professors teaching the psychology of solicitation, comparative cultural solicitation, business leadership, legal and medical problems of solicitation. Their only requirement was that they selected the pimps as teacher and set up the courses. What would you think of me as an educator if I chose that?"

"Oh, you consider it a moral question, don't you?"

"Yes."

"Isn't it unfair to ROTC to compare it to pimps?"

"Rather, it is unfair to the pimps to compare them to ROTC. They don't endanger the world as much as the military does. They have no government subsidy. They don't pretend to be moral." It was interesting to me that the student didn't see that I considered it a moral issue until I put it in terms of sex.

As the campaign to oust ROTC gained momentum, more than a dozen gathered daily during lunch hour to pray the rosary outside the ROTC office. After joining them, I thought I should go in and assure the Colonel (who directed the program) that my presence meant no disrespect for him personally, only our opposition to the military on campus. I knocked on the door. It opened just a crack, and an officer curtly asked what I wanted. Receiving the Colonel's approval, I was ushered into the office and the door quickly shut. Two young lieutenants remained to guard the door.

Our visit soon took on a friendly tone, and the Colonel offered an intriguing perspective in support of ROTC: "Father, why can't you see that a Georgetown education will help humanize the army?" he asked. I rebutted, "There is merit in your argument. However, the size and resource of the military are so great that it is more likely that the army may militarize the students than the students will change the military." Our dialogue was most educational, giving me insight into the pro-military education mindset. We parted with a handshake.

Back when I first arrived at Georgetown, three first-year students came to see me because they had formed a club to promote a debate on the issue of ROTC on campus. I suggested that the topic should be: "Resolved: that military training should not be on a Catholic school campus." But I added my opinion that surely the ROTC would never debate that. They were already on campus. They couldn't win anything by engaging in the debate. Even discussion of the topic would be a loss for them. Sure enough, the debate promoters failed for three years to get the military to agree to a forum. In their fourth year they succeeded in getting the ROTC Colonel to agree to debate me about the Vietnam War.

About two-hundred students, almost evenly mixed between those opposed to and those who supported ROTC, attended the forum. Surprisingly, the Colonel opened with, "I am a Christian and I know war is wrong. I also know God will forgive me, so I go right ahead." Amazingly, he was backed-up during the question-and-answer period by a ROTC student who stated, "I agree with the Colonel. In war you put morality in the back seat and you just get in the front seat and drive." Military men rarely admit that war is wrong and certainly don't concede the moral position in debate. These two were making the point for me and made "winning" the debate easy.

— ❖ ❖ ❖ —

ROTC used to have what was called "War Day" at Georgetown: A day when classes were canceled so ROTC units could parade before parents and other spectators and receive prizes from the dean. The event took place on a field located at the edge of campus. Membership in ROTC was up to seven-hundred because belonging to it meant an exemption from the Vietnam draft. Students for peace organized about thirty-five picketers who carried signs at each entrance to the field. Friends in ROTC told us of the advice given to them before the parade: "Don't panic if those peaceniks surround the football field and try to block our entrance; the police will remove them" — as if the thirty-five of us could surround the entire football field.

As the troops marched through the gates and on to the field, we sang, "Ain't gonna study war no more." Inside, they marched past the reviewing stand with their flags and guns. Medals were presented to the best battalions, to sharpshooters and to outstanding cadets.

Next came a display by Special Forces units. At mid-field a small hut was guarded by students impersonating VietCong dressed in black pajamas. The plan was for the rangers to sneak up on the VietCong and strangle them one by one with small cords. As the rangers began the slow process of squirming on their bellies across the field toward the "VietCong," in full view of the audience an instantaneous cemetery materialized just outside the wire fence. A hundred white crosses were set up on a mound of dirt created by a construction project. A huge sign that read: "How Many More Must Die?" was hung from the fence nearest the rangers. Simultaneously, nearly fifty people also dressed in black pajamas climbed over the fence and started running across the field toward the hut. They quickly passed the crawling rangers and mixed with the ten fake VietCong near the hut. When the rangers reached them and told them they were dead, the protesters refused to play dead. University security was ordered to remove "those people in black pajamas." Of course, security couldn't tell the difference between protesters and ROTC members. The resulting confusion was illustrative of the Vietnam War in which the enemy and civilians were indistinguishable. That is what impressed the audience instead of a cleverly staged killing of "the enemy" by well-trained rangers.

Next on the program was a close order drill performed by the "Pershing Rifles," a battalion that practiced all year to march, counter-march and throw bayoneted rifles to each other with precise timing.

As the drill began, I watched at the end of the field far from the grandstand. Next to me a student said, "Now is the time to call in the helicopter." Another student with a walkie-talkie radio sent the message. The military air transport near National Airport rented helicopters (at the cost of a dollar a minute). Within a few minutes a helicopter flew above the marchers. It descended close to them and dropped fake napalm (leaflets that read: "If you can read this, your face and chest have been burned away"). Disrupted by the menacing helicopter, it became impossible to continue their exercise. The Washington Post ran a photo in the next day's edition that showed the helicopter over troops in disarray.

I'm sorry to say I had nothing to do with arranging the helicopter "napalm" drop nor with the black pajama group that climbed over the fence. They were a surprise to me, a pleasant surprise, representing the creativity of the Georgetown University student peace group.

When I entered the main gate of the university at about 2 p.m. the same day, the campus police told me, "The vice-president wants to see you." I went as ordered.

"Dick, I want you to make those peace people who are dancing on the front lawn leave."

"I can take you to the committee that organized the peace celebration, but I have no power to tell them what to do," I replied. "They decided to have a peace celebration to show their opposition to the War Day celebration."

He accompanied me to meet the committee. He told them to move the celebration to the lower field or else the police would be called to remove them.

At that point a student from the committee countered, "We know why you are trying to remove us from Copley lawn. You don't want the parents of the freshmen who are due to arrive this evening to see Georgetown students in jeans and bare feet dancing for peace. If you do move us off, we will surround the parents and tell them what a hell of a place Georgetown is. We can have a War Day celebration but no Peace Day celebration."

As we walked away from the students, I said, "The peace groups on the lawn are from all over the city. Neither they nor the Georgetown students with them are afraid of the police. They face the draft and death in a war they oppose. The women among them face losing their friends. If you let them stay where they are, they will stay there and play their music and films. If you drive them off, they will start up again in some other part of the university. It is not good for public relations for the university to block a peace demonstration on the same day they officially sponsor a war demonstration." He let them stay. That was the last War Day Georgetown ever had.

Besides making life difficult for ROTC supporters, I also had the opportunity to counsel students about their decision to become conscientious objectors. A Georgetown student asked my advice about quitting ROTC. "I am a senior, and I am beginning to think I should quit ROTC because I don't believe in killing people. On the other hand, I could go ahead with ROTC and just stop when I am asked to kill."

"The longer you are in, the more difficult it will be to get out," I said. "If you apply to quit ROTC, they probably will refuse to accept your application and order you to report an as enlisted man to an army base. If you graduate and get commissioned as an officer, there is less chance they would believe your request for conscientious objection."

"My conscience is not quite so clear that I can say I am a conscientious objector. I still have to think about it."

"Tonight Phil Berrigan is speaking here," I said. "Suppose I introduce him to you and see if he has a moment to talk to you? He is very informed about conscience and war."

Next day I asked what happened. "Father Berrigan listened to my doubts then he said, 'Your doubts make it clear that you don't have enough evidence yet to make an informed judgment about leaving ROTC or staying. Don't make any decision until you are sure. Continue to collect information and experience on what military life is, then make your decision.'

"That means you will continue in ROTC until you are ready to decide?"

"Right."

He graduated and was commissioned a second lieutenant. About three months later he returned to Georgetown looking for me. "Right now I am absent without leave from the Army. I want your advice."

We sat on a hill overlooking the Potomac River as we talked about his future. "I have fully made up my mind now. I'm not going on in the military. I've been driven almost out of my mind. In boot camp, at target practice I found I could shoot okay until they put a human form in front of me as the target. My arms and fingers just wouldn't function, so I kept missing. The sergeant yelled at me. When I explained that I just could not bring myself to shoot human beings, he screamed at me.

When I got back to the tent, one of my tent mates called me a coward. He grabbed me from behind in a headlock and pushed his pistol against the side of my head, 'You son of a bitch. You are going to kill or be killed.' I thought for sure he was going to shoot me. He kept saying he would shoot me unless I said I would kill. He held the pistol to my head for forty minutes. By that time a lieutenant came into the tent, saw what was going on and pulled him away from me. I think he was pretty out of his head, but God spoke to me during that experience. I am going to have nothing more to do with the military. I need some advice on what to do."

"I can put you in contact with a lawyer familiar with military law who can help with the legal issues of applying for conscientious objection release from the military. More importantly, turn to God and thank Him for clearing up your conscience and ask God's help to follow what your conscience now tells you."

Vicariously sharing the experiences of this student helped confirm my view of life in the military. I later learned that he got out of the military.

Another conscientious objector who asked for my help was Pat Moran. He phoned me from boot camp and said, "I told the captain at the recruiting office that I was a Catholic. I had worked with the poor at the Catholic Worker and I wouldn't mind working in the army, but I didn't want to kill anybody. He told me there were lots of jobs in the army and promised to use his influence to get me a non-combat job. So I joined.

"At boot camp, when they told me to begin target practice, I told them I had been promised a non-combat job. They laughed. I phoned the captain. He said he was just a lowly captain and had no power to help me. So I applied for conscientious objector status. It looks like they will refuse me. I know I am not going to kill. I don't know what the army is going to do. My wife and child will need help." I offered to help his family in case he was jailed.

About two weeks later his wife Linda arrived in Washington, D.C. with her one-year-old child. "Pat has gone to Sweden," she told me. "He left during a furlough to visit his family in New York." I was able to find her a place to stay with friends of mine. I also helped her get a job as a waitress so she could save enough money for the trip to Sweden. More on their story of life in Sweden later in the book.

I admired the faith, the strength of the young objectors I met. I felt sorry for America when fine intelligent young men told me of their plan to escape to Canada or Sweden. I considered them some of the very best of our young people.

Soon my schedule was full. In addition to my teaching duties, I was picketing and speaking at anti-war rallies. I helped organize an evening of war resistance symbolized by the burning of draft cards on the stage of the Hall of Nations at Georgetown University. I spoke on the right not to kill. A philosophy professor, Jack Ostrowski, encouraged all young men to refuse conscription. About a dozen young men came up and burned their draft cards before the audience.

This event was covered on television and in newspapers. A Jesuit in my community said, "I would have laid down on the ground and blocked the door if I knew what you were going to do except that I have a bad heart."

In support of these resisters, I joined a group of a thousand or more in an anti-draft demonstration at the Selective Service headquarters on G Street in D.C. Five of us were allowed to go inside to present our grievances to General Hershey, head of Selective Service. He spoke to us like a grandfather to his children. Because he used up all the time talking of his experiences in World War I, we hardly got a chance to say anything. Much later I learned that an FBI agent had been following me as I went in and out of this meeting and reported to FBI headquarters that I had visited General Hershey.

I also went with a small delegation to the Justice Department to deliver hundreds of draft cards given to us by students who refused to carry them. When we met with the assistant attorney general, he listened, but refused to accept the draft cards. We left them behind on his window sill.

When we first entered the building, a group of FBI agents had walked with us. I recognized one agent whom I had met several times at the Kennedy home. He quipped, "It is a different world now, father. Before I was protecting you, now I'm protecting others from you."

16 ✢ *Assassination, again*

Throughout this time period, my relationship with the Democratic Party continued. While I actively opposed Johnson's execution of the Vietnam War, I supported the Party's policies on civil rights and poverty.

In 1968 Eugene McCarthy beat Lyndon Johnson in the New Hampshire primary. While this seemed promising, I was convinced that McCarthy didn't have the organizational muscle to win. On the other hand, Robert Kennedy did. I wrote to him and urged him to join the presidential race. Many others did the same. Before McCarthy returned to D.C., Robert had announced his decision to run.

As soon as he opened a D.C. campaign office, I volunteered to help. My job: enlisting clergy support. I offered my name as a delegate and was elected as an alternate to the national convention. I spent my free time, the little I had, at the Kennedy headquarters phoning clergy to support Kennedy. Certainly, Kennedy would win the Democratic nomination.

The night of the California primary, I was in his headquarters watching the television reports with much of his staff. Victory in California assured him of enough electoral votes to get the nomination. It was past midnight when the news of his victory was aired. I left to go home before he made his acceptance speech.

About two hours later I was asleep when I got a phone call from California. "Sorry to bother you at this hour, but Mrs. Kennedy wonders if you would go over to McLean to be with the children. You know their father was shot?"

I did not know. I drove immediately to the Kennedy home. Police surrounded the house and the grounds, but quickly let me in. Some of the younger children were still asleep. Some were in California. There was not much to say, just a few prayers for Bobby's recovery. The medical news was uncertain, but I had hope and tried to share this with the children.

Next morning I offered Mass in the parlor for family and friends. Later in the morning I saw Bobby Jr. ducking behind some bushes on the lawn. "Where are you going?" I asked him.

"Trying to avoid photographers." They were all along the front and side hedges of the house. "I am going out through a neighbor's yard. I have to go to the store to get a dark suit for my trip to California."

I could understand his problem and offered my assistance. We talked for a minute about one hundred yards from the hedge. The photographers didn't miss it. The *Washington Post* ran a picture captioned: "Consultation in a time of grief."

"I will get a car and meet you as you come out of the neighbor's property," I told Bobby, Jr.

When I picked him up, one of his brothers and a sister were with him, also wanting to shop. Bobby, Jr. left the store before the rest of us. When I got back to the car, he said, "The radio says he is doing better this morning." As he listened, he was visibly cheered by the news.

"Let's pray for a swift and complete recovery if it be God's will," I replied.

The second morning I again offered Mass in the parlor. Later in the morning in discussion with several Kennedy friends, including John Glenn and Nicolas Katzenbach, I was asked, "Do you know the seating capacity of the cathedral in Washington?"

No," I replied.

"Is there any other Catholic church in Washington with more capacity?" someone asked.

These questions unsettled me.

"I think you are very pessimistic to be planning a funeral when there is a good chance he will live."

"We are sorry. We didn't tell you. There is no hope. We need to plan the funeral. The news will soon be public." This news hit hard.

I said nothing more. I wanted to be with myself and God. A few hours later the radio announced his death.

"Do you have any experience in selecting coffins?" I was asked. "We need someone to help with this."

I never had selected a coffin for anyone, and I didn't want to select one for my friend Bobby Kennedy. But I did go — receiving only one instruction — "Any place will do except the one that charged six-thousand dollars for President Kennedy's bronze casket. We don't deal with that undertaker." We visited a half a dozen undertakers and looked at all kinds of caskets. They were lined up with price tags on them like automobiles for sale. Each undertaker treated us with a great respect. It was obvious they wanted the job. We selected no one. We just got information which Ethel could use to decide when she arrived from California.

When we returned, someone said that Michael was alone upstairs in his room crying. "Should someone go upstairs and talk with him?"

"No," said John Glenn, "The children are all different ages. Each of them has to understand the news in his own way. Leave him alone until he decides he wants to talk to somebody." The truth of what he said was illustrated when Ethel arrived at the airport and the child in her arms cheerfully told her brothers and sisters, "Daddy died." She was too young to understand what she was saying.

Since Robert was a senator from New York, the family decided that the funeral Mass would be at St. Patrick's Cathedral on Fifth Avenue. Ethel wanted me to have a part in the Mass. I flew to New York on a private flight with Ethel, the children and family friends.

At St. Patrick's I went to the priest's residence looking for the place to vest for the Mass. I walked in and found a man in an otherwise empty parlor. Seeing me in clerical dress, he supposed I lived there and said, "I'm Andy Williams. I'm going to sing at the Mass. Can you tell me where I can find a phone?" I had seen a phone in another parlor and led him to it. In the sacristy I looked for the master of ceremonies and told him that Ethel Kennedy had asked me to be part of the ceremony. "All right, you can read the epistle. If you wish, go out on the altar and read over the passage and test the microphone." Back in the sacristy I found my name on the vestments laid out. I vested and joined Cardinal Cooke, the main celebrant.

President Johnson, Lady Bird, and many federal, state, and local officials attended the Mass. During the homily Cardinal Cooke said, "It was not two-hundred fifty million people who pulled the trigger that killed Bob Kennedy. It was just one crazed man."

From the cathedral the funeral procession inched its way to Penn Station to board a special train for its slow, sad journey to Washington, D.C. In the cities and towns along the tracks thousands of people stood in silent tribute. Inside the train, politicians and celebrities, unshielded by secretaries or assistants, moved from car to car.

As I talked with the family and friends, they expressed displeasure with Cardinal Cooke's remark that the murder was the work of one man. "We were all responsible because of the climate of violence and militarism in our society."

A bit later I passed Cardinal Cooke, sitting right on the aisle. I stopped and said, "Cardinal, I have been talking with some friends of the family. They liked your talk, except for . . . [I repeated the line]. That seems to excuse everyone else. But we are all guilty for our culture of violence."

"Well, Father, when the President of the United States is there listening to you, you don't want to say anything to offend him."

I said something more and started to walk away. But the man in the seat behind Cooke grabbed my sleeve and pulled me back. It was Cardinal Cushing of Boston.

"Did you straighten out the archbishop?" he asked in a very loud voice making sure Cardinal Cooke could hear him.

"I tried to."

"It is impossible," he blared out in a deep, heavy voice. "Once he has been made archbishop, it's too late. He will never learn." Cooke turned around, looked at him and they both laughed.

In Washington, the funeral procession wound slowly through the crowds at Union Station and across Memorial Bridge to Arlington Cemetary. Ethel had decided that Bobby should be buried next to John. Cardinal Cushing gave the blessing at the grave. From his voice, it was clear that he shared deeply in the sorrow. The deep base tones of his prayer that God would care for the family and for Robert brought comfort and consolation to all the mourners.

I returned to Georgetown and to a city and world that seemed black and empty. To know that Bobby was gone, with all the high hopes he inspired, left me desolate and weary.

Since I was elected as an alternate Kennedy delegate to the Democratic National Convention, I went to Chicago to represent his ideals as best I could. That 1968 convention was dominated by Mayor Daley. Police barricades surrounded the hall. Police beat demonstrators in the streets and in a city park. To enter the convention, we had to run through a gauntlet of police and other security. At the door our admission cards, different for each day, had to be inserted into a metal box. If a green light appeared, you could enter; if red, no.

One of our delegation had a lot of Humphrey signs and asked me to carry some for him. The policeman at the entrance said to me, "No signs allowed."

"Who says so?" I asked.

"The FBI"

"What right do they have to decide? I am an elected delegate. Mayor Daley has thousands of signs stacked inside."

"No signs."

I picked up the signs and walked past him.

"I will call the FBI," he said.

"Go ahead. I'm going in."

Inside there was much talk and hope that Edward Kennedy would be willing to enter the race in place of his brother. I was convinced that Edward Kennedy could beat Nixon, but very doubtful about Humphrey; so I made a lapel sign reading "NIXON BEATS HUMPHREY" and wore it into an area where the Illinois delegates were cheering for Humphrey.

After Kennedy refused to run, the voting began; but it was soon suspended when the chairwoman of the New York delegation announced that New York would not take part in the voting until the chairman of the New Hampshire delegation was released from jail. He had been arrested for saying that Mayor Daley's admission system to the convention was a fake. He had put a business card into the entrance door and the light had turned green. "Any card will do it," he said.

With New York refusing to vote or even caucus, the convention came to a halt. In about twenty minutes the chairman of the New Hampshire delegation was back with us and the voting continued. Of course, Humphrey won.

When Humphrey came to Washington to ask for votes, I joined other protest groups who walked out of the church just after he started speaking. He was Lyndon Johnson's vice president; he supported the war.

When Humphrey wrote to all the delegates asking for support, I answered that I would vote for him, but, unless he spoke out publicly against the war, I would not ask others to vote for him. He replied that he thought he had disassociated himself from the war. I answered, "Not clearly enough."

Humphrey lost to Richard Nixon by a small margin. Some friends of mine blamed me and the peace movement for the defeat. I blame Humphrey and his support for the Vietnam War. Nixon won and the Vietnam War continued.

17 ❖ *From Protest to Resistance*

In 1968, various national peace groups tried to close down the Pentagon by surrounding it with people. The demonstration began with one-hundred thousand people gathered on the Mall to hear speeches. Then we marched across the Potomac to the Pentagon. As we marched, troops with bayonets surrounded the Pentagon to protect it from us. I marched with the crowd right up to the bayonets, even talking with several stern soldiers. Some in our group put flowers in the barrel of the rifles.

I had helped arrange for some demonstrators to sleep in the Georgetown gym, so while events at the Pentagon were at a standstill, I bicycled back to Georgetown to check on arrangements. On campus I coasted down the steep hill into the parking lot; I figured the speed of the bike would carry me across the lot to the gym. Wrong. Security police had strung a cable across the road. Though the cable missed the bicycle, it caught me in the stomach. It seems I spun around the cable several times before my head finally hit the ground. I was taken semi-conscious to the university hospital and released that evening. The next day people noticed my bandaged head and asked if I'd been wounded at the Pentagon.

Before we marched to the Pentagon, Philip Berrigan and I sat half-listening to rally speeches on the Mall as we carried on a private conversation. He told me enthusiastically, "Keep your eyes on Baltimore." I found this a bit cryptic — a week later I would learn what he meant. He called my room one evening. "Dick, I would like to talk with you."

"Sure, go ahead and talk."

"Can we meet and talk. It is not something I want to talk about on the phone."

I figured he thought the FBI might have tapped his phone. "I understand. When shall we meet?"

"Tonight."

"Are you coming to Georgetown?"

"No. Let's meet at my friend's house at sixteenth and Q."

"What time? It's already 9:30 and I go to sleep by 10:30."

"This is important."

"Okay, I'll meet you there by ten."

"I'm just leaving Baltimore, so it will be more like 10:30." I was amazed. He wasn't even in D.C. Though this seemed quite an inconvenience, I agreed to meet him.

On Q Street I found a half a dozen people in the parlor, but not Phil. I recognized Tom Lewis so I told him, "I came here to see Phil. He phoned and said it was important. Where is he?" I was annoyed at not finding him there.

"Let's walk down to the corner and get some cigarettes," Tom said.

"I don't smoke."

"Will you walk me down? Phil will be here in a minute."

As we walked, Tom clued me in, "Phil is talking with a group of people in the basement. We want to talk about an action we are planning, but we want some people who are not part of it to leave before we can talk. There may be informers in this group. Just wait out here awhile and then we can go down and see Phil."

When we finally got to the basement, I found about ten people around a table with Phil.

"Welcome, Dick, ol' buddy. Thanks for coming. Did you hear what we are planning?"

"Not yet."

"Do you know everybody?" He introduced me. "All of us and a few others, we hope, are going to join in a draft file action. At a draft board office near Baltimore we plan to get A-1 draft files and burn them. We have very good information on the place. No one will be harmed, just the draft files. We are wondering if you would like to join us?"

"When?"

"The day after tomorrow."

"This means you will be arrested?"

"We are not trying to avoid arrest. We will stay after the files are burned until the police come."

"Where will you burn the files?"

"Outside the office on the parking lot."

"Do I have to give an answer tonight?"

"No, but there isn't much time."

At the time my teaching commitments seemed paramount, so I hesitated although the action was certainly worth considering. I also learned that some others were still uncertain, including Daniel Berrigan. Apparently, Phil expected to talk him into it.

I was completely surprised by the invitation to join the action. I was teaching courses in war and peace. Arrest could mean a substantial prison sentence. Would I do more for peace by going to prison than by continuing to teach? I didn't know the answer. Going to prison was difficult, but it would be a dramatic peace witness. Teaching peace in a university would be respectable, comfortable. Was that the deciding influence in my decision to say no? I had a contract with the university. If I broke it, I could not hope to be reinstated.

I learned later that Daniel finally made up his mind to join the group after hours of discussion with Phil. The decisive element in his decision to join was this: "I have been thinking too much of saving my own sweet skin." I did not see it that way, but I may have been influenced more by saving my own skin than I realized.

Daniel overcame that uncertainty when he put his own comfort aside at the Catonsville, Maryland draft office. Nine people, dubbed the Catonsville Nine, removed the A-1 draft records, took them out to the parking lot, placed them in wire baskets and burned them with homemade napalm: a mixture of soap chips and gasoline. They prayed and sang about fifteen minutes while they waited for the police to arrest them. A friend of theirs from NBC had been invited ahead of time to film the event. He made an eleven-minute film before the police arrived. He took it to NBC to air it, but the FBI threatened to sue NBC as an accomplice in crime if they showed it. It was not shown.

At the trial of the Catonsville Nine I tried to imagine what it would have been like if I had been on trial instead of in the audience. After years in jail for draft card burning, Daniel and Philip Berrigan continued to protest the war with civil disobedience and returned to jail many times. As writers, priests, and prisoners, these brothers had a great influence on stopping the Vietnam War. All three elements increased the impact of their peace witness. Did I do as much by continuing to teach peace theology? Three decades after the event, I have no clear answer. Daniel has continued to teach year after year at many universities. Maybe I could have done that also. Maybe a prison experience like theirs would have made me a better teacher.

I remember going to visit Phil in the Arlington, Virginia county jail. At the visitor counter I asked if I could leave books for Phil Berrigan.

"Those Berrigans are always asking for books. We haven't had a college graduate in jail in the last ten years. Why do they want more books?" said the clerk.

Behind me, a black man in line asked me, "Is Fr. Berrigan in this jail?"

"Yes," I answered.

"I admire him. I wish I could meet him."

The policeman at the counter heard the visitor's remark and replied, "Those Berrigans give us more trouble than any of the other prisoners. They could set the whole place in revolt. The other day one of them refused to stand up for cell inspection. That message went all through the jail. I wish they were out of here."

Several times I visited Dan in jail. Once in the old D.C. jail, Dan talked to me from behind bars. "Dick," he said, "I think this is a good time for someone like you on the Georgetown faculty to give the university something to think about by going to jail for opposing the war."

"But Dan, you're a well-known author of more than thirty books; you're welcome as a teacher in many universities. It's not the same with me. If I get a prison sentence, I think I'll be out of teaching and won't be able to get back."

"Oh, that's the way it is, is it?" Dan commented. He clearly didn't think much of my argument.

In the late seventies I went to pick up Dan Berrigan, as he was being released from the Alexandria, Virginia jail. At the sheriff's office I asked, "Is Father Berrigan released yet?"

"We don't have any Father Berrigan. What is his first name and what did he do?"

His first name is Daniel, and he threw blood on the temple of death."

"What does that mean?"

"You ought to know. You've been holding him here."

About that time, Dan appeared, and I introduced him to my niece who had accompanied me to the jail because she was keen to meet him. As we drove along, my niece asked, "Dan, why do you do those acts that get you arrested?"

Dan turned to her and replied, "If you are a follower of Christ, you read in the gospel how he was suspect by both the church and the state. Then you look at your own life and see if you, too, are suspect by church and state. If you are not, you may ask yourself, 'Am I really a follower of Christ?'"

"But what good does it do to throw blood on the walls of the Pentagon?"

Dan replied, "People often take a long time to understand things. I remember a Jesuit who told me, 'Dan, I agree that destroying draft cards at Catonsville makes sense, but your opposition to nuclear weapons is crazy.'"

Dan continued, "As a Catholic priest throwing blood on the Pentagon, I symbolize the opposition of the Catholic faith to what goes on in the Pentagon. Many Catholics' first reaction is anger. But after a while, if they are reading the scriptures, they may see the action in scriptural terms."

Now, nearly thirty years after the Catonsville action, it's obvious that Dan has succeeded in converting at least some of the Jesuit officials of the New York Province, his home base, to agree with him.

In the mid-eighties the general superior of the Society of Jesus, on a visit to the United States, visited Dan in jail. All Jesuits have been influenced more than we realize by Dan's writings and the example of his life. His work has paved the way for the Jesuit order to declare that the mission today is faith at the service of justice and international peace. He has lived according to the gospel of peace and preached that gospel at the cost of many years in prison.

He has paid the price in other ways as well. For example, after being scheduled to speak at a Jesuit university, he was disinvited. A Jesuit friend told him, "Dan, you are the most pro-life Jesuit writer and poet. You would be most welcome at any of the twenty-eight U.S. Jesuit colleges if you would just stop talking about peace." Not everyone is converted.

Dan replied, "What would I talk about?"

Indeed, the role of Catholics is to be in the service of justice and international peace. In an effort to do just that, a group of Catholics opposed to the war initiated an effort to collect funds for the war victims. They asked me to help. This meant standing outside the doors of various local Catholic churches on Sundays. At first I felt rather strange soliciting money in clerical dress. I soon got used to it. We handed out leaflets explaining that we were collecting for the victims on both sides of the war. At some churches, pastors ordered us off the steps, so we retreated to curbside. At St. Stephen's on Pennsylvania Avenue, after we had moved to the sidewalk, the pastor came up to me and asked, "Who gave you permission to be here?"

From my pocket I pulled out a D.C. beggar's license and showed it to him. He did not say anything, just walked away. At another church a group of young men surrounded me and asked, "Are you a real priest?"

"Would a real priest be interested in the victims of war?" is what I thought they should be asking. Their question helped convince me that God wanted me to be there.

During those years, as the Vietnam War intensified, so did the efforts to end it. I became an active participant in several of the major demonstrations against the war, and I moved from protest to active nonviolent resistance. When I picketed at the White House sidewalk, I wore clerical dress so as to be identified with the Church. I remember once I was in a crowd at Lafayette park across the street from the White House. I was holding a ten-foot high image of President Nixon. A policeman came up to me and said, "You're not allowed to have demonstrations in the park."

"Isn't he allowed to be here?" I asked looking up at Nixon.

"I'll go find out," he said and departed, but never returned.

A Harvard-trained attorney named Charles Butterworth, who worked in my Dad's law office, invited me to join a group of Quakers who had walked from Philadelphia to Washington to protest the killing. We spoke to the powers-that-be in the place of power: the Pentagon. About thirty of us sat on the floor in front of the door marked "War Room." When the building was closed at 5 p.m., we refused to leave. Word came from Secretary of Defense Robert McNamara that we would not be permitted to enter the building again once we left. The police allowed us to use a restroom fifty feet down the hall, but blocked us from going anywhere else in the building.

The media reported our sit-in in progress. The police had a television going right near us, so we were able to see the coverage as we sat there. Many of the Quakers, prepared to stay all night, had brought sleeping bags and food with them. It was my first association with such serious and prepared protesters.

I didn't stay the night, but did return the next morning. At about 9 a.m. the police ordered us down the steps of the building and said we could stay on the veranda outside the door. Some refused to leave the steps and were carried out.

At about 10 a.m. we were ordered off the veranda. Those who refused to go were carried out and deposited on the lawn. Most of them promptly walked back and sat on the veranda again. The police carried them down to the grass again. This continued until about noon. Many were carried to the lawn five or six times, yet they continued to return. Apparently, McNamara wanted to avoid arresting us. But by noon the police began to arrest the protesters.

This was one of my first experiences with civil disobedience. I admired the Quakers in their witness for peace. I was now ready for more.

In the Capitol Rotunda I knelt to pray with more than one-hundred fifty clergy. We demanded that the Senate pass a bill outlawing the bombing of Cambodia. We were arrested for that act of conscience.

My second arrest in the Capitol took place in a hallway with two-hundred other citizens. Together we sought redress of grievances against an undeclared war. We refused to leave and were kept overnight in the D.C. jail.

I was in a filthy cell with Dr. Spock, the famous seven-foot-tall baby doctor. When the group in the cell block discovered Spock was among them, they started shouting for advice. I quipped, "All requests for advice for Dr. Spock will cost ten dollars in advance."

There was only one bed, nothing more than a metal shelf hanging by chains from the wall. The floor was wet and dirty, no seats. I told Dr. Spock, "You sleep for a couple hours, then I'll sleep for a couple hours."

"No," said Spock, "I know anatomy. I will direct you on how the two of us can lay down together at the same time."

But we never slept; the crowd in the cell block stayed up and entertained one another all night. They sang, they laughed. We were almost all professionals: artists, clergy, lawyers, journalists and doctors.

When we lined up to be processed, I heard the policeman ask the man ahead of me, "Do you use drugs?"

"Yes," he replied.

"What drugs do you use?"

"Just the regular American drugs: coffee, cigarettes, beer, aspirin, wine, liquor."

"No, I mean drugs."

"They are drugs."

The policeman stopped asking and took his fingerprints.

It was a day to remember: May 1, 1971. The People's Coalition for Peace and Justice organized the "May Days" actions to shut down "business as usual" in

Washington. They planned to block the streets during rush hour. The night before, I slept outside with about three-thousand students in Potomac Park. At about 7 a.m. the police surrounded us and ordered us to leave or be arrested. One of the leaders announced by loud speaker, "The local universities: Georgetown, George Washington, Catholic University and American University invite you to hospitality on their campuses."

"What a wonderful message," I thought, pleased that Georgetown welcomed everyone. Later I learned that the invitation came from students, not the administration. But the crowd didn't know that.

Georgetown was soon jammed. Visitors slept in the hallways, lounges, lawn, classrooms. The president was away. I went to the acting president and asked him not to call the police to eject the visitors. He was friendly and concerned, but didn't give me a definite answer. "It will not be good for Georgetown's reputation to call the police. Students from all over the country are here on a life-and-death issue: the continuing war that they may be forced to join"

"But we can't have classes with people sleeping in the hallways and classrooms?" he replied.

"It is going to be difficult to have classes if you try to get them out."

I started back to my room. On the way a student told me that the police were chasing students on the lower baseball field. I went to a place where I could see the field. There a single D.C. policeman on a small motorbike was trying to catch up with a student who was evading him by running a twisting circle. I quickly got my bicycle and rode after the policeman. I was dressed in my black clerical suit. I called out to the policeman, "Who let you in here?"

He stopped and said that the student was blocking the road.

"This is private property. You have no business being here unless you're invited. Who invited you?"

By this time the student had disappeared. So I left the policeman and started out the front gate on my bike to join the blockade in some way. I was about two blocks on the way when I started coughing because of a stinging sensation in my lungs. It was tear gas. I turned back to the university. On the university grounds at the edge of a steep hill that drops down to the highway I found three policemen wearing tear gas masks. I bicycled up to them. "What are you doing here?" I asked.

Without removing their masks, they mumbled something I could not understand. Then one took off the mask and said, "We're stopping students from rolling rocks down the hill onto the road."

"But there are no students doing that."

"That's because we're here."

It reminded me of the story of the man who visited his friend in a psychiatric hospital. He found his friend sitting in the corner of a room continually waving his arm in front of him. "Why do you keep waving your arm?" he asked.

"To keep away the elephants."

"But there are no elephants here."

"Of course there are none here, I'm waving my arms."

Meanwhile, in other parts of the city, traffic blockades consisting of old, stalled, and abandoned cars were met by police with many tow trucks. The federal government asked workers to come to work in shifts to lessen the rush hour crush. Police arrested groups that sat down on bridges. But the tens of thousands of May Days peacemakers were too much for the police.

I went with the crowds to the Justice Department. The streets between Constitution and Pennsylvania Avenues were completely filled with people. A watchful Attorney General Mitchell was on the roof puffing a pipe like Sherlock Holmes. Along with many others, I spoke that day, standing on a flat-bed truck equipped with loudspeakers. During the speeches, resisters, many of whom I knew, chained themselves to the iron grill doors of the Justice Department building. Ringed by police with shotguns, Mitchell directed the arrest of thousands from the roof top. Police formed lines at both ends of the streets and started loading people into buses to take them to jail — an illegal mass arrest

Due to the size of the crowd, there was no way to get protesters onto buses, let alone distinguish them from bystanders or government workers. After awhile the police gave up. The crowd, including me, marched on to the Capitol where we completely covered the East steps. Police, shoulder to shoulder in riot gear, surrounded the crowd but didn't ask us to leave.

I had particular reason to be afraid of arrest. My pockets were full of the protesters' IDs. Many military in the crowd had given me their IDs in case they were arrested; they were not allowed to protest the war. As I saw the police surrounding the steps, I told my friend Tom King, an ex-Peace Corps volunteer whom I first met in a small town in Africa, "I can't get arrested with all these cards in my pocket. I have to leave." Dressed in my black shirt and Roman collar, I demanded that the police let me through the line.

"No. You're under arrest," an police officer told me.

"You cannot arrest us without first ordering us to leave," I told him. "I heard no order."

"Clear out your ears," he said. But he did not stop me as I pushed by him.

Outside the cordon of police, a crowd of thousands of protesters hooted the police and cheered those who were arrested and loaded into buses to be driven off to jail. I saw police take the wallets, money, and papers out of the pockets of those arrested and spill them out onto the pavement. I went over and picked up as much as I could so I could later return the items.

Later, Tom King told me that he and his buddy, when arrested, were put into a packed bus guarded by one policeman in the front with the driver. When the bus stopped at a red light, Tom said to his buddy, "Look here, the sign says, 'To open door for an emergency, pull down this handle.' This is an emergency. Let's go." They opened the door and escaped. They went back to the Capitol steps. Arrested again, they were taken to a football stadium filled with arrestees They. enjoyed each others company for a few hours, then police started moving the crowd. Tom and his friend hid under a tarpaulin until the crowd was gone, then escaped for the second time in one day.

At trial, the arresting officers did not know whom they had arrested. They could identify no one. No proof of any charge was possible The mass arrests were all illegal and thrown out of court. Later those arrested sued for false arrest and won their case along with compensation. Despite this fact, President Nixon went out of his way to invite the chief of the D.C. police to his office and have his picture taken as he was congratulated on a job well-done.

V

Travels Abroad

18 ✤ *Sabbatical*

England

While on sabbatical from Georgetown in 1969-70, I visited several peace groups and individual activists in Europe, Africa, South America and the United States to better understand what they were doing and to learn from them.

I carried in my pocket *The World Peace Diary*, a small pocket calendar plus directory of sixteen-hundred peace organizations listed by country. Beyond some addresses I already had, I used this to make contacts. When I came into a country, I would visit the Friends (Quakers) or find the Fellowship of Reconciliation office and ask who were the most important people for me to visit during my short stay in country. I trusted their opinions and, of course, they always steered me to the right people.

My first stop was England and while there I lodged at the Jesuit residence on Farm Street in London. There I met Archbishop Roberts, S.J. the recently retired Archbishop of Bombay, India. He made a deal with the Vatican for him to take early retirement and guaranteed the Vatican would appoint a native Indian as archbishop. He was very active — writing and lecturing on conscience and obedience.

He sat relaxed and smoking at his desk while I sat in a chair beside him. A gas fire warmed the room, and I considered our conversation one of the great opportunities of my life. He was one of the eminent men in the Church, one who had already lived a long life of service. He had shared with many his vision of how to serve God in peacemaking and in following conscience.

Although our exchange covered a wide range of topics, I was most interested in discussing an assertion that had been made by Archbishop Roberts: Because the Church has failed massively since the fourth century to speak out against war (and has no intention of doing so), it has found itself looking for some other way to demonstrate its moral responsibility.

He had taken up the issue of Church moral teaching in his book *The Diary of Bathsheba*, a story that features the woman who stole the heart of King David from his wife and his thousand concubines. She comes back to earth and visits an agnostic psychiatrist. Their colloquy is an allegory for Archbishop Roberts' own challenge to the Church to face up to and repent for: Augustine's Just War Theory; the crusades (led by popes); and the weakening of conscience by the abuse of Church authority. Points like this come to life in the revelations delivered by Bathsheba to the psychiatrist. As the archbishop spoke of the story, he often chuckled, "I can say the things I want to through the mouth of Bathsheba."

In another book, *Black Popes*, he develops the theme that obedience, by its wisdom, should commend itself even to outsiders. The book outlines the history of use and misuse of authority in the Church and follows the theory that authority should be so used that any examination of its use would find that it is well used.

Roberts' main view on peace was that a Christian can never accept the idea of "kill on order." He or she must always follow individual conscience. An example of the archbishop's active faith and peacemaking was the Mass he celebrated at Notre Dame University during which draft cards were collected at the offertory. He noted that one of the best features of the Mass was the fact that many university officials, including President Father Theodore Hesburg, were part of the ceremony.

In a speech delivered in the United States, Roberts made himself perfectly clear: "As an American citizen, I will no longer allow my government, in my name, to order anyone to kill against his conscience, nor will I allow the government to direct my thinking. . . . The image of America is badly damaged by the limitation of choices to one of three alternatives: murder by order, long imprisonment, or freedom outside the U.S. . . ."

I brought up the argument that there is some objection to this on the grounds that selective objection would make war impossible. He confidently answered, "This is what we are looking for, isn't it?"

He summarized his view with the phrase, "NO KILLING BY GOVERNMENT ORDER, NO THINKING BY ORDER."

Archbishop Roberts spoke and lived this out in a hundred ways before his death in 1975. (*The Life of Archbishop Roberts*, by David Hearn, is published in England by Dart, Longmans and Todd.)

After my visit with Roberts, I met with another great man — Monsignor Bruce Kent. From the Farm Street residence, I found my way to the University of London where Kent served as the chaplain. He also functioned as the secretary in England for Pax Christi. Monsignor Kent had previously served as secretary to Cardinal Heenan, head of the hierarchy in England.

Kent lived in a large four-story building on Gower Street that housed seventy students, including foreigners and non-Catholics. Several nuns worked there full-time with him. A handsome young man, six foot, strong and husky, Kent talked with me for hours and invited me to lunch with his staff. He gave an interesting account of his correspondence in the London *Times* on the launching of the Polaris Submarine named HMS Resolution. His letter was critical of the fact that a senior Roman Catholic chaplain helped commission the nuclear submarine. He questioned, "Is it that the use of the Polaris Missile is thought not to involve the type of active war which is condemned by Vatican II? Do we really intend not to use these missiles even if we are ordered to do so?" The series of letters which followed from bishops, admirals and chaplains rehashed many of the arguments that come up whenever the idea of military chaplaincy is mentioned.

In another article Kent pointed out that the Quakers, with twenty-thousand members in the United Kingdom, planned to spend about fifty-thousand dollars that year for peace. If the Catholic Church were to proportionally match that effort, it would have a massive effect. This was a good argument; it gave Catholics a standard by which to measure their peace interest. Are we as interested in true peacemaking as are the Quakers? In the article he quotes the Dutch Bishops' joint pastoral of January 1969 entitled *Banning War* in which they say that many people think war is unavoidable, "on a par with the thunderstorms and the cycle of seasons." This sense of inevitability was rejected absolutely by the bishops. Looking for peace means "giving peace work a real place, not only as a pious wish on our lips, but in our thoughts, our interests, in our educational work, in our political convictions, in our faith, in our prayer, and in our budget." What impressed me the most was that the Dutch Bishops' letter was a genuine call to do something in this world, not just wait for pie in the sky.

After leaving Monsignor Kent, I went to the Conflict Research Institute which operated in the Psychology Department at the University of London. It had little to do with the active peace movement, but was a research project on the social psychology of conflict. It did not reach into the undergraduate departments, but did have some effect on the graduate course lectures in psychology. However, there were no credits given for this. Considering the immense size of London University, it was unfortunate that only an appendix-type program was available. Georgetown and Notre Dame suddenly looked much better to me because both had credited undergraduate peace courses.

There are three categories of peace work that seem the most important to me: First, there is research; second, faith-related programs; and third, action groups (not listed in the order of importance). Like the Pentagon triad of "defense" — land, sea and air — this is the peace triad. Ideally, a group process that includes all three of these components — research, faith and action — will yield the best results. Illustrative of this praxis was the Ark Community in France and the Quaker Action groups, both very active in the late 60s and early 70s. The Conflict Research Institute exemplified the inadequacy of concentrating on only one aspect of the problem. Few knew about it, and its influence appeared to be minimal. It had become lost in the web of academia.

Another peace priest in London was Benedictine Father Simon Blake. When I told one of the Jesuits at Farm Street Residence that I was on my way to visit Simon, he said, "Oh, you may hear something of Vietnam over in the priory (the Benedictine residence), but I wonder if they still believe in the Nicean Creed" — a sad commentary indeed on how interested that Jesuit and others like him were in peacemaking. But it convinced me that Simon was worth visiting.

Simon was dressed in a black suit and a black turtleneck sweater when I met him in the community room of the Benedictine priory. I told him what the Jesuit had said. He commented, "What does the Creed mean today? In a united world, to use nuclear weapons is suicide. To be concerned with the main moral problem of today is no neglect of the Creed." He also acted as the Vice-Chairman of the Campaign for Nuclear Disarmament which held an annual demonstration at Aldermaston where nuclear weapons were produced. It was out of the first demonstration in March 1958 that the peace symbol developed: a straight vertical line with two horizontal arms falling off from it, both enclosed in a circle. This symbol was selected to combine the two hand semaphore signals for the letters "N"(nuclear), the vertical line, and "D" (disarmament), the arms pointing down. The circle enclosing them symbolizes the world.

Simon had become involved with peacemaking because his brother, who was in the Naval Air Corps, was very concerned about indiscriminate bombing. The nuclear weapons used at Hiroshima and Nagasaki intensified his concern about weapons of mass destruction. We talked for hours and then went into the dining room, an old monastic-type room with bare tables laid out along the rectangular

1930 family portrait — from left to right, Front Row: Therese, Marge, Paul, Mary; Middle Row: Richard, John, Winifred holding baby Anne, Joe, Frank; Back Row: Jim, Eleanore, Patrick. Not Pictured: Rita (mother), Richard (dad), Rosemary (youngest sibling).

Poughkeepsie, New York - 1933 Richard McSorley as a Jesuit novice at St. Andrew on the Hudson.

Naga, Philippines — 1940 Richard McSorley, center front, with boys enjoying a snack on the steps to the boxing ring.

Left:
Lingayen, Philippines —
April 1945
McSorley brothers meet in
army chaplain's tent near
Manila. Left to right:
Richard, Frank, John.

Bottom:
Woodstock College —
First Mass, 1946
Richard T. McSorley, S.J.

Left:
South America —
1970
Richard McSorley
with shanty town
children.

Bottom Left:
Richard McSorley
circa 1980.

Bottom Right:
Georgetown — 1968
Richard McSorley
picketing against
ROTC.

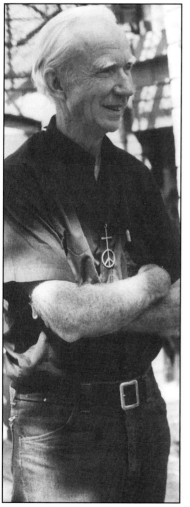

Would **YOU** be proud of "A" in R.O.T.C. ?

photo by J. Russell Lawrence, Georgetown Univ. News Service

Georgetown University — 1980
Richard McSorley and Bill Clinton, after Georgetown University commencement exercises.

Georgetown University — May 1995
Bill Clinton and Richard McSorley at Georgetown University, after Memorial Prayer for the
Dead of the Class of 1968.

walls and servers in the center. There were about thirty present; none of them seemed young. All wore white robes, while Simon and I were in black.

We continued to share stories of our work for peace. In France, Simon had led an interesting demonstration protesting France's nuclear weapons program. The group received a lot of attention when they carried a heavy cross for a long distance. He also told me of the picketing of Porton, the center which manufactures chemical and biological weapons. The United States worked very closely with the British on these weapons. In one of the demonstrations, four-hundred soldiers came out to protect the plant against one-hundred picketers. That reaction impressed upon me how the imagination of warmakers exaggerates the power of the peacemakers.

The peace marchers also used their imagination. They danced before the gates of Porton and then they all fell down. Simon explained that the children's game: "Ring around the rosy; A pocket full of posies; Ashes, ashes; We all fall down;" has its origin in the times of the black plague when people carried roses to overcome the awful smell of the dead around them. *All Fall Down* is also the name of a book on chemical warfare. Simon noted that humor is very important because the seriousness of the peace issue can be paralyzing.

He told me about John Collins of St. Paul's Cathedral who worked very actively against racism in America. Fr. Collins had lost his chance of becoming dean of St. Paul's and then head of the Church of England because he was very open in his opposition to apartheid in South Africa and to capital punishment. Also, he did not hide his opposition to the British government's nuclear deterrence policy. Simon gave me a copy of Collins' book *Faith Under Fire*, and I found it very worth the reading.

Simon contrasted Fr Collins' defiance with the action of the local bishop. The Campaign for Nuclear Disarmament wanted to have a service at the church near Porton, close to the chemical-biological military establishment. The march would end with a Mass. They were anxious to show the Catholic Church's interest in the march for peace. However, the local bishop insisted that the Director of the Porton military plant approve of the permission to use the church. This was an amazing example of Church subservience to the military.

Just when I thought I had heard it all, Simon educated me about some (more) ugly Church history: The persecution of the Jews began with the Crusades. On the way to the Crusades, the knights slaughtered German Jews on the Rhine and Eastern Rite Christians who did not use the Latin Mass — one of the worst examples of the sanctification of killing.

I asked Simon about the assertion of Fr. Courtney Murray that if there exists any doubt about whether a war is just or not, the benefit of the doubt must always be given to the state. This argument is often used to show that anyone who dissents from a war must prove that they have a clear case against the state. Otherwise, the presumption is that the state is correct in its judgment that war should be waged.

Simon responded that the presumption of the gospel is that the rich or those who rule the state are in danger of losing their souls because of their riches. He further commented that if two states are making war, both cannot be presumed to be right. Yet both invoke the name of God to support their argument. He argued that the idea of just war is academic in a nuclear world: War today is so destructive that you cannot presume that it is ever right. Also, Simon observed that the kind of authority that is needed today would be an authority that stands above the conflict, a transnational organization. National states no longer represent the common good.

He added that at the Nuremburg trials, the defendants all claimed they were only following orders, obeying the state. I suggested that even if the state may be presumed to be correct on some issues, when it comes to the issue of killing or ordering citizens to kill, it is on very shaky ground. Even by the standards of the Just War Theory, the right of the state to wage war is considered the exception to the gospel, allowed only on fulfillment of very rigid conditions.

Although Simon put no time limit on our conversation, finally, with a great deal of reluctance, I had to say good-bye and move on to my next appointment.

I visited the London branch of the Fellowship of Reconciliation (FOR). The Fellowship began in 1914 when two Christian ministers saw World War I as evidence that the gospel of peace was not believed. Its members oppose all killing on a scriptural basis. At the office I met Leslie Tarlton who invited me to come that very evening to a yearly re-dedication service of FOR members at St. Martin of the Fields Church near Trafalgar Square.

When I arrived at St. Martin's, a church often used by the royal family, a few hundred people had gathered for the service in which the members re-dedicate themselves to their basic belief: "In order to establish a world order based on love, it is incumbent on those who believe in this principle to accept it fully both for themselves and in relation to others and to take the risks involved in doing so in a world which does not as yet accept it. That, therefore, as Christians, we are forbidden to wage war, and that our loyalty to our country, to humanity, to the Church Universal and to Jesus Christ our Lord and Master, calls us instead to a life of service for the enthronement of love in personal, social, commercial, and national life."

An Anglican minister, George Mitchell, gave the sermon. Using a story from the Book of Chronicles, he talked about how Solomon had built a temple and a palace built with slave labor. Solomon thought that the palace and the temple would unite the people, but the power which was built on slavery did not unite. The people revolted against the son of Solomon. Those who led the revolt were the Sumerians who refused to own slaves and wanted to free them. Judah went to war and lost. So the question that was asked then, and in every war, is: "Whose side is God on?" The point was made that the presumption in the question is that God is on one side. But in fact, the whole question is wrong. The question should be: "Are we on God's side when we are waging war?"

Reverend Mitchell pointed out that God is the Father of all VietCong, of all Englishmen, and even the Father of Americans. He asked the rhetorical question we should ask ourselves: "Are there any good VietCong? Good Chinese? Good Communists? Good Americans? Are there any good Japanese?"

During a return visit with Archbishop Roberts, we discussed the beliefs of the Fellowship of Reconciliation. He said that he could not agree with their stand against all war because it would rule out even a police force. I answered that it did not rule out a police force, it just ruled out killing. A United Nations force or an international police force that stopped short of killing would be possible. In view of the capacity of our technology to supply us with incapacitating weapons, there is no need to kill in order to capture or immobilize criminals.

Archbishop Roberts also argued that death is not as bad as life in slavery and that you must allow for slaves to throw off the yoke of their masters. I pointed out that theoretically this might be allowed, but in practice the slaves would likely bring on more bloodshed and more slavery and give the tyrant wider support in the community. As a matter of fact, in the history of throwing off the yoke of slavery there were always more than just a few people killed. Killing begets more killing.

I continued to say, in support of my case, that the Just War Theory on which this idea of throwing off the yoke of slavery is based, is a very complex theory with many conditions that must be fulfilled. It is doubtful that they can be fulfilled in a revolutionary situation. Furthermore, the ordinary person on the street does not always understand or care about such complex theories. If you are going to reduce the gospel to something that can only be understood by the learned and the informed, then it cannot be for the masses who are likely to be the slaves. Archbishop Roberts answered that life is complex and that a certain amount of complexity is necessary if you are going to deal with life. I retorted that the characteristics of war today — the mass killings, the psychological mobilization of the people to hate each other, and the momentum in every war which carries it to a savagery that was unplanned — make every war a violation of any kind of Just War Theory.

I was impressed with Roberts' willingness to listen and to consider what he heard. He was approachable and mellow, and he was also a Jesuit — that was a bond between us.

Archbishop Roberts had been in India during Gandhi's time and thought Gandhi just as bad on the issues of sex as Pope Paul. He also said that Gandhi was too idealistic about the use of Indian cloth and that he is not followed in India today on that point, but repudiated. I started to defend Gandhi, but the Archbishop replied that he liked Steven King-Hall better.

Steven King-Hall was a commander in the British Navy who proposed that the military system should be court-martialed for not following the rules. King-Hall, author of some thirty publications, asserted that weapons of mass destruction have made war obsolete. War is not won simply by killing people. He believed that education was the key to the military's future. First, all must believe in some basic values; no one will win a war they do not believe in. If there is no set of values there is no chance of winning. Instead of victory by mass murder, you must try to convert your opponent to your values, make them believe you have a better set of values to offer. War is essentially a conflict of ideas.

Archbishop Roberts concluded that King-Hall's approach is a fully commonsensical one, but that Gandhi's is quasi-mystical. King-Hall asks the question: "How can the Navy be useful today?" His idea is that the whole approach must change and that weapons of universal destruction have made that change necessary.

King-Hall maintained that the root cause of war is the maldistribution of wealth and that the cost of nuclear weapons only aggravates this injustice. In *In Defense in the Nuclear Age*, King-Hall argues that military strategists who prepare England to become a radioactive ash-heap, are not defending the country. Since any nuclear war would do this, he prepared a whole new concept of war fighting which renounces nuclear, then conventional weapons, and substitutes a strategy of resistance to death, even after occupation. There is some hope in this plan, but none in nuclear weapons.

On November 13, I went back to the University of London to talk with Bruce Kent. We set out with his large gray Labrador retriever for a walk in the park and talked about peace issues in the Church and the world. He was so intrigued with my peace course, War and Peace, that he thought a similar course should be offered at the Jesuit seminary, Heathrop Seminary, which was in the process of moving into the city in order to affiliate with the university.

Before I left, we phoned Father Copleston, Dean of the Heathrop Seminary and a famous writer of philosophy, about meeting with him to discuss the possibility of introducing a peace course. However, Father Copleston was not the least bit interested. No meeting. No peace course. End of phone call.

Bruce said that Copleston reacted to the word "peace" as if the word "spinach" had been used. If Monsignor Bruce Kent, former secretary to the Cardinal Primate, Chaplain at prestigious London University, got a put-off like that, what would happen to someone less famous?

I pointed out that the ordinary Jesuit (and Copleston might be one of them) goes from one academic experience to another. He goes from seminary to graduate school and then on to teaching at a university. This often leaves him without practical experience in judging how academic decisions affect human life. He lives in a small and artificial world of academics.

I told Bruce that chaplaincy is better than academic bureaucracy. As chaplain he can be concerned with the human side of life, not just the university which is separated from much of life and is depersonalized. The chaplain has to solve problems in the human context; this usually results in a set of priorities which puts the human first, while the impersonal, structural, academic view often relegates human values to second place.

My own awareness of human values developed when I was pastor of a racially-mixed parish in a segregated area. I had the chance to see the higher priority of human values over racist theory. I believe that without that experience I wouldn't have been nearly as sure of my priorities. Nor would I have felt such a kinship with Bruce Kent or Simon Blake.

On November 15,1969, I participated in the British moratorium against the Vietnam War in front of the U.S. Embassy at Grosvenor Square in London. Even the appearance of the Embassy stressed the over-exaggerated nature of U.S. power. A gigantic spread eagle emblem about eight or ten feet wide dominated the front of the building. Unlike other embassies where the flag flies from the roof, two flags hung inside the glassed-in front of this building. The building itself took up one entire side of the square, and the total effect of the architecture and decor said to passers-by, "America is the biggest and greatest power on the globe." Both the effect and the scale were out of tune with the subtle, more gentle architecture that graced most of London.

On that day in November about five-hundred people, both English and Americans, were meeting to express their sorrow at U.S. misuse of power in Vietnam. Other demonstrations took place that same day in Birmingham, Manchester, Liverpool, Glasgow, Edinburgh, Bristol, Brighton, and other places. These actions supported similar efforts in the United States.

As I approached the square, several hundred people had already begun to march. The crowd walked around the sidewalk which ringed the outside of the park. Most of them carried signs which read, "Americans out of Vietnam; Bring our boys home; Withdraw American Troops; Stop the Injustice." Some of the banners carried by our marchers gave the names of places destroyed by American firepower in Vietnam. Other large posters carried the heads of skeletons with a black hat on top. When you drew closer, you could see that the eyes and other black parts of the skull were made up of pictures of dead Americans cut from magazines.

Each marcher carried a card on which was written the name of a dead soldier and the city and state from which he came. As each passed around the square to the front of the embassy, he or she read the name of the dead soldier on a loudspeaker pointed toward the embassy, then deposited the card in a small coffin that lay on the ground across the street. Around the coffin, five or six young men lay in the street pretending to be dead. Bobbies lined both sides of the street. More police waited in parked cars and a bus.

In contrast to U.S. demonstrations, the police had a relaxed attitude. They did not wear guns or carry sticks. They were friendly and cooperative when spoken to. The crowd in turn made no remarks attacking the police. Throughout the afternoon, even though some militant groups arrived, the relationship between the crowd and the police never worsened. All of the demonstrators wore black armbands and were well directed by the stewards who marched them around the square.

In the middle of the afternoon, a group from the moratorium marched up Bond Street to the Swedish Embassy to show appreciation for the Swedish government providing a haven to war resisters.

After three hours one of the women who was handing out names of the dead said to me, "I've been here since 1:30 p.m. giving out these cards and look how many I still have to give out. There are so many dead!" Although she only heard names and held papers, her heart, mind, and imagination reached to recall the golden youth who would never sing or laugh or run or love again. Why? We believed there was no good answer to that question, only bad answers: false and lying answers!

As the hours wore on and name after name was read with the word "dead" spoken after each, the impression of the horror of this war grew. About the middle of the afternoon, a boy with a drum began to beat a muffled beat between the readings of each name. This continued for the rest of the afternoon.

For awhile I talked with a young English woman of twenty who worked in a newspaper office. I asked her how she got interested in the peace movement. She answered, "I just continued to get more and more angry as I read the newspaper reports of what is going on in Vietnam. I do not pretend to be a scholar, but the situation there is so bad that I just couldn't help but do something about it."

Toward evening a large number of additional police arrived; the reason was soon clear. Up the street and into the square marched a group of sixty to seventy young men who were representatives of the Communist Party. The procession was led by a sound truck broadcasting a speech against the war. After the police forced them to stop using the sound truck, they joined us in the march. Soon some of the communists began to heckle the other marchers, "You aren't giving political education about the evils of imperialism, you are just reading off the names of the dead. You aren't getting into the reason why these people are dead and you're not reading the names of any of the Vietnamese dead."

I answered that the U.S. government and the rest of the world saw our actions as a call to end the war. Then I asked one of them, "If you agree that the war should be ended, why do you come with speech that divides the marchers?" He didn't answer the questions, but continued with his same argument.

Some of the people in the march told me that communists were a problem for the British peace movement. There were only a few thousand communists, but they were very zealous, often confronting gatherings like this to make it difficult for the peacemakers to carry out a program without their interference.

When it grew dark, we read names by candle-light for an hour or more before we finally came to the end of the names. We had received word from the embassy that they would not allow the small coffin to be brought in the door, so the thousands of names were transferred to plastic bags, and a group started to move across the street to the U.S. Embassy. At this point, a nearby policeman started pushing against me and telling the crowd to move back. I noted that he did not lay his hands on me; he just pushed his stomach against me. I asked him, "How do you expect me to move back with all these people behind me? Do you want me to push against them?" He just kept mumbling something like, "Let's move back there now; let's be agreeable; let's move back."

The question with the police was soon settled — they allowed six people to take the names of the dead into the embassy. The six carried torches and candles as they walked slowly across the street. BBC television took pictures of the crowd bathed in candle light and singing, "We Shall Overcome."

As we were leaving, a young American announced through the loudspeaker that on the next day, there would be an interdenominational service to urge the immediate withdrawal of all American troops from Vietnam.

The next day I joined with several hundred other people for at St. Mark's Anglican Church near the square. Most of the participants were young, and many of them were Americans. As I was waiting for the ceremony to begin, Bill Clinton, then a Georgetown student and a Rhodes Scholar at Oxford, came up to give me a warm welcome. He was one of the organizers and asked me to open the service with a prayer.

All of the presenters at the memorial service were young people. Although it was a sad day, I was encouraged and comforted by the determination of these young women and men who would stand against the evils of war.

I was also glad to see a Georgetown student leading the religious service for peace. After the service Bill introduced me to some of his friends. With them, I paraded to the U.S. Embassy; we each carried a white wooden cross about one foot high. At the embassy we left the crosses as an indication of our desire to end the agony of Vietnam.

Coastal France

In England I boarded a triple-deck tourist boat bound for France. From the top deck I looked up at the chalk cliffs: the solid white walls, about one-hundred feet high, that rise straight up from the beach. Out in the Channel the boat began to rock and seemed to be riding sideways on the waves, and I soon felt the seasickness so often chronicled by Channel voyagers. I watched the waves from the window of the boat's restaurant and thought of the young men who had sailed this sea to their death in World War II.

In three hours I was at the town of Dieppe, population twenty-thousand. As the boat sailed into the harbor, I could see a lovely church high on the cliff. Dominating the landscape, the image of the church reminded me of the days when the Church dominated Europe. I wondered how history might have been if the English Church had not broken away from Rome. How would this have affected the history of the United States? Religion and faith should unify the world just as war divides it. But when religion is allied with war, the world loses its best chance for unity and peace.

The business district of Dieppe was just off the pier. At the tourist bureau, Syndicat d'Intiatiative (Union of Initiative), I got a map and a pamphlet with the story of the Canadian landing here in World War II. I drove six miles inland on the Paris Road. As the sun dipped low in the horizon, I came upon a small walled-in military cemetery, about the area of one city block, enclosed by a low fence. Surrounded by gentle hills and farms, the cemetery was shielded from view. This especially morbid burial ground was created specifically for this Canadian group; no one else will join them. The war had separated them even in death from their loved ones. I counted one thousand graves, close together in lines of sixty, all almost too neatly kept. I recalled what Daniel Berrigan had said to me as we rode through Arlington Cemetery, "It's all so antiseptic, all so well-arranged. It makes war look like that was well-arranged too."

In these thousand graves there is nothing of the agony, nothing of the gory reality, nothing of the frustration and stupidity of coming onto a beach that was so heavily armed. There's nothing here to remind us of the cries of anguish that rose up in the thousand homes at the news of these young men's deaths. There's nothing about the suffering of the broken families who struggled to repair their lives.

Governments keep military graves in such good order that military cemeteries become, in some minds, one of the glories of war. Thought of in this way, graves become an invitation to die in the same way in another war. They become a step in removing the stigma, the fear and the knowledge of the horror of war.

By the time I left, the sun had set. It was a dark, cold and dead November night. The young victims of war's solution to human problems lay quiet and unattended. Only their graves spoke out to me this silent night about the futility of war, about the irrationality of war, and about the inhumanity of war. I was there alone to receive their message. I pass it on to you.

I drove back to the hotel through dark streets. Because of a strike, the power was off. In the gloom, the atmosphere evoked a sense of life in the Middle Ages. I was led to my room by the hotel manager with a candle.

In the morning I drove along narrow roads that wound their way through lush farmland to the town of Puys. Here too, a Canadian regiment had landed where now the road drops to the coast, between two high palisades. Now the scene was peaceful. Family dairy farms made up most of the town. Waves broke rhythmically along the rocky shore. From these cliffs the German Army had smashed the Canadians, and the survivors withdrew. Above the beach is a monument on which is inscribed:

> On this beach, officers and men of the Royal Regiment of
> Canada died at dawn, 19th August, 1942, striving to reach the
> heights beyond. You, who are alive on this beach, remember

that these men died far from home so that others, here and everywhere, might freely enjoy life in God's mercy.

In front of the plaque sits a large stone grave marker in remembrance of the Canadian fighters whose bodies were never recovered. An inscription, in French, reads:

"Les anciens prisonniers de guerre Neuville les Dieppe reconaissants 19 aug. 1960." (The former prisoners of war of Neuville remember the men of Dieppe on the 19th of August, 1960.)

The message of the inscription for the general public is that war is honorable, that death in war is honorable, and that everybody should be prepared to participate in this honor if called upon. This brand of grand propaganda emphasizes sacrifice, but ignores the primary purpose of war: to kill, to force your will through violence.

I drove up the coast three miles to Belville, a small farming village high on a cliff. I looked out over the edge and down to the surf. The roar of the waves seemed greater here than on the other side of the Atlantic. As I stood there, I thought of how bodies of water connect all the shores of all lands, and thus all people.

My thoughts then turned to how equally divisive war is. It is essentially irrational to solve by force that which we cannot or will not solve by rational argument. Any theory that makes war look good; any human work that makes war look worthwhile, as these monuments try to do, is an attempt to make rational what is essentially irrational.

Monuments of war take a marginal element, the undesired death of war's victims, and turn it around to make it look glorious — as though these young men had chosen death or revealed the highest of human achievements in obeying unwise orders. Their orders were not to die, but to kill.

We are told in the poem *The Charge of the Light Brigade*, which immortalized a battle of the Crimean War, "Theirs was not to reason why, theirs is but to do and die." When the idea expressed here is accepted, you've taken God out of your life and out of your plans and made a God out of the state. Such a position is idolatry, a form of madness.

In the film *King of Hearts,* a commentary on the insanity of war, when people from the mental institution are placed in a war situation, they are more at home than the soldiers. Nonetheless they prefer to go back to their crazy house than to live among the army.

— ❖ ❖ ❖ —

The Netherlands

I traveled by train through France and into Belgium. After an overnight stay in Brussels, I continued by train to the Hague. Once there, through the assistance of Mr. C. Termaat, International Secretary of Pax Christi, I got an appointment to see Cardinal Alfrink, a leader in the European peace movement. Eight Dutch bishops, under the leadership of Cardinal Alfrink, had published the pastoral letter titled *Banning War*. This document gave a strong message of peace, rejected Augustine's Just War Theory and called people to work together in very specific ways. In part it said, "As in our time mankind is facing the possibility of total destruction by war, we must develop an attitude toward war that is completely different from the way we looked on it in the past."

The document went on to state that the story of Cain's fratricide is not the last word of the Bible. The disturbed relations between peoples is not the final truth. The deepest truth concerning humankind is the reconciliation in Jesus Christ. Armaments and local conflicts that spread and develop into a world conflict, make war senseless. Resignation to the inevitability of war diverts us from the road to peace. The legacy left behind by Gandhi, Martin Luther King, Jr. and other pioneers of nonviolence shows us that political action against injustice and oppression must be administered carefully and made to bear fruit. This kind of resistance finds its support not in military power, but in spiritual power. Peace work offers as many opportunities to be a hero as does war.

The Dutch Bishops' letter was hammered out in a thorough dialogue between the bishops and laity who were delegates to the Council. In both a forthright attitude toward peace and in promotion of dialogue between the bishops and the people, Cardinal Alfrink proved himself a world leader. Alfrink was the International President of Pax Christi, the Catholic peace organization dedicated to the ideal that Christians should form the avant-garde striving for peace.

The Pax Christ movement came into existence in 1944 when its founder Monsignor Theas, a prisoner of the Nazis, had the courage to proclaim to fellow prisoners the Gospel charge that they should love even these enemies. He felt war was caused by both sides and that a clearing of the air was of primary importance. He chose a rapprochement between France and Germany as his first task. The first phase, marked by this idea of reconciliation, gradually attracted more countries.

Cardinal Felton, primate of France, gave the movement a program based on three elements: prayer, study and action. Later Pax Christi tried to promote the spiritual testimony of Pope John XXIII. It adopted *Pacem en Terris*, the peace letter of Pope John, as its charter. Under the leadership of Cardinal Alfrink, Pax Christi promoted: peace on every level of existence, particularly in world relations; and a sense of personal responsibility in world events. The movement cooperates, to the greatest possible extent, with other forces and organizations like the U.N. which are devoted to the cause of peace. In a variety of ways — publications, conferences, centers for study — it promotes peace.

Pax Christi is not just a paper organization, a pretense of the Church doing something, but rather is the Church in action, organized together with peace groups from other Christian denominations. Pax Christi works to change the structure of governments where they need to be changed and to create the political atmosphere in which peace can exist. I think it offers a model for all Christians who are interested in peace.

Cardinal Alfrink agreed to see me two days after my initial phone call. It was unusual to be able to make an appointment with a high Church official so easily. Due to travel difficulties I missed the appointment by several hours, but a phone call reinstated the appointment for the next day. I could think of no cardinal in the United States who would offer the same courtesy to an unknown Dutch priest who had missed an appointment.

Cardinal Alfrink lived in a row house on an ordinary residential street — no grand palace with a fence around it. A pleasant housekeeper opened the door and asked me to sit in the parlor. After a few minutes, a middle-aged man with gray hair and a firm face and shoulders, warmly greeted me, "Welcome, Father McSorley." I looked for the cardinal's red or some sign of rank, but there was nothing. He wore only a simple black suit with a roman collar.

We sat together at a small table as friends might. We spoke at length about the Dutch Bishops' pastoral letter on peace, and I gave him a report on conscientious objection in the United States. I also told him of my interest in Pax Christi. He was amazed to learn that no U.S. bishop was interested enough in peace to lead a U.S. chapter of Pax Christi. (Today, of course, that situation is changed. Today ninety-two U.S bishops are active members of Pax Christi.) But he was heartened to hear about the role played by Church leaders in Clergy and Laity Concerned About Vietnam.

I was honored that a cardinal would make so much time for me, and I was impressed by his lifestyle, by his manner and by the peace message spoken through it all. I left his home with a deepened commitment to work for peace and an increased hope that the Church could be the instrument of peace that Christ intended.

— ❖ ❖ ❖ —

After my visit with Cardinal Alfrink, I traveled just eight miles from Utrecht to Drieburgen. There I caught the last day of a conference called "Peace Week" sponsored by an ecumenical peace group, Church in the World. Peace Week, a study and action program started in 1965, brought together Catholics and Protestants to evaluate accomplishments of various committees in the educational, political and religious sectors of society.

Although the entire discussion was in Dutch, John Barry translated for me while Mr. Termaat provided explanations. One report demonstrated how youth organizations were doing more than the churches to promote peace. In response to this, participants discussed outreach efforts to unions and young socialists. At least some church outreach was working because one Church in the World questionnaire showed that fifty percent of the general (Dutch) population had heard about Peace Week.

Another example of the leadership Catholics gave to the peace movement was Cardinal Alfrink's letter, published in *Pax Christi* magazine, asking the Dutch military to recognize conscientious objectors who morally oppose participation in the Dutch Army when it is under NATO command.

Peace Week ended with a beautiful ecumenical liturgy at which Catholic Bishop Moller participated with Dr. A. van Leuden, the director of Church in the World.

With the work of organizing Peace Week behind him, Dr. Eterman, chairman of the International Fellowship of Reconciliation, had time to meet with me. While visiting in his parlor, he told me that even though Peace Week was doing wonderful work, he was disappointed that it tolerated those who kill with a good conscience just as it tolerated and encouraged those who refuse to kill. After all, FOR is a pacifist organization.

As we drank tea, I felt a strong community bond with him. He was about forty, vigorous, with brown hair and a mustache. He obviously was committed to his work and, although a busy man, was willing to interrupt his lunch to be hospitable to me. Enjoying the family hospitality, I met his wife and eight (!) children (three adopted).

At the Jesuit college in Amsterdam I had supper with a roomful of seminarians. None were wearing a Roman collar or religious dress, although a few wore gold lapel crosses. This was a new experience for me and reminded me of how conventional American Jesuits are.

After a half-hour train ride from Amsterdam, I arrived in Heiloo and went to the home of Otto Boetes. This peacemaker also had served in the Dutch parliament. The earmarks of an individualist were apparent in his parlor. There was a large, thick plank hanging from the ceiling by four heavy chains. This formed a low table which gave the entire parlor the appearance of a ship. The ceiling was made of rafters; wicker chairs added to the marine atmosphere.

Once, the police had raided his house. They were looking for leaflets and stickers used in the campaign that Otto organized to publicize the fact that, according to Nuremberg principles, President Johnson was a war criminal. Apparently it was against the law in Holland to make unfavorable remarks about the heads of friendly nations.

Otto and his wife worked to find safe havens for American deserters in exile. In Holland the government sent U.S. deserters back to the country they had come from. Typically, within a few hours after arrest the deserter was back on the plane. This prevented appeals from anti-war parliamentarians, like Otto, who demanded that the whole case be examined before returning the deserter.

Only recently resigned from parliament, Otto left the legislative body because he felt crushed by the weight of the majority. Besides all his other activities, he had organized monthly anti-Vietnam marches. In addition to politics, he had served as clerk of the Quaker yearly meeting. Since this religious group doesn't have a hierarchy, the yearly meeting serves as the decision-making entity. He resigned when some Quakers questioned his holding an anti-Vietnam War meeting in a church, an action some considered too political.

Because he saw me as a companion in peacemaking, he welcomed me into his home. He illustrated, in one person and in one family, what the Quaker community in the world illustrates: namely, one person with a belief is equal to a force of ninety-nine who have only interests. His belief was so strong that he risked his government job and even risked his family's security

Seven years later I again met Otto and his wife at the Movement for a New Society in Philadelphia, where they spent a year learning new ways of bringing peace to their country and to the world. People like the Boetes do more to change the world than any generals or military heroes.

Sunday morning I attended a liturgy at the Dominican priory in Amsterdam. I could not understand the sermon, but I did hear the words Vietnam, Biafra and Dubcek. I later learned that this inclusion of politics in the sermon was not unusual. The topic of the sermon had been discussed beforehand with the people. After the sermon, a mimeographed copy of the previous Sunday's sermon was distributed in the back of the church. The congregation, seven hundred people in the lower part and more in the two balconies, sang and participated fully in the ceremonies.

In Gronegen I visited the Institute of Peace Research and met the director, Dr. Bert Roling, one of the most influential voices for peace in Holland. In his regular television program he discussed international politics, nuclear armaments, armament expenditures and how all of these relate to the individual. He wanted to move people in the right direction, if only a little bit.

This gray-haired and dignified man of sixty had a busy schedule which included a meeting with the former economics minister of Czechoslovakia the next morning. He had formed the Institute in 1952, which received funding from the government, although was not controlled by the government. Roling also lectured on international law at the University of Groningen.

During our visit I asked him about the possibility of thermonuclear war. He thought it could not happen because the Soviet Union and the United States had too great a fear of each other. (Time has proved him right in that.) I commented on the fact that this was no satisfactory basis for building peace. He replied, "No, but it is all we have."

Roling invited me to critique the institute. My only question: "You state in your brochure that your purpose is to promote peace through research and action and that in doing this you use the expertise of leading authorities in the fields of sociology, psychology, international law and other sciences. Why do you not have someone to represent theology?"

He leaned back in his chair and laughed heartily, his whole head shaking. When he recovered, I asked him what was so funny. "Because theology has contributed more to war than toward peace."

"I admit that," I said, "but if that's true, there should be some exposure of that fact through research so that theology can stop being a force for war. Religious leaders do not admit they support war; they see themselves as peacemakers. If research could convince them that they have contributed to war, they might stop supporting it. Let me put the question more broadly," I continued. "Your brochure nowhere directly or indirectly mentions God. Do you imply that you can get peace without God?"

"Of course not. Organized religion is one of the greatest influences on people. It could be of great help in creating a peaceful world."

Ben Terveer drove me to the home of Foppert Benedictus, a conscientious objector, who filled me in on the process for obtaining CO status in Holland. A central board sets standards that oblige local boards to grant CO status to any applicant who fulfills the requirements. This is just the opposite of the American system during the Vietnam era which let local boards exercise their own discretion. With no uniform standard in the United States, the 4,092 draft boards operating during the Vietnam War tended to grant CO status arbitrarily. Holland's conscientious objectors were assigned to work in hospitals and in government jobs as traffic directors or office secretaries.

I left Groningen enlightened by all that I had learned about what was being done for peace, but with a new sense of the endless job ahead. I ended my time in Holland at Assem with Tom Bossman, one of the best-known lion tamers in Europe and a member of Fellowship of Reconciliation. I found this unique individual at work in the provincial museum. He put away his carpenter's tools and sat down to visit with me. Half-facetiously I asked if he saw any relationship between lion taming and taming the war machine. He took a minute to absorb my question and then laughed heartily.

He told me his story: At age sixteen, while working with large animals at a zoo, he grew fond of the lions and discovered they were not violent, although they could be dangerous. They only killed when they felt threatened or needed food. He left his job at the zoo to work with lions at the circus. While many lion tamers used a whip or a club, Tom only used a bamboo stick to give food to the lions. In this way he tried to win the cooperation of the lions, rather than control them. Although retired from lion training, through FOR he continued working with the more difficult problem of taming people.

Scandinavia

From Holland I traveled on to Stockholm where the effects of U.S. foreign policy appeared to me from a very different perspective and in sharp focus. As I walked from the train, I saw Swedish soldiers guarding an American office building with large glass windows that had been broken many times. I learned that many American firms had the same military protection for their buildings.

President Nixon, without explanation, had delayed assigning an ambassador to Sweden for many months. It seemed obvious that this was due to Swedish Prime Minister Palme's criticism of the United States' war in Vietnam

I found my friend, Tom Hayes, in his second-floor apartment with his two daughters and three other American expatriates. Tom, an American and an Episcopal minister, was sponsored by Catholic, Protestant, and Jewish groups to be chaplain to the four-hundred or so American deserters in Sweden. I was unfamiliar with the term "deserter" and learned that they intentionally used this term, rejecting the Pentagon's "defector'" label which implied that they had gone over to the other side. They also rejected the term AWOL, absent without leave, used by the U.S. Embassy and State Department. The deserters no longer considered themselves to be part of the military. The men compared their experience to a forced exile, to that of the Jews wandering in the desert for forty years.

I had supper with three deserters: George Meals, Gerry Condon, and Dan Porlock. Later Richard Pauley and Michael Baker came in. They were critical and suspicious of me. If I had not been the guest of Hayes, they would have thought I was an agent sent to spy on them. While we were eating, Charles Cutlip and his wife came in.

Tom Hayes told me there was almost every imaginable type of person among the American deserters in Sweden: Australians, Puerto Ricans, even some Englishmen. According to U.S. law, any visitor was eligible to be drafted after six-months residence in the United States. Before deserting, they had served an average of twenty-two months in the U.S. Armed Forces.

The day after I arrived, I met a British citizen named Desmond. Drafted into the U.S. Army, he refused to serve and instead came to Sweden. The British government told him that if he returned to England, the British courts would be obligated by a treaty with the United States to turn him over to U.S. authorities.

Gerry Condon had been a Green Beret. He finished serving his time in Vietnam and returned to California where he spoke against the war to the press. He was immediately dropped by the Green Berets and ordered to go back to Vietnam in the regular army. He refused and came to Sweden. Here, in Stockholm, he was visited by a Catholic army chaplain who argued for hours that he should go into the military as a non-combatant. Gerry said, "The chaplain claimed he had never met anyone with whom he was so diametrically opposed."

Gerry's case was typical of how the army deals with the issue of conscience. Gerry did not leave the United States immediately. First, he was court-martialed. His lawyers told him he was facing five to ten years in prison. So he got a passport and spent the next seven months hitch-hiking around Europe. In Germany he phoned his mother who told him the authorities were searching for him there. So he headed for Stockholm. In 1977 he finally came back to the United States with a good conduct discharge and worked for amnesty through Clergy and Laity Concerned.

After supper, the crowd at the apartment continued to grow. That night I slept at the Hayes' home along with many others. But this scene was soon to end;

Tom was planning to return to the United States. The next morning he gave a farewell television interview about the work he had been doing with the deserters. One reporter questioned why there was no replacement. Tom answered that he had done himself out of a job. The idea of a chaplain was to help Americans in Stockholm integrate their lives into the life and culture of the country. He felt a start had been made and the job could better be done by Swedes and people like Jim Walsh, who was living there and actively helping Americans. Tom noted that, for the first time in our history, Americans were fleeing the United States and seeking political asylum from American militarists — the end of the role of America as a haven for those wanting to live by freedom of conscience.

Besides meeting deserters, I also learned a lot about life in Sweden. One distinctive feature of Sweden is the great national prejudice against drinking, a response to a history of over-drinking, perhaps caused by the prolonged cold and dark in winter. Bars were strictly controlled, and young people had no place to go at night. Their elders stressed that their place is at home. Consequently, people took refuge in meetings and lengthy political discussions. I found the people to be politically sophisticated.

Tom Hayes took me to the home of Dick Pytok, another deserter, who lived in a very poor section of Stockholm on Kocksgatan Street. He had hunted for six months to find a place to live. To get housing in Stockholm you submit your name to the housing bureau, and then you wait, sometimes years, depending on your priority designation. Those with children have higher priority. Consequently, Dick turned to the black market; he paid nine hundred dollars to rent his very poor apartment with no shower, flimsy walls, and heated only by a kerosene stove in the bedroom. For bathing, he and his wife went to nearby friends or used the public shower, including a sauna, for twelve cents. The floor, eight inches above the earth, had no heat under it; not the best situation in cold Stockholm winters. In the first six months, the landlord could evict without cause. Sounds like the United States.

Most landlords wouldn't even rent to foreigners. Dick and his wife were fortunate because she had dual Icelandic and English citizenship. All Scandinavian countries recognize the citizenship of Iceland, Norway, Finland and Denmark.

Although the housing situation was bad, other government services were good. Richard and Desmond, another deserter, took a course on computer programming, paid for by the government. The government also helped with the rent and medical bills.

Although satisfied with his new life in Sweden, Dick expressed frustration with U.S. journalists' depiction of it. The deserters were tired of pouring their hearts out, telling American journalists why they left the United States, only to find the journalists concentrating on small details like the number of deserters arrested on drug charges — not even mentioning the deserters' deep-felt opposition to the war.

Some American journalists, former CIA employees, wrote biased reports. For example, one journalist claimed that each of the hundred deserters he met wanted to return to the States. Although most of the deserters did indeed want to return home to see friends and family, many didn't want to live under or participate in the American empire. Many insisted that until the whole idea of the United States' "policing" the world was rejected, they would not return. This was a commonly-shared opinion among all the deserters I met.

"In five more years we can be Swedish citizens," said Desmond. "Then we could go to Germany for Octoberfest, we could go anywhere — except the U.S. We'll be ready to help American deserters from the war — in Thailand or Brazil or South Africa. . . ."

My last glimpse of a few of my deserter friends was in the subway. It was not easy to leave them, exiles for the sake of conscience. I wondered why more of us were not with them and reflected on what Chuck Cutlip had told me: "We have got to make it on our own." They gave very concrete evidence of the ability of some men and women to say "no" to a quality of life distorted by its dependence on the combination of the military and industrial spending for war.

I took the train bound for Uppsala, traveling through a landscape that looked like a Christmas card, the trees freshly frosted with snow. In Uppsala I met with Reverend James Jones, a Baptist chaplain at the International Student House. An American married to a Swede, he ran a dormitory and provided the chaplaincy services for the international students. I boarded for five days in his office where he had a spare bed.

Eighteen American deserters were enrolled at the state university in Uppsala. Although Jim was not appointed to serve as chaplain for them, he provided strong support. Because of his work with deserters, some in his own church withdrew their support of his ministry.

Jim invited me to join him at the Holy Spirit Chapel for a performance by the magnificent International Student Choir. The heavy wooden pews, candle-light, chandeliers, green and gold angels painted on the ceiling in that ancient cathedral created an other-worldly atmosphere. A robed minister gave a sermon and made announcements including one about a benefit for the aged, co-sponsored by the American deserters.

At the university, I attended a seminar on peace research led by Dr. B. Weimark. A student reported on six months of peace research in the United States at Yale and Stanford — programs funded by the Navy. One program analyzed U.N. votes related to the trade practices of those countries; the other related economic theory to international conflict. The student, when questioned, found no correlation between the topics researched and the source of the money for research.

I asked him, "Was there anything in the research critical of the war, massive nuclear retaliation, or Selective Service?"

When he answered, "No," I continued. "Do you think that your funding would have been continued if the research had been critical of any part of military policy?" The student did not know what to answer. I explained that the Defense Department pretends to work for peace by funding what they call peace research. It is true that some of these projects might actually help in peacemaking, but they do not deal with the priority questions. Also, they usually draw conclusions which are critical of other countries.

I went on to comment that our basic mistake is that we think peace can be achieved by military means. The means used will determine the end. Violent means cannot bring a peaceful resolution. This was painfully evident in Vietnam.

I met Pat Downey and his wife, Linda. Pat had been in the Catholic Peace Fellowship. Although Pat and Linda Downey were young, they had a different understanding of their relationship to church and state than most Catholics. Pat remembered that in his Catholic grade school he was taught very basic, simple things — not to kill and to be good to your fellow man. Once drafted, he didn't apply immediately for conscientious objection because he thought he could work out a deal with the army. The first week he had a personal interview with his company commander. He told the commander that he would not kill anyone, ever. It was against his principles, it was against his religion. The commander said he would work something out, a vague answer.

At the end of eight weeks of basic training, he just handed Pat his orders: Report to Fort Ord California for artillery training. The night before graduation, Pat decided he would refuse the direct order to do military training.

Pat explained to me that he had not applied for conscientious objector status because he was ignorant of the process. The first eight weeks he had put his trust in this one man, the commander, and then it was too late to say he was a conscientious objector because it would appear as though he had just waited for orders and then chickened out.

The military assigned a guard to point an M-16 at Pat's back and march him off to the stockade to await a court martial. On his second day in the stockade a chaplain helped Pat with the CO application process. Finally, after much red-tape, he was released. They placed him in an office position pending the outcome of his application — a five-month wait.

In the end, the military refused to grant him status as a conscientious objector. They stated that there wasn't enough information even though a Catholic priest wrote on Pat's behalf, along with a lawyer from his hometown, and other professional people.

Not only was he denied CO status, but a sergeant from the Military Personnel Division made sure he was assigned duty in Vietnam. The sergeant said, "That son of a bitch will shoot or be killed." Pat held firm to his beliefs. With no options left, he headed for Sweden — AWOL — and joined the growing group of resisters. His wife was able to join him and they started a new life.

— ❖ ❖ ❖ —

After visiting with Pat and Linda, they thought I should meet Father Henri Roel. A Dutch priest studying theology at Uppsala University, he was the lone Catholic living in a community of Lutherans. In their home was a small chapel where we joined together for vespers and evening prayer.

Father Roel showed me around and introduced me to the six other men with whom he lived in a dormitory-style room. They seemed pleased to have another Catholic priest among them. Over tea and coffee, we talked about how long it had taken for Catholics and Lutherans to dialogue, in a constructive way, about theology. During our time together I began to realize the far-reaching influence of the Lutheran Church as the state religion. Although these men represented the Lutheran Church, their salaries were paid by the state. Therefore, they could not seriously disagree with the state if they wanted to keep their jobs.

The mode of state control in the United States is not as apparent: In our nation, where we tout separation of church and state, the Church seldom publicly disagrees with a U.S. foreign policy that promotes war, the arms race, and arms exports. Not only does the Church silently accept — or openly approve of — national military policy, but it even silences (or tries to silence) any priest, like Daniel Berrigan, who publicly criticizes U.S. policy. It is much more effective and less risky for the state to have religious authorities act as their surrogate in quashing dissent.

Although we enjoy tax-exemption for religious purposes, this privilege is used by the state to threaten church activities it feels are too political. Furthermore, the Catholic Church has a military archdiocesan ordinate, and many priests don a military uniform as well as their priestly robes. I cannot imagine Jesus doing that!

Next I visited Harold Reisenfelt, professor of New Testament theology at the university. A small man with a bright and cheerful personality, he told me something that has influenced my thinking deeply in the ensuing years. "There is no way of interpreting the New Testament except as pacifistic, against war," He agreed that the failure to speak against war has helped to weaken the Lutheran Church's authority to speak against abortion. I saw this as another example of the difficulty endemic to a church-state union.

A familiar face greeted me in the train station at Oslo: Bill Clinton. Serendipity — we had been on the same train. During our meeting in London, there had been no time to visit or to get to know one another. When he learned I was going to visit the Oslo Institute for Peace Research and other peace groups, he asked to come along. Our time together was intellectually stimulating as well as congenial. It was no surprise to me when Bill Clinton went on to serve as Arkansas' youngest governor, and then rose to be a two-term President of the United States.

At the Institute, the assistant director showed us around the facility — housed within a very lovely reconditioned Victorian mansion. While there, we visited three Norwegian conscientious objectors who objected to their nation's role in NATO — a new rap for us. Together we toured Oslo University campus. I lunched with one of the professors while Bill visited a friend from Arkansas. Later we continued our "peace tour" including a stop at a peace center founded by two actors. Bill agreed that this was a good way to see the country: While you see as much as a tourist, you have an important subject to talk about with the people you meet, and you learn something of the process of working for peace.

Following supper together, Bill and I parted ways. I headed on to the seaport town of Malmo where a two-hour ferry sails to Denmark. On the ferry a festive graduation party was in progress. Across Europe I found that many people travel to neighboring countries for short holidays and celebrations. Except for those of us who live on the Mexican or Canadian borders, Americans miss this, and it makes us less internationally-minded.

I spent my one afternoon in Copenhagen with Anders Baserud at the Institute for Peace Research which had ten people on the staff! One-third of the institute's budget came from the Danish government, the result of an arrangement made when the institute began in 1965. Partial funding came through research grants to the university.

West Germany

An overnight train took me to Munich where my priest brother, Jim, had an apartment in the McGraw Cacern (barracks), a massive structure of heavy concrete that formerly housed Hitler's Gestapo. Jim had a comfortable place with a study room, parlor, bedroom and kitchen. Though Jim worked as a civilian under contract with the army, he served as an assistant to an army chaplain. Because of this position, most of Jim's friends supported militarism and the Vietnam War. Now I was conversing with people whose positions contrasted greatly with those of my other European contacts.

Jim steered me to Dr. Ed Crowley, director of the Institute of Soviet Studies. Rather than converting me to his viewpoint, after several hours of conversation, Crowley's perspective only served to reinforce my opposition to militarism and the Vietnam War. Amazingly, Crowley backed up President Johnson's ongoing lies about the progress of the war. However, he did agree that the administration lied about the purpose of the war: to secure an economic advantage. The United States wanted to ensure a supply of tin, tungsten and oil. Vietnam was the gateway to control of those resources. When I asked if he thought the American people would support the war in Vietnam if they knew the truth, he gave no answer.

In the course of the evening's discussion I argued that the United States was supporting a South Vietnamese government that had no support among its own citizenry. In response, he asserted that likewise, no government in the East enjoyed the support of its people; furthermore, if the United States stayed in Vietnam long enough, the government there would gain support by virtue of staying power alone. I, of course, voiced my skepticism.

Jim told me later that Ed Crowley was keen to have me attend a briefing by the CIA. I told Jim that, although my conversation with Crowley was friendly, I was convinced that he was for all the wrong things and against all the right things. He was against the United Nations, against labor unions, against the civil rights movement in the United States; he was for the Vietnam War and for an increased military. He believed that the United States should police the world. I wondered how much Crowley's views were associated with the needs of his job. After all, it was his job to train Americans, mostly officers, in U.S.-Soviet relations. He may have been an expert on communism, but he was not an expert on the other issues we discussed.

Another friend of Jim's, Dean Connolly, a Georgetown graduate, was deputy director of the base hospital. During our conversation, he told me the U.S. military maintained twelve hospitals in Europe. Each was fully equipped, some even with helicopter landing pads. This led me to comment on the cost of our military presence in Germany so many years after the end of World War II. At the time (1969) the U.S. military had two-hundred fifty-thousand troops stationed throughout the continent. One soldier and his support personnel cost approximately eighty-thousand dollars per year.

One of the most interesting parts of my visit to Germany was seeing my old friend Ed Doherty. After many years in the U.S. State Department, he was the American Consul-General in Munich. He was bypassed in his State Department career because he criticized the U.S. nuclear stance: the intent to reply with massive nuclear destruction if we were attacked with nuclear weapons.

I visited him in his lovely home in the Bogenhausen section of Munich. The whole area sparkled with a light frosting of snow. We talked about the war, and I showed him the manuscript for the book I was planning, *Kill for Peace?* I wanted him to answer the question: "What is the relation between the Just War Theory and the gospel?" He said that the Just War Theory had an ethical value and some usefulness, but that it was not related to the gospel.

"If it is not related to the gospel, then can it have moral meaning for a Christian?" I asked. He skirted the question and instead told me that there was no political viability for a theory which did not allow for some kind of war. I replied that neither was there any political viability in the United States today for a nuclear pacifist.

This was another stop along my path to peace and justice: a long road which ultimately led me to reject the Just War Theory. Other incidents: an increased knowledge of nuclear weaponry, a closer look at the gospel and at the theory itself, all helped convince me that the theory is morally bankrupt. Once that conviction was reached, I had only the gospel to guide me. Even Augustine admits that the gospel forbids war. The gospel makes sense and stands by itself. Even a child can understand it. Once one understands that the Just War Theory is useless, nothing is in the way of understanding the peace message of the gospel.

Another instance comes to mind: I was explaining these points to Reverend Philip Solem one day after we had both spoken to a group at the University of Minnesota. A young man listening to us said, "When I hear clergymen like you speak, I'm glad I'm an atheist!"

"Why?" I asked.

"Because I don't need all those conditions and all that argument to know that the war is wrong!"

"How do you know it is wrong?"

"It's just inhuman!"

I thought this over and found merit in what he said. If, on a matter of life and death, the gospel can only be understood though intricate and sophisticated reasoning, then the gospel is not for the masses, only for the specially educated. This doesn't make sense; the gospels are for the masses, especially the poor and oppressed. Although the Just War Theory stresses the primacy of individual conscience, there is disagreement among theologians and scholars about the conditions for and application of the theory.

Where is the unity and simplicity of faith in such a vital matter? The reasonings of the Just War Theory contradict the text: "Unless you become as little children, you will not enter into the kingdom of heaven." Are God's children only learned theologians?

My brother Patrick, also a civilian chaplain, and I loaded into an army truck for a tour of the eleventh-century town of Augsburg. On the way, we passed the former concentration camp at Dachau. We stopped at a U.S. Army base, separated from the infamous camp by only a wire fence. I was looking through the fence, lost in thought, when a couple of soldiers called out for me to come with them to see the commanding officer. I simply refused. I refused, I suppose, with such confidence and assurance that one of the soldiers said to the other, "Leave him alone. He's an officer."

On New Year's Day, 1970, I concelebrated Mass with Jim in an army chapel. Jim made a little oasis of humanity among the rigidity of army rules. For instance, believing that his door should be open, he left the key to his apartment on the ledge above the door. In my two weeks with him, there was hardly a night when there wasn't an extra person, a soldier or friend, staying with us. He had a tape library on theology which he used to pique the interest of the soldiers and introduce new ideas.

The next day he drove me to the trolley line, and as I said good-bye to him, he said, "Let me know if there is anything I can do for you." As the train carried me to the Alps, I realized that I was wearing his sweater and his socks.

Switzerland

I went on from Germany to Geneva, Switzerland and visited the United Nations buildings. I was impressed by the beauty of the setting: a stunning lake shore. The buildings, attractive and roomy, housed the older part of the United Nations: the Secretariate of the U.N. Conference on Trade and Development, the Economic Commission for Europe, the office of the High Commissioner for Refugees, the Division of Narcotic Drugs, the permanent Central Narcotics Board and the Drug Supervisory Board.

The Palais de Nations here was built originally for the League of Nations by the cooperative effort of all the member states. It was turned over to the U.N. after World War II, August 1, 1946, symbolic of a worldwide urge to aid international cooperation. One of the most famous parts of the Palais is Assembly Hall which is reserved for large international conferences. Accommodations are provided for eighteen-hundred people, including seven-hundred in the Press and Gallery. Many important conferences, including ones on disarmament, have been held here, like the Geneva Conference of 1954 which partitioned Vietnam into temporary military zones.

The murals around the Council Chamber, a gift from Spain, were done in gold and sepia. The murals represent successive stages in humanity's advance. On the ceiling five figures, representing the five continents, join hands — their union an allegory for the United Nations itself.

Paris and Southern France

My travels continued, and by train I left Geneva and headed for Paris. I took a small room at Hotel Du Progres in Paris and set out to visit peace groups. One of my first stops was a visit with Ron Cruse, French National Director of the Fellowship of Reconciliation. Obviously, he had given considerable thought to the question of national defense:

> "When you talk about defending a country as a justification of war, you should ask yourself: 1) What kind of society are we defending? 2) Against whom are we defending it? Against what? 3) By what means are we defending it? Answers should be given to these questions before any conclusion is reached."

Ron told me that the Bishop of Orleans defended conscientious objectors. He also brought to my attention the true nature of the Magnifcat — the poem of Mary, mother of Jesus — an almost revolutionary document: "He has put down the mighty and exalted the lowly."

I visited the Movement for Peace with a small office in the business district of Paris. They published the magazine, *COMBAT pour la Paix*. This organization had its beginnings at a world peace conference in Paris and in response to a 1950 call from Stockholm to oppose the development of nuclear weapons. Since then, they worked on the Geneva Accords to end the Vietnam War, the independence of Algeria and an end to the nuclear arms race. The Movement for Peace enjoyed great popularity throughout France. The National Secretariat of the movement was made up of prominent clergy, and figures, like Jean Paul Sartre, sat on the National Board.

At the Quaker International Center in Paris I met an American couple who were in charge of the facility. I was surprised to learn that, at the time, there were are about two-hundred thousand Quakers world-wide. I was so surprised because, relative to their numbers, the Quakers have immense influence, for example, their impact on our Selective Service Law in the United States. Because of their focus on peace, because of their belief that "there is something of God in each person," the Quakers give witness to a great truth: that the peace issue is so central to the Christian faith that when you touch on it, you are important even if you are small in number. Because of the Quakers and the other peace churches, it can be said that at least some Christians have given witness to these truths: that Christ came to bring peace, that Christians should be peacemakers and that peacemakers are God's children. The Quakers do this without the unity that comes from a hierarchy. Their unity is based on each individual's direct relationship with God. This has the advantage of not restricting any individual Quaker who wishes to work for peace.

I was strolling around Paris one night and stopped at the corner of Sebastopol and Rue St. Denis to check my map. A man came up and asked if he could help. Thinking he wanted me to pay for his assistance, I said, "I only want to take a walk."

"Where?"

"Around this area."

"Can I accompany you?"

I decided to trust him, but told him I couldn't pay. He suggested that we ride in his car to the Champs D'Elysee, Notre Dame, and to other famous landmarks so that I could see Paris at night. I agreed, warning him again that I couldn't pay. As we rode along, he told me he had just had a fight with his girlfriend and was feeling depressed and alone. He really wanted to talk to somebody. We passed the theatre district, drove slowly along the crowded boulevards, passed the Opera House, the Champs D'Elysee, Etoile, the Louvre, along the Seine, and back again to where we started. With a very friendly native Parisian showing the sights with obvious pride, the trip was far more than just a mere tour. It was a person-to-person education.

Feeling rather ashamed now that I had so obviously not trusted him at the beginning, I thought the least I could do was to buy him a beer. I was thinking this over when he said, "Can I buy you a beer?" I told him it should be my treat, and we went to a bar together and talked a little longer before parting. It was a lesson to me — you miss a great deal in a foreign country or anywhere if you do not trust others.

That next Sunday I attended Mass at the Church of Sainte Michel. In the center of the church five concelebrants gathered at the altar, and a large crowd filled in on all four sides of the altar. At the church the Comitee Catholique Contre La Faim et Pour Le Development (Committee Against Hunger and for Development) set up an exposition on world poverty and the concentration of wealth in the Church. The theme, Christian obligation to join in the revolution to change the global maldistribution of wealth was also stressed in both liturgy and the sermon. During the Mass, a man shouted out two or three times criticizing what was said. No one paid much attention, and when I talked to one of the priests afterward, he didn't seem very concerned.

On the way home from Mass I met Jacques Denny from the Cameroons, a Black man studying at the University of Paris. He invited me to his ten-by-four-foot room on the sixth floor of his apartment building. In this small room he had a bed, a basin, books, tools, a radio and two or three friends. They were about to have a celebration with oysters and white wine, rice and beef and red wine, and coffee and liquors, all prepared in that small space. The whole shabby room conveyed an atmosphere of enjoyment. Music came from under a shelf with speakers mounted near the ceiling. Every move required skill lest you knock over something or somebody. The room was lighted only by a skylight and had no windows. When the cigarette smoke got heavy, you had to open the door. This was the way I had heard that students at the university lived — now I saw it in real life.

One morning at breakfast in my hotel, I talked with two Indians, B.B. Gupah and his wife about nonviolence. Gupah said. "It is better to err on the side of not killing, even not killing animals, than to err on the side of killing any living being." It occurred to me that the link that connects all to God is respect for life. When that link is broken, the connection to God is gone. Some links may still exist in the chain, but the connection with the Divine is no more.

I took a morning train to Tours to visit Robert McAfee Brown who was director of a group of students on Stanford University's year abroad. As a divinity professor, he was naturally interested in peace theology. He suggested that Christians need to look again at the Barman Confession by the Protestant Confessing Churches — forged to oppose Hitler's effort to gain control of the church..

Karl Barth, a co-author of the Barman Confession made a 1959 statement to the European Congress For Outlawing Atomic Weapons. In it he raised the idea that the congress should invite people to refuse service in military units that employ atomic weapons. Barth's statement had special weight because he had had the vision that all churches should take a stand against Hitler. He also had the courage to act on what he believed.

Robert and I talked about his article in *Look* magazine in which he said, "I must break the law [meaning the draft law] for conscience's sake." He told me that when students question the Vietnam War, they soon find themselves turning against all killing and all war; their conscientious objection leads to pacifism. We also found encouragement in the way youths were able to see how self-imposed obstacles, such as Dad's real estate deals, prevented their parents from opposing the war. He thought it would be very difficult for any future president to create enthusiasm amongst youth for any war. Sadly, this appears a mistaken idea.

I took an evening train for Beziers in southern France. As I got off the train in the early morning light, I noticed an ornate war memorial across the street. The inscription read:

> A ses morts glorieatix
> A Ville de Beziers rconnaissantes
> 2 Octobre 1914, 3 Septembre 1939
> 11 Novenibre 1918, 8 Mai 1945
> [To their glorious deaths / The village of Beziers pays its recognition]

A long list of war dead was engraved on the monument. It was like any other monument, in any other city, in any other country: glorifying war, but omitting the stupidities, the conscription, the killing, the deceit and the failures that are part of war. A step toward peace would be the removal of monuments like this and their replacement by living memorials — ones that help people learn how to work for peace.

From Beziers I traveled north by a one-car train to the station of Boire-Noble. I was the only one getting off the car, the only passenger at the station, and the station was the only building around. I asked the station master how to find the Community of the Ark. He said he would show me when he finished closing up the station. We walked across the train tracks, and he showed me a footpath leading into the woods. "Follow this for ten or fifteen minutes, and you will come to it."

Carrying my luggage, I trudged along the path for ten minutes and then saw a couple of stone houses perched up on a hill and surrounded by tilled lands. As I approached one of the houses, I could see someone working in the kitchen. Her name was Susanna, and she was from Montevideo, Argentina. She greeted me and led me to the community dining room. There I met Lanza del Vasto. He looked as if he had just stepped out of the Old Testament — long white beard, white hair, and dressed in home-made clothes. In place of a shirt he wore something like a Roman tunic.. As he sat on a window sill, he whittled on a large walking staff; he continued to carve as we chatted. He welcomed me and explained a bit about the wood-carving. We found we had much to talk about; he knew many of the people whom I had already visited and others whom I planned to visit.

Lanza founded the Community of the Ark some seventeen years earlier in the outskirts of Paris. After a couple of years experimenting there, he found that a great deal of the community's time was taken up with visitors, and they were unable to get organized. They wanted to do more than hospitality; they wanted their entire life to be a witness to peace. So they moved away from Paris and settled at Boire Noble in the province of Herault, France, about an hour and a half by (a very slow) train from the Spanish Mediterranean border. The community was made up of one hundred people, married and single, who lived by working with their hands.

As a principle of a peaceful life, the community had a goal of absolute economic independence, and they came close to it. However, this independence did not mean isolation. They devoted a great deal of energy to contacts with the outside in a variety of ways: helping local farmers, providing hospitality to visitors, corresponding with families and friends, speaking on tours in France and abroad, creating and supporting groups of friends living in urban areas (Friends of the Ark), training people in nonviolence, and organizing and supporting nonviolent direct action in cooperation with the Action Civique Nonviolente. For example, they protested the war in Algeria and the build-up of nuclear weapons.

They lived in two groups of houses which were about a mile apart. They made their own clothes, grew their own food, and built their own houses. They lived voluntarily under conditions similar to those in the Third World — non-industrialized. Twice a week, whole-meal bread was made by hand and baked in a brick oven. Fields and gardens produced cereal grains, fruits, and vegetables; their dairy produced milk, eggs, and cheese. Furniture and cloth were made in workshops.

Lanza introduced me to eighteen-year-old Girald Chirole from Verde Valley, Arizona, at that time the only American in the community. She showed me the residences. In the single women's dormitory each person had a separate room and use of a common room for reading and relaxation. She showed me the kitchen with its wood stove and the bakery which was built into the basement of the house. The door above the oven had a wood relief carving of Christ with the words, "I am the bread of life" written in Latin. She also showed me the chapel, a converted chicken coop with white-washed walls. They had a wood-carved altar and candlesticks, and even some carved chairs. As we walked through the farmland that surrounded the houses, I felt a personal peace — the kind that such a pastoral setting never fails to provide.

Later I joined Natacha Bethus, an eighteen-year-old from Nice, to visit the other community houses. I saw the women spinning and weaving and the men building a section of the house. Through these tours I learned that in its agricultural practices, the community avoided chemical fertilizers or pesticides. I also grew to appreciate their simple, peaceful communitarian life: All property was held in common. They had one car for the entire community.

Since they had no ice box, in the wintertime they cooled food outside. They washed clothes by hand in an open shed, where water was heated by a wood fire under a cauldron. Clothes were soaked in hot suds and scrubbed on a board. They were double-rinsed in cold water flowing from the mountains and then hung out under a roofed-in drying area. The water continually flowed into large stone basins: an inextricable link between the community and the earth — a source of community life.

Some of the bedrooms had a wood stove, others did not. While there I slept in an unheated room — under four blankets! In an unusual set-up, a single sheet on the bed was sewn into a kind of sleeping bag.

I found this lifestyle intriguing and not as uncomfortable as one might imagine. After observing the manner in which the community met their needs, I was curious about their attitude toward technology. When I asked about this, one member commented, "When technology becomes a necessity, it becomes a master."

I also asked Lanza, "Why no machinery?"

"We create inventions without weighing their effect on humans. Adam's original sin was to try to get the fruit without doing the work. To the banker this is profit. Most men seek power over others and force them to do their will. The desire for money drives this. Machine production pushes all these trends. Machinery withdraws men from work and the purification of life that goes with it. Power and riches are the two horns of the devil." (More on this theme can be found in Lanza del Vasto's book, *Free Man and a Wild Donkey*, where he links freedom, obedience, and authority.)

I was interested in what Lanza thought about those who insisted that Gandhi was against progress because he promoted the use of the spinning wheel. Lanza replied, "People with such ideas are probably full of Western prejudice in favor of technology." He added that "technology is neither a search for truth, nor a finding of it. It is a manipulation of matter such as one does when one plays chess; it is a game. You play according to the rules; you just learn the maneuvers. There is nothing about truth . . . or God in it. Machines aim generally at power and control, not at the betterment of man. They are not neutral; they do not tell you anything more about man's nature or purpose or about truth." Lanza became more emphatic as he told me that Christ did not say, "Make machine." Yet God knew humans could make machines if we wanted to.

Without the benefit of technological creature comforts, the daily routine at the community contrasted greatly with that of most Americans. The schedule of the day went something like this: a cold shower with water from buckets at about 6:00 a.m. — or 5:30 a.m. if you want to join in the yoga meditation. Morning prayers were sung together, followed by a personal "good morning" from each member of the community to one another. Breakfast was at seven. From eight until noon, the people worked in the fields, the bakery, the laundry, and all the other activities. Each hour a bell was rung to give people opportunity for a minute of silent reflection on the purpose of life. At every two-hour period a longer time of prayer was recommended, again at the ringing of the bell. Those near the main house came into the cool of the stone-walled chapel for five minutes of silent prayer. At noon, if the sun was shining and it was not cold, there was about ten minutes of reading and comment on the news of the day on the steps outside the kitchen. The noon meal began at 12:30 p.m.. Afterward there was relaxation. There was another four-hour work period from two until six, supper at seven, and then evening prayers at about eight-thirty. Children at the Ark spent their days busy at primary school which was provided by community members. Following primary education, they typically went to the lyceum and then the university.

Several times a week there were community programs: a special meeting, singing and dancing, or a community conference. After the evening prayers, sung by candlelight, there was time for visiting in the apartments or rooms.

The prayers used at the Ark — the Beatitudes, the peace prayer of St. Francis of Assisi, etc. — were general enough to suit all denominations. Each religious group at the Ark was encouraged to have its own ceremonies. I had the pleasure of hearing beautiful Gregorian chants sung in Latin.

In the eight days I was at the Ark, I took a shine to it. I had some good discussions with groups as we sat around in the candlelight, sipping thyme tea. Many interesting stories were told by unusual people; the company was good, even extraordinary. The candlelight and the tea added to the deep, peaceful atmosphere, that had a timeless quality.

The soft glow of candlelight aided the good conversation; two candles are enough for reading. The setting was nearly surreal as Lanza del Vasto, named Shantidas (peacemaker) by Gandhi, sat at the table speaking to the community. His face was bathed in candlelight. Around him sat thirty or so others: some knitting, some carving as they listened to him speak on philosophy. I heard him talk on the Aristotelian-Thomistic philosophy. He spoke about the human soul, how it is spiritual; he described the three types of souls: the vegetable, the sentient, and the intellectual or substantial human soul. I never would have dreamed I would be hearing this in a peace community. I appreciated seeing the link between monasticism and peace activism.

Lanza del Vasto a Sicilian with a Ph.D. from the University of Paris, had twenty-six books to his name. One of his books, *Pilerinage Au Source*, tells of his trip to see Gandhi in India. (The English translation of the book, titled *Return to the Source,* was published in 1972.) During this visit Gandhi encouraged him to found the Community.

It was clear that Lanza was the leader in this community. Not long after I arrived, he commented, "You know, many people come here asking what makes the community go, and I think that an essential element for any community is authority. Some people think that I am joking. They feel, especially young people, that community can be built on friendliness or common dispositions. But when they find that I am serious, they don't stay long." He explained to me that the Community of the Ark has a patriarchal structure. The patriarch, like the head of the tribe among Jewish people, is the leader.

While this community was patriarchal, all the important decisions were made by consensus among the adult members. If unanimity could not be reached, discussions did not go on forever. Silence was observed for some time in order to quiet down excitement and to cool arguments. Then fasting was added to the silence. If the matter could not be decided then, it was not decided at all.

The commitments to the community by those willing to accept the life were sealed by seven vows, which began as follows: "We vow to devote our lives to the service of our brethren which begins by working with our hands so that at least we do not rely on others in order to find for ourselves and others an end to misery, abuse, servitude, and the troubles of our time." The other six vows were responsibility and co-responsibility; truthfulness, the practice of nonviolence, self-purification, poverty, and obedience. Children were not eligible to take the vows and thus achieve full membership until they turned twenty-one.

The companions of the Ark saw their life as a permanent nonviolent direct action. It was the simple life: natural, wholesome, fraternal and within the capacity of everyone, a living witness to the possibility of social life without violence. They gave an example to the two-thirds of the world who did not have technological benefits: You can live a decent, developing human life without much technology. To the rich nations they gave an example of a voluntary yielding up of the so-called comforts of life, and they showed that a happy, personable human life can be led without those comforts. They put aside a society based on competition, the art of social multiplication of needs, and the pursuit of profits. Companions of the Ark did not ask for salary, advantages, protection, or help. They were thus free to offer civil disobedience — protesting against laws which are unjust or offensive to human dignity. They did not accept many of the benefits the government offered children. They returned a small portion of these benefits in land taxes and gave the rest to the poor. They owned the land. But since it was not very valuable, the tax was small.

Community members were obliged by the vow of responsibility and co-responsibility to amend their own faults, publicly if the fault was public, and privately if no one else knew about it. Co-responsibility meant that, for example, if one companion found that another was not doing his fair share of labor, she brought it to his attention. If the companion still refused to do the work, she would admonish him and do the work in his place. This appeal to the heart was a pearl of their structure.

About two-thirds of the members of the Ark were married. Some took the vow to remain single. Girald commented that she saw how marriage separated one from the service of the larger community. Family members stayed more to themselves and spent more time with their children. Each family had a separate apartment or a separate house. Rooms were added as the family grew. Everyone usually came to the midday meal. They had breakfast and supper in their own residences. Yet, the families added much to the community in the way of stability.

While I was there, plans were being made for the marriage of Nicole, at the Ark for four years, to Michel, there for five years. Although marriage was a cause for big celebration in the community, it didn't make as big a change in each individual's life as it does elsewhere. The residence changed, but the work and the economic base went virtually unchanged.

One of the members of the Ark was Joe Pyronnet, the author of a book on nonviolence and former professor at the University of Paris. With his wife and five children he moved into the Ark. I asked him why: "I was very active in the political affiliate of the Ark, "L'Action Civique Nonviolente." Many times the Companions of the Ark joined with us for peace actions. I began to reflect that working for peace should not just be an occasional thing, but that it should be twenty-four hours a day. I asked my wife and children about it; they agreed, so we came."

His choice was nonviolence through living at the Community of the Ark. "No doubt one can be a Christian without being opposed to personal use of weapons and vice versa: one can be a Christian and be opposed to firearms. But every Christian should realize that Christ represents a power and a struggle in which the logic is contrary to the logic of the military battle. The time for a choice has come."

He continued, "One of the fundamental bases for modern life is: First you earn your living, and then you try to find a purpose in it. This is just contrary to what the gospel says, 'Seek you first the Kingdom of God and its justice and the rest will be given to you.'"

After hearing all this, I couldn't help but draw a comparison (one that I'm sure was not lost on this community) to Noah's Ark. Long ago Noah gathered a few believers and their animals into an ark to protect them from the flood. This new ark aimed to protect humans from the disaster which lies ahead from technology, especially nuclear technology.

The people in the Ark tried to live out the Gandhian ideals: politics without violence, production without machines, a society without exploitation, a religion without bigotry. They advocated a return to craftsmanship, to manual work, to the simple life with the accent on the common base of all religions. Their truthfulness was borne out in their dress, their manners, their buildings, in the forms and patterns in their lives, the physical form of their products and their fields, the markings they left upon the surface of the earth. Their creations did not jar, deface or mask the great Creation. They blended humbly and peacefully with the earth which is their source.

Italy

Upon leaving the Ark, I took the train along the Riviera and into Italy. After my arrival in Rome, I contacted Fabricio Fabrini, a conscientious objector from the Italian military. During our time together he told me a disturbing tale of the consequences of standing on the gospel opposition to war. When Fabricio was drafted into the air force in the late 60s, he asked to be released from duty on grounds of conscience: a near impossibility because conscientious objection was not recognized by the Italian authorities. Fabricio consulted the chaplain about this dilemma. The chaplain responded by refusing him Holy Communion and by telling him that an act against the state is a sin. Fabricio went to the bishop who only instructed Fabricio to go to confession.

Finally, after fourteen months in the air force, he refused further service. Fabricio was arrested and jailed in a stinking, rat-infested underground prison. Fortunately, under the general amnesty given all prisoners with sentences under five years, he was released after six months. Amnesty was granted by the parliament in honor of the anniversary of the Republic.

His story of defiance continued: Not long after his release, he was at Mass at a church in Rome. While a Franciscan was preaching that the Jews were justly persecuted because they killed Christ, Fabricio yelled out, "Racist, this is opposed to the statement of the Council." A loud dialogue continued between the two of them. Meanwhile, another Franciscan priest called the police. Fabricio was arrested again and sentenced to two months in prison.

These trials did not cause Fabricio to give up. He was strengthened in his convictions by an outspoken priest, Father Valuducci, who got a two-week suspended sentence for supporting Fabricio and for saying that a law was needed to allow room for conscience.

Fabricio told me about other conscientious objectors in Italy. Guissepi Gozzini took his stand in 1965 and was jailed a few months before amnesty was granted. Georgio Vilea spent six months in prison in 1967. Another jailed CO was Enzo Beletato. In 1969 Giovani Gistoi was jailed, and the numbers swelled. In all, there had been about one-hundred fifty jailed, seventy during my visit in 1970. Most of the jailed objectors in Italy were Jehovah's Witnesses.

By 1965 Vatican II had called on all nations to make allowances for those who could not, in conscience, accept active military service. But Italy was intransigent.

I questioned one objector, Limo Taschini, "How did you become an objector?" He answered, "I analyzed the function of the army in Italy. I found it to be an institution aimed at sustaining a political system with which the Church is allied. This means the Church has compromised Christ and the gospel. It sustains the state and joins Christ to it. I also object to the army because it is part of the way the wealthy oppress the working class. It adds to the division between the people who think and people who work. I am against all armies because they serve the interests of the ruling classes."

Giorgio LaPira had served as mayor of Florence for most of the 60s and had become world-famous for his attempts to mediate an end to the Vietnam War. He went to visit Ho Chi Minh, and then met with Bobby Kennedy in Paris with a proposal to end the war. President Johnson turned this down very harshly.

I spoke with LaPira about nuclear weapons and peace — he beamed with intense conviction. He smiled, then he spoke, "Peace is inevitable. When Kruschev, Kennedy, and Pope John were all alive at the same time, they realized that war was obsolete because of the nature of the modern weapons. Since that time, no wars have been ended. In fact, . . . since 1945 when the nuclear age began, . . . no war started after that time has ended. They just keep a stalemate. The reason is that many of the weapons cannot be used. But politicians are so accustomed to gaining political power by talking about the danger of war, that they still play the game. They do not tell the people that war is ended and peace is inevitable." Given that we were in the throes of the Cold War, I found his analysis incisive.

It seemed to me that Mayor LaPira was working on the theme that we must learn to cooperate or else perish together. Given that, we are forced to cooperate since the alternative is not really viable. He built this up with examples. Since he was a professor of International Law at the University of Florence and had a long record of service in politics, he spoke on the subject with great authority.

However, most of all, Giorgio LaPira was a most hospitable man; we shared dinner and an evening of conversation at his apartment. We saw one another as kindred spirits.

I took the train to Bergamo and then a bus to Sotto El Monte, a small town of eighty people. The bus stopped near a sign which read "Casa Natale di Giovanni 23" (the birthplace of John XXIII). It was dark when I arrived. I found a restaurant at the intersection of the road and went in to telephone. While phoning, I glanced over to a table where a man sat — he looked just like Pope John! Not quite, but in fact he turned out to be his older brother, Xavier.

I sat at the table and had a cup of coffee with him. He told me that he still worked on the family farm There, talking to Pope John's brother, I learned that I could go up to the top of the mountain above the village to spend the night. In an old monastery, visited by Pope John when he came home, I found an ecumenical retreat center.

In the morning I came down the mountain and visited the home of Pope John. There was no doubt that this was a home of the poor: The family lived on the second floor above a stable. The room in which Pope John was born had been converted into a chapel. In it I felt that I was on holy ground. I stood and reflected on the change that had come from this humble place. From here, a farmer, faithful to his Church and to his vision of God, reached out to the whole world and broke through the barriers that divide humankind: He encouraged ecumenism. He advocated the gospel of peace in a way that was understandable to all nations. He gave a vision of brotherhood and sisterhood under one God to the human family threatened by thermonuclear war.

Adjoining Pope John's family home, a seminary had been built in his honor. Through the years thousands have made the pilgrimage to see the humble origins of a man who moved the world. There is still hope for the Church and for the world when a man of the poor, a man of great vision, can become Pope.

Pope John's position on peace was influenced by the history of the twentieth century. During World War I, when ideologically-driven hostilities began to make war irreconcilable with the Just War Theory, the Vatican began to speak out against war as never before. Though the popes, especially Pius the X and Pius the XII, condemned area bombing, the bombing of Germany, and the bombing of Hiroshima, they never did it with a clarion call condemning war in general or calling for peace in clear terms.

But Pope John did — particularly in his encyclical *Pacem en Terra* (Peace on Earth), and he did it from a pulpit that no other Pope ever had, that is, a world-wide acceptance of himself as a human figure. He saw himself, and he was seen by others, which is more important, as the one world-wide figure that had a loving interest in everyone. He spoke in clear tones: opposing war, opposing nuclear weapons, and taking a position that went much further than Vatican II. Vatican II took in some of the vision of Pope John, but equivocated on the issue of self-defense.

I returned to Rome, arriving at night. It was interesting to visit St. Peter's when nothing was going on. The main plaza was empty. It was just like any other deserted church. Next day, I went back to the Vatican and walked around the Papal gardens in the back of St. Peter's. One of the fountains there caught my eye: In the center of it was a model of a battleship with water coming out of its miniature cannons — hardly a symbol of peace. A sign over it read: "Pius Sextus Pontifex Maximus Fontem Rusticam Antea a Paulo IV, Extructani, in Elgontiorem hanc Splendidioramque Fornam Restituit. Anno Domino. MDCCLXXIX. Pontiff Sui V." (Pius the Sixth, the Supreme Pontiff, the fifth year of his pontificate restored this fountain in a more elegant and splendid way, this fountain was built by Pope Paul IV. In the year of our Lord 1779.) I recalled that 1779 was a time when Black slavery was widespread among Christians. It was a bit discouraging to see this kind of decoration in the residence of the representatives of Jesus.

I watched as workers toiled to finish a large addition to the Vatican Museum. This caused me to wonder what these construction workers, with their modest pay, think about the Catholic Church. Since the worker is most likely Catholic and in Italy possibly a communist, how can he, without difficulty, relate the gospel of Christ to the ownership, management and construction of such a museum in an age of great human need? True, many of the art treasures are worth preserving. But should the followers of the materially-impoverished, but spiritually-rich Jesus act as the custodians and owners of these riches? The fact that these treasures have been donated to the Vatican over the ages is not the point. As St. Theresa of Avila said to the Pope, "In as much as you are dressed in silks and satins and ornaments of gold, you do not represent the poor Jesus." The same idea applies to the museum.

The Vatican has vast property holdings in Rome, believed by some to amount to twenty-five per cent of the real estate in the city. This ownership makes it more difficult to understand the gospel message of Christ.

I next visited a slum area (in contrast to the Vatican) outside of Rome. Father Gerald Lutte and several co-workers had been serving the poor here for four years. At the time, about one thousand people lived in this slum in an area known as Mantasacio Pato Rotondo. They were a small part of the sixty thousand poor who lived in the suburbs of Rome. Most of the people simply squatted here with no permission from the government. Initially, they lacked electricity and phone service. However, once the houses were finished, the power company was obliged, by law, to supply power.

Father Lutte used to teach, but he was suspended from his duties as a Salesian at the University of Rome because he gave so much time to the poor of Mantasacio Pato Rotondo and encouraged others to do the same. Church officials were afraid that Father Lutte and his supporters might start a maverick parish because the assigned parish priest, while known by the slum people, was not enthusiastic in his service to them.

Heidi Vaccaro, National Director of the Italian Fellowship of Reconciliation, helped arrange an appointment for me to meet at the Vatican with Bishop Ferari Tonioloa. He had participated in some of the peace marches in Italy, so I was keen to meet and talk peace with him. After about three hours of discussion about the morality of killing, he said, "I agree with you theoretically, that under no circumstances is killing allowed, but practically, you have to allow it."

I answered, "If you say that the theory of the gospel cannot he lived out in practice, you are continuing a division that has gone on since Constantine's time, a division that is disastrous to the Church. The masses of the people will never see the light of the gospel in a religion like that. If you say that under some conditions, certain fixed conditions, some amount of killing, even a little bit, is allowed, then you are doing just what Augustine did in the fourth Century. You see the result. The Church is identified everywhere with every war in which Christians have fought. No where are Roman Catholic Christians seen as opposing war. Our faith is opposed to war, but our practice is not. This is certainly not what Jesus wants or what the Church should be."

He listened sympathetically to all of this. He did not say he agreed, neither did he disagree.

Heidi Vaccaro, mother of three and a Christian pacifist, had arranged almost all of my visits in Rome. She spent several days showing me around and even arranged a television interview for me. She did all this spontaneously and at such an energetic pace that I had a hard time keeping up with her. She herself was not a Catholic, but instead a Waldensian, a group that started as pacifist, many of whom died for their beliefs. Although she had a doctorate in mathematics, she quit teaching and lived on a reduced income so that she could focus full-time on peace work, primarily with the Fellowship of Reconciliation.

I continued by train south to Sicily. After a night on the train, I awakened to the deep and intense blue of the Mediterranean Sea. The rock formations along the shore caused the waves to break a long distance out. I was going to visit Danilo Dolci, a social reformer from Northern Italy. There he had worked with orphans left homeless by World War II in a community called Nomodelfia located in the old Axis concentration camp at Fossoli. He saw that work as a bandage on a painful wound, but inadequate to remedy the evils of the world.

Dolci had set out for Trappeto, Sicily, without knowing why and found it to be the most wretched country he had ever seen. "I found myself, while still in Europe, in one of the most miserable areas in the world with tremendous unemployment, widespread illiteracy, and Mafia violence reaching nearly everywhere." The people were discontented, but not committed to change. They said, "It has always been like this, and it will always be." People had no idea that life could proceed at a different pace or in a different direction from what they saw around them. Here Dolci learned that he must work with the people to create "new facts" so through their own experience they learn to see that change is possible. Dolci emphasized that communication is needed between persons from many different backgrounds and walks of life.

The Italian state had responded to the half-starving and desperate population by imprisoning or killing those who protested instead of providing employment and schools. The state treated those in the peasant movement demanding possession of uncultivated land the same as criminals. The police themselves became like outlaws in their brutality and dirty tactics, while Mafia leaders became friends of highly-placed politicians and police.

From 1952 until 1958, Dolci attracted others to his work, and they shared in the life of the poor in the heart of this tragic situation in Sicily. In 1958 Dolci and his comrades established the Center for Study and Initiative. *Outlaws of Patenico* by Dolci described how so-called development (in the conventional sense) killed instead of cured. It became increasingly clear to him as he wrote this book that evil in the world must be everywhere identified, denounced, and stamped out. He asked himself how it was possible to transform a region when most of the local population will do nothing to help and are either unemployed or engaged in unproductive work.

A later book, *A Report from Palermo*, tried to explain to the people the tragedy of makework and to help them understand this phenomenon in other parts of the world. True development comes from people working according to their own needs and convictions. When the masses of people are hungry and afflicted, exploiters, old and new, suck their blood. People who are idle are glad to do work to bring progress if they know what to do.

The problems in western Sicily were so bad after so many centuries of neglect, that material assistance and exposure of the situation were not enough. The Center for Study and Initiative set out a more comprehensive plan: First: study the causes and symptoms of backwardness because facts and theories must be verified before action can be taken. Second: set up a pilot scheme outlining patient, practical, everyday work in order to experiment and demonstrate possible solutions to the problems. Third: to overcome certain intolerable situations, pressure the relevant authorities with nonviolent, democratic action to stimulate them to a greater sense of responsibility and to encourage other local people to participate in the concern.

These theories were developed out of Dolci's own experience. Before he started the Center he was the organizer of the "Trapetto Fast" and the "Strike in Reverse" aimed at giving employment and a voice to the people. His actions led to his arrest and to the arrest of trade unionists, but the trial that followed helped to call public attention, in Italy and around the world, to the misery of western Sicily.

The first element of his plan, study of the socio-economic situation, was worked out with a small group of friends. When the key points of a pilot scheme had been drawn up, study centers were set up in three areas: a hilly zone in the interior, a stretch of the southwestern coast and at the Gulf of Castel Mare. Partenico, Corleone, Roccamena and Menfi were the towns chosen. Agricultural technicians, social workers, teachers and young volunteers began to work.

The three rivers in the area provided 150,000,000 cubic meters of exploitable water which would be of fundamental importance for sound economic and social development in the area. Harnessing this resource became the goal of the Center. A reservoir was built on the River Carboi. Construction of a dam on the Jato River and canalization began. Plans for a dam on the Bellise river were started. Other projects followed, for instance a large co-op that was developed in the southwestern zone. Additionally, the Center started a co-op for the production and sale of wine "el progresso" at Menfi.

The Center was housed in a rambling, two-story structure. I arrived at siesta time; the place was locked. After much knocking, a young boy opened the window and told me the place would stay closed for an hour. He took my luggage while I went on a walk through the narrow streets of the town. I went into a store to buy lunch, and the people were very curious and obviously not used to strangers. When I returned to the Center, I talked with some small children. Their teacher came by and told me that Dolci would be there soon. He came into the room and was an impressive figure. He wore a white turtleneck sweater and looked, to me, like a Roman official. He was tall, well-built, and a bit on the heavy side. He spoke English well, but was more at ease with French, and of course Sicilian or Italian. Since I was not very familiar with his work, he advised me to take a tour and then come back to talk.

Kevin Seitz, a twenty-year-old American, who was in his second year as an intern, showed me around. We went to see the Jato Dam. The concrete dam glittered in the sunlight and looked almost like snow. Though it would take another year for water to completely filled the dam, the people could see progress. Already the struggle for use of the water had begun. The problem of political control of the water would have to be solved. But the dam was tangible evidence that things could change. On the way to Trappeto we drove along a mountain road overlooking the Gulf of Castel Mare. There we saw a construction wall built by the Mafia which was of no functional value. It was a clear example of misuse of funds even as people starved. At Alcolel and Gibel Lina we saw the damage, still not repaired, of the 1968 earthquake. Dolci's group, along with the people and a group of experts, had been working on plans for appropriate development in this region.

At Trappeto we went to the study center high above the sea. It was an attractive one-story-high quadrangle built by local workers and with local materials. Teachers came from all over Sicily to the Center to take seminars lasting from three to ten days. Seminar topics included: cooperatives, lineographing, activity with youth, irrigation, and study of flora. The idea was to stir-up the imagination of the teachers and equip them to do things in a different and better way.

I was impressed by a mural in the auditorium which depicted the local history of the Mafia and its cronies: The Mafia leader stands in the middle handing out money. Cardinal Ruffini of Palermo is giving a letter to one of the Mafia. People are dying, police are killing, and others are buying votes. Another mural shows the initiative of a small group pictured as though it were a growing flower. The death of the Mafia results. In another mural as the police kill innocent citizens, the police themselves become animalized.   Their dehumanizing treatment of others has left them dehumanized as well.

At the Center I met Lorenzo Borellia, who told me about an initiative by a group of about fifty youths who refused to join the army because the government ignored the plight of the poor. The youths' position was that if the state won't help them, they won't help the state. They wrote letters to various officials such as the Minister of Defense, the President of the Republic, and various parliamentary groups stating that since the government was not reconstructing houses (some twenty-five thousand destroyed and another twenty-five thousand in need of repair after the earthquake) as required by a law passed in 1968, they considered themselves exonerated from military service. A post-script by the Center members said, "We, the undersigned citizens of Partania, agree with these youths, and we have urged them to not join the military."

After the tour I had much to discuss with Dolci. Though I had heard much support of his programs, I also had learned that the political parties objected to his active nonviolence which included civil disobedience. I talked for some time with Dolci about his plans. At his desk he charted for me what he considered the heart of his program: breaking apart the "Mafia-client relationship." He drew a circle, put a hub in the middle of it, and then drew dots inside the circle near the rim. "You see the ordinary relationship is expressed in this circle. The head of the Mafia is the hub. He deals with these points near the inside of the rim. The people are outside of the rim." He made a lot more dots outside. "All dealings, especially money dealing and voting, is between people on the inside edge and those on the outside. The people don't deal directly with the top man. What I want to do is develop all kinds of relationships so that there is a direct relationship between the clients themselves, between the client and the center-man, and between the client and the assistant middle-man, so that these intermediate relationships are broken." He showed this by grouping the points into combinations on the chart. As these small groups are made, the large

Mafia-client relationship is broken. All the action is promoted by revolutionary nonviolence.

I asked him why he didn't include a faith component in his program. He replied, "Of course, I understand that God is in the program, but in Italy, the people tend to confuse God with the pope." He was in full agreement with Gandhi and Lanza del Vasto, who was his friend, that the very rock and center of the program is a belief in God. His comments caused me to reflect on the caution that is needed in the forms taken to express the spirit of God.

I said farewell to Danilo Dolci with respect for him, with new hope, and with joy to have met him and his friends. Here was a man who, with a small band of companions, was doing work that could be modeled by any individual or group who struggle to create a more fair distribution of wealth in the world.

Other books by Dolci include *The Man Who Plays Alone*, (McGibbon and Key, London, 1968) and *A New World in the Making*, (McGibbon and Key, 1965).

Next I set out for Riesi, a town located in south central Sicily. There, a Christian community called Servicio Christiano (Christian Service) was committed to bringing the message of the "New World" of Christ's Kingdom. They sought to demonstrate that Christ is the savior of each one and that the world of "agape" or love which He preached and incarnated is different from the world in which we live and is the ultimate reality to which each is called. Without Christ there is domination, a senseless search for prestige, and exploitation of others. Christ's world is one of giving, one where service and gratitude prevail. This is not only a theological truth, but also a political and economic truth necessary to build the Kingdom. True politics is a matter of service, not strength, and all rulers are called by Jesus to be servants. True economics should not be considered in the narrow frame of profits and debits, but from the point of view of sharing the world's resources. Everyone should participate in the abundant riches of this world. This concept of agape must enter into our lives in all its manifestations since nothing in itself is sacred and nothing is profane, but everything is true in Christ and false outside of Him.

To the people of Riesi, Servicio Christiano brings the message: To the extent that you exploit, dominate, live for your own well-being, you destroy the town; to the extent that you cooperate with one another, you truly build a town.

The foundational work of Servicio Christiano grew out of the teaching of Tullio Vinay, a Protestant pastor who began his work after World War II in northern Italy. An ecumenical center was founded and from there the witness was realized in the creation of intentional communities and voluntary work camps. In 1948 the work focused on economically depressed areas with the greatest need. When Danilo Dolci began his work in 1952, some in the Servicio Christiano movement went to his aid.

In 1961, a Servicio Christiano community was established in Riesi — a town in great need. Community members had their commitment tested immediately: They were robbed on the way, and the little they had was taken from them.

A few days following their arrival in town, they heard a great noise from a large crowd gathered around a woman and two children. They learned that the crowd wanted to run her out of town to avoid a scandal because she was a prostitute. To diffuse the situation, the Christian Service workers took the woman and the children to safety, fed them, and paid their fare home. This was how they first got to know the people of the town.

They soon learned that the story of the town was poverty. Anxious families shared with them a litany of concerns ranging from high infant mortality to worries that the local mine would go out of business, leaving hundreds unemployed.

On the outskirts of the city in a pleasant grove of olive trees, Christian Service community members built their center. One of their first struggles was aimed at the custom of annual rent charges, a practice going back to feudal times. Local barons levied high annual charges, even though the peasants had been improving the land for centuries. The peasants also paid state taxes. The issue was fought in court, and despite several losses there, a new law was passed to make land reform easier.

Steadily, the community grew, and there were twenty members when I was there. Their projects were impressive: A Swiss pediatrician served as a community volunteer in the pediatric clinic. An agricultural center planned experimental plots and developed planting information for local farmers. An embroidery workshop grew into a cooperative of fourteen workers who sold articles all over Europe. This generated income for women in the region who typically were unable to work outside the home. The community began schools: a kindergarten, a training center for machinists, and a school to train medical workers. After training leaders, the community turned control of the schools over to the local people.

By 1968, structures included community houses, a meeting hall, a library, a house for the night watch, three large barns for chickens, and a tool shed containing a feed-grinding mill. A transformer house provided electricity for the community. With much trouble, a well was dug. A vegetable garden produced food for the staff and the students — a crowd of about three-hundred at the noon meal. All of this was developed despite many problems and a great deal of opposition.

While some of the projects generated income, they still had to be subsidized: The community received donations from individuals (they sent a newsletter to eight-thousand subscribers) and received grants from the World Council of Churches and the Van Leer Foundation of Holland.

At supper I was honored to meet sixty-year-old Tullio Vinay. His friendly, wrinkled, tan face was topped with bushy gray hair. A big man, he was the moving spirit of the community. He spoke English, French, Italian, and Sicilian. He was of Waldensian background, a pacifist sect. Many Waldensians were killed by Catholics in the twelfth century. The survivors fled to the Alps.

In the evening, over tea, crackers, and wine, I had a leisurely visit with Theodore and Heidi Buss. This Swiss couple, he, a Protestant minister, she, a former airline hostess, planned to spend two years in service with the community. Of particular interest to me was the story of how Theodore had led the public petition effort to have the Jesuits readmitted to Switzerland.

Next day Tullio drove me to the train station forty miles away. Theodore and Heidi came along for the ride. Running late, we had to pick up the pace; we took curves sharply and came close to hitting other cars. Our small car was deceptively fast. I was shaken a bit by the fast ride, but I made it to the train without a moment to spare.

The train took me over the mountains and back to Palermo. There I waited a few days for a ship to Tunis. While eating lunch in a restaurant, I met two French sailors on shore leave from an escort destroyer that had just come into the harbor. Graciously, they invited me to their ship for lunch the following day.

I met them at the gangplank., and they introduced me to their shipmates, most of them in work clothes, who were already lined-up for chow. We sat at iron tables in the dining room located in the bottom of the ship. It was very noisy, crowded and stuffy — hardly an appetizing atmosphere. When lunch was over, the crew gathered around the table for a general discussion on the immorality of war, especially as waged with nuclear weapons. We agreed on the stupidity of the Vietnam War and the economic motivation for the U.S. intervention after the French withdrawal. Each of the crew members I met spoke of low morale and insisted that nine out of ten of the men didn't like naval life. On deck I met the captain of the ship and the other officers, who gave me a cordial welcome. I had a photograph taken with my two new friends and departed.

As I left, I was struck by the contrast between the community at Riesi and this iron-clad body of men who had been organized for the purpose of killing: one group trying to bring life, even Divine life, the other prepared to bring death. The gospel group was committed and happy in their work. The military group was hassled and discontented.

This contrast illustrates the difference between the process of war and the process of peace. In the community at Riesi the members worked freely among the poor, but the men on the destroyer were packed into their little boat and placed in uniforms to be marked as separate from the people. The community at Riesi transcended national barriers to spread the gospel of peace. The sailors on the destroyer were part of a nationalistic build-up — the kind that prevents world peace.

Northern Africa

A half-hour before my ship was to sail from Palermo, a U.S. Embassy official read my mail to me over the phone since there was no time to pick it up. With no unsettling news, I prepared to enjoy the ocean voyage; but one hour out to sea the small ship began to roll. By the time another hour had passed most of the people were sea sick. Having heard that fresh air is one of the best antidotes, I tried spending the trip on deck. No luck, ten hours later I was still sick. I spent most of the time sprawled out in a lounge chair with a coat over my eyes so 1 couldn't see the walls moving. Everything seemed to rattle and nobody talked. This was not a vacation!

We arrived in Tunisia at 10:30 p.m., stranded six miles from the city of Tunis and half a mile from the train station. Once at the station we found the trains didn't run until morning. Fortunately, a kindly Tunisian with a station wagon stopped and in the wee hours of the morning took nine of us, free of charge, into the city where we found a hotel for three dollars each.

In looking forward to my Africa visit, I discovered from my reading that there were few peace leaders or peace communities to visit there. Primarily, my interest was to study the relationship of colonialism and slavery to war and peace. From experience and through reading, I noted a comprehensive parallel between racism and war. Both are built on the same kind of false theology, supported by the same types of arguments. Both separate people from one another; both depend on fear, hatred and lies.

Getting around Tunis was a breeze. A Georgetown student's father lent me his car and his chauffeur who acted as my guide. We drove to the site of the ancient city of Carthage —twice leveled in Twentieth Century wars. Once a powerful city, it had been a rival of Rome. The Romans had the adage: "Delendum est Carthagum" (Carthage must be destroyed.) From Carthage, Hannibal led his army, using elephants, over the Alps to attack Rome. Rome resolved to destroy Carthage and did. Cruel fate, the city was destroyed for good during World War II. It became, instead of a city of the living, a city of the dead — a memorial of rival empires. What struck me most painfully was for almost as far as I could see, there were graves. They were divided into American and French sections. No doubt there were German sections too, though I didn't see them.

I went on to the American Peace Corps Headquarters in the suburbs of Tunis. Although I could get no official information from the staff there about where to find Peace Corps volunteers, some friendly secretaries let me know that they could be found at the Cafe de Paris and that they could be recognized by their long hair. By the time I managed to find the café, I was glad to get inside where it was warm. I found the "long-haired" Americans I was looking for and struck up a conversation.

Apparently, just a week before, a visit by Secretary of State Rogers had caused some friction: These Peace Corps volunteers strongly disagreed with U.S. policy toward Israel. They were outraged that Israeli fighter jets, bought from the United States, were used to kill people with whom they worked. When the volunteers were ordered to attend the address by Rogers, eight of them sat in the front row, their backs turned to Rogers while others booed him at regular intervals.

Later, they were admonished that the Secretary's address was no place for protest, that such rudeness was out of place. How strange to fixate on rudeness when the real issue was the crime of taking innocent lives. Is it rude to turn your back on the official of your country who helps kill the people you serve?

My travels took me next to Algiers where I was supposed to catch a connecting flight to Rabat. Procuring flight information, let alone a place to stay, proved nearly impossible. Yet out of all this frustration, I learned something: Algerians are not in a hurry. Fatalism, even when it is not formally recognized, seemed pervasive — an attitude that "Allah takes care of all things." In this way, the people relate patience directly with God.

I finally learned that it would be very difficult to get to Rabat. So I changed my plans and booked a flight to Casablanca. The difficulties I experienced in trying to get to Rabat (located on the Mediterranean coast) were a holdover from colonial times in Algeria. The transport routes in colonial times did not go from town to town, but were direct lines from the interior to the coast and then on to the mother country.

As I walked through the streets of Algiers, I thought of the Battle of Algiers: Muslims bombing French stores and the French torturing Muslims to find guerrillas hidden in the Casbah. One evening, in a restaurant, I talked to young Frenchmen who were part of the French remnant. They told me that the French population in the country was down to one-hundred-thousand and that it had been a million at the time of the war. I also met an Algerian college student at the post office who offered to take me on a tour of the Casbah and other sites significant in the war for independence. We walked through the winding village streets, too small for autos, and full of steps and stairs.

The Casbah was built on the side of a mountain at the edge of the sea. Most of the architecture is Turkish, but some of it is French. The Turks used rocks, earth, and many arches in their construction. Markets and stores were everywhere. Foodmakers, barbers cutting hair on the sidewalks, children playing in two feet of space, all created a lively scene.

When I expressed interest in the Turkish baths, we went down to a cellar where we were given a towel, left our clothes, went down some more stairs, through a door into a large, steam room. There was a stone massage table in the center of the room, steam pipes in the ceiling, and spigots of hot and cold water pouring into some stone basins along the walls. We soaped up using handfuls of fibers as wash-rags and then poured hot water over ourselves with plastic bowls. After we washed and rinsed off, we were given two large towels: one for the head and shoulders, like a hood, and the other for around the waist. We went back upstairs and lay down on mattresses. There an attendant covered us with another large towel. It was easy to sleep. At the time, these popular public baths cost about seventy-five cents.

On March 1, 1970, I arrived in Casablanca via Air Tunis. Most of the city was gaily decorated for the coming anniversary of the coronation of the king. In contrast, in the slum section of the city, the Medina, living conditions were poor: houses without water, families crowded into one small room, streets a few feet wide.

During the day I sat in the park; palm trees lined the walks and flowers were blooming. I was content to sit .and watch the people — women with veils over their nose and mouth, men wearing a headpiece and long clothing that reached to the ground. The clothing of the adults was mostly white, gray, brown, blue or green. In contrast, the children wore multi-colored robes. While little more half the men wore this traditional Arab dress, most of the women did. I saw one man walk by with four veiled women and many children — out for a family stroll. Rich men can have as many as ten wives. The games of the children were like those of children everywhere: I watched a three-year-old who kept eluding her father's efforts to make her sit quietly on a bench beside him and provided amusement for the watching adults.

I talked with university students who told me they were anxious to leave Morocco because there were no jobs. Like so many poor countries, Morocco was experiencing a brain drain. The best educated left because of lack of opportunity to use their skills.

At night there were firecrackers, further celebration of the anniversary of the king's coronation. Parents enjoyed the their children's excitement as the multi-colored rockets filled the air. Further along the street, a less joyful scene: women sat begging with children in their laps.

I took an Air Morocco jet to Dakar, Senegal, another port city, the closest part of Africa to South America. Dakar, located on the seacoast, has a tropical climate. Unlike the other major North African cities, Dakar had a very visible European population. On the way into the city, the bus I was riding passed shanty towns along the roads screened by high bushes. Here the crowds of hidden poor lived close together.

There were many signs of poverty in the city. Taxis followed me along the street trying to get me to take a ride. Boys on the corners everywhere tried to shine my shoes. I was amazed that they kept asking me for a shine even though I was wearing sandals. Most of the people wear sandals, so anyone with shoes was followed. I saw a child of eight, with torn shorts as his only clothing. He had open cuts standing out against his black skin. Along the streets, men used English and French to sell their wares. They had big smiles and no jobs. Women sat or lay on the sidewalks, sometimes suckling babies at their breasts.

On Sunday, as the faithful came out of a church, I saw a group of five beggars came up the steps to meet them. I noticed that a couple of them had hands and arms disfigured by leprosy. One of them was blind. Here was poverty, disease and disability, all concentrated.

Such poverty made the idea of a "vacation" here painful. Anyone who rides in a plane is rich in comparison to the people here. They told me, "All Americans are rich." I heard this phrase repeated often, and, by global standards, it's true.

A young man named Baba, whom I met on the street, agreed to take me to hear the native drummers. He told me that the way to find them was just to listen. We did, and the sound led us to a group of several hundred people formed into circle at a street corner. In the center, five drummers beat on tom-toms of different sizes and shapes; a woman danced as they played. As a part of the dance, she increased the tempo; the drummers responded by beating even faster — each intent on outracing the other. The women took turns dancing, and when it was all over, the crowd gave money to the dancers who shared it with the drummers. The dancing continued for most of the night.

I went to visit the Peace Corps headquarters in a large compound that once was a Protestant mission. I got a friendly welcome and caught up on the news. Peace Corps volunteers were coming in from various places. One was Sharon Altus of New York who invited me to visit her in Bombay!! I wondered if she expected me to go to India, but learned that Bombay (Senegal) was only about three hours away by bus.

I went to Bombay, population three-thousand, with Marion Rahman, a young American woman. We traveled by inter-city car service with six Africans who kept the windows closed to keep out the dust. The ground along the road was parched and cracked. Herds of light brown cows with large horns ate only brush because there was no grass. At every stop, vendors offered their wares: cabbages, eggs and peanuts. Since the road was good, we arrived in Bombay in just two hours.

Sharon Altus was the only Peace Corps volunteer in town; the other woman who was supposed to help her got sick. Sharon had a full plate: She ran the social center in town, taught sixth grade and kindergarten, held a sewing class, and helped in the local hospital by teaching prenatal and postpartum care. The first floor of the house in which she lived was a store and an assembly room for her social center.

With Sharon I visited the home of a Bombay family, who spoke only the local dialect. Mother, father and six children lived in two rooms: one a bedroom, the other a combination kitchen, parlor and dining room. We sat on the floor around a tin basin (like a wash basin) full of white rice. When they poured a peanut soup over the rice, we all were invited to eat from the dish — with our fingers. The soup had soaked through about two inches of the rice. When we reached the remaining white rice on the bottom, it was saved for later in the meal. The next course was a black meat stew: an extravagant item for a poor family. It was served in honor of meat-eating Americans. I do not eat meat, so I told them I follow Gandhi's principle not to eat what dies in pain at the hands of men. This provoked a discussion on Gandhi. They were pleased to find an American following Gandhi, and I was glad they accepted my excuse. Since the meat stew was very black and there is little refrigeration in Bombay, this dish did not tempt me. After the meat stew was finished, the dessert of unpasteurized goat's milk was poured over the remainder of the white rice. I asked Sharon if it was safe (in English). She told me to pass — I could get all kinds of disease from it.

I noticed that the children were very quiet and obedient throughout the meal. Even the smallest ones sat quietly and watched us. They did not eat.

In Senegal, rice and peanuts were the staple foods: unchanged since colonial days when there was little freedom to grow anything else.

We visited the hospital, a group of one-story buildings forming three sides of a square. Although the wards were crowded, there was no doctor. For emergency care or surgery, they had to take the patients fifty miles to the nearest doctor. Here, in human faces, you could see what lack of medical care means. At the time, the United States had one doctor for every nine-hundred persons, and many poor countries had one doctor for every ten-thousand people. Nonetheless, many doctors from the poor countries came (and still come) to North America where the pay is more lucrative.

I decided to go further south to Gambia. Because planes and boats only went every two weeks and land travel was cut off by a war between Portugal and Portuguese Guinea, I chose to hitchhike. Janice, an American friend, had some free time and asked if she could go with me. I was delighted. She was fine company and made the hitchhiking much easier. We traveled along the Gambia River, with swamps full of crocodiles. At Bramba-Tenda we caught a ferry and then made our way to Pacalingding where we found the house of Jim Martin, a Peace Corps volunteer. Although the Africans in this village lived in poverty, they had a strong community spirit. For example, they had an elaborate litany of greetings when they met.

Jim Martin worked at the Government Agricultural School for a salary of one-hundred sixty-five dollars a month from the Peace Corps, and he paid five dollars and sixty cents in rent. His salary was minimal by American standards.

However, most of the people in the area lived on less than thirty dollars a month.

The school had many demonstration projects designed to solve local problems. Many times these problems were a result of poverty, lack of supplies, government or Peace Corps obstacles, and slowness to accept change on the part of the people: a common phenomena in most cultures. Jim's current effort was to devise better ways to store peanuts..

Jim told us that lots of resources go unused because of lack of development money: The water in the river cannot be used to irrigate crops for lack of a twenty-five-dollar pump. Food, such as tomatoes and lettuce, which Jim was growing, failed to interest people because they weren't used to eating them and couldn't sell them.

And nature provided her own set of challenges: Monkeys, traveling in groups as large as twenty, were a problem. They destroyed gardens and raided crops of oranges, grapefruits, lemons and limes.

Near the elementary school, an eight-foot mound of hardened mud marked the home of white ants, termites! It had an irregular shape like a large cactus plant. During the hot season the ants traveled underground over an area of three-hundred feet. There they attacked the underground wood fence posts and building foundations. In the wet season, they would continue their blight on the surface. We asked Kebba, the teacher, why he didn't remove it. He said it would take two or three days work, plus the cost of an exterminator to burn out the termites with gasoline. As it was, they didn't have money for chalk, paper or books, let alone an exterminator.

Besides showing us around the community, Jim went with us, by ferry, to an island which formerly served as the embarkation point for slaves bound for the Americas. This small island, about half a mile wide and a little more than half a mile long was first "owned" by the Portuguese, then the Dutch, the English, and finally the French in successive waves of colonization. Unused now except as a tourist attraction, much of the island remained as it was in the days of colonialism. The slave house, on the edge of the water, had double steps which led up to the front porch. The second floor had been the residence of a family, and the ground floor had been a prison for slaves. The rooms were so small that the slaves had to lay on the floor with head and toe touching the side walls. There were even rooms of different sizes to accommodate slaves of different sizes: men, women, and children — a system designed for efficiency, not human decency.

Slave buyers looked over the slaves on the front porch. Then the slaves were taken down a set of steps, led out through a narrow passage to the back of the building, put in small boats, and ferried out to the waiting ships. It was almost impossible to escape from the island. We were shown around by an African who put leg chains on himself to make us understand a little better how the system worked. I wondered what he thought of white westerners as they looked at this museum. From the eleventh to the nineteenth century, this "system" stole about forty million Africans from their homelands. Six million perished from the cruel treatment and inhuman travel conditions. The slave trade ended in the old French colonies in 1848.

Janice and I headed back to Dakar filled with a fresh perspective on the tragedy of slavery and its legacy. The efforts of the Peace Corps were small compared to the devastation wrought by the system of slavery. Yet, I was inspired by the dedication of the young Peace Corps volunteers, often working in conditions that could easily evoke despair. The Peace Corps experience changed the lives of these young people. Many returned to the United States with a new vision.

Yet, there was much about the Peace Corps that was disturbing. President Kennedy had founded the Peace Corps with the hope that the idealism of young Americans might promote international goodwill and thus peace. However, some saw the Peace Corps as a structure through which to promote business interests and U.S. foreign policy. The Nixon Administration was not enthusiastic about the Peace Corps. Its appointees reflected more of a business interest than the community-organizing emphasis of the Kennedy days. The Peace Corps director in Senegal told me he was resigning because business attitudes were replacing the ideals of peacemaking.

These conflicts became clear to me in another instance: Purely by accident, on the streets in Dakar I ran into Tom Garvey. He was from Georgetown University. We headed for a local café to catch up on news and were soon joined by three other Peace Corps friends. They doubted that the Peace Corps could last. One of them, Toni Barber, had been working in Zuiganshore, a town in Senegal near Portuguese Guinea where they were threatened with bombing. Half the territory of Portuguese Guinea was held by the guerrillas and half by Portugal which got money and military equipment from the United States. This undermined Tom's work because the country he represented was helping to kill Africans.

Despite the pressure to promote U.S. business, the volunteers I met were more committed to the original Peace Corps emphasis. The four friends at the café all planned to apply for conscientious objector status because of their opposition to the Vietnam War. Jim Martin came home from the Peace Corps and joined the peace movement and worked against the Vietnam War. I was on the steps of the Capitol with him and his friend, Jim Good, when the whole group was arrested in the May Day protest of 1971.

It was difficult to leave the pleasant climate and small-town atmosphere of Dakar. It had been nice to meet old friends there and easy to make new ones. As I left Africa, I reflected on what I had seen. Because the lifespan of the average African was about forty-five years, I saw few old people. I had seen not only poverty, but also parties. The colorful dress, the street dances, the tom-toms, the frequent laughter, all were pleasant memories; but the heritage of colonialism continued. Economic control, poverty, subservience in trade relations and racism are all scars left over from slavery and colonialism. The subservience to the white man seemed forever entrenched. Black drivers did not even pick up other Blacks who hitch; they only pick up whites.

I had found little mood for change. It seemed that the people, lovable and friendly, with a melody in their laughter, had accepted their fate.

Brazil

I left Dakar by plane, flying against the rotation of the earth to my destination: Rio de Janeiro. My first impression of the city was the relentless stream of buses: passing at break-neck speed in the congested traffic and filling the air with diesel fumes.

It was nearly as oppressive as the Brazilian government of the time. My first taste of the regime's tyrannical nature came during my visit with Maria Bandira, secretary general of the non-governmental rural basic education program. On the way to her office I passed the U.S. ambassador's residence, a palatial embassy with big iron gates and a very visible military guard. As we visited, Maria told me that the government considered any kind of nonviolence a subtle type of subversion and sedition against the state. Arrest and prison awaited those caught advocating it. A young man from her office had been arrested six months before and remained in jail. All of this because he had held some meetings in his home to talk about nonviolence. Since fear and intimidation were pervasive, this was not the last I heard about such violations of human and civil rights.

My temporary residence was a room at St. Ignatius College, a Jesuit secondary school. From my window I could see the famous Christ the Redeemer statue on the mountain above. Along the mountainside, just behind the college was a *favella*, a settlement of flimsy shacks, called Santa Maria. In Rio nearly half a million people lived in favellas despite government threats to move them out.

At breakfast the next morning my "education" about the situation in Brazil continued. An elderly priest and I discussed the kidnapping by guerrillas of the German ambassador to Brazil. I asserted that the best resolution to this crisis would be for the government to grant the demands of the kidnappers, thus saving the life of the ambassador.

"But they [the guerrillas] are subversives," he said.

"So was Jesus called a subversive," I replied.

This led us into what I hoped would be a dialogue about one of greatest gifts of Christ: forgiveness and reconciliation. But instead, the priest insisted that the Bible sanctions killing of the guilty. I reminded him that Christ never sanctioned murder. At this point the priest became so angry that he spoke loudly in Portuguese (which I couldn't understand). Finally, he asked, "Do you think that the Church could err in a substantial matter?"

I answered, "In theory, the Church has never said that killing is allowed, but in practice it has been complicit in killing."

In the fashion of a skilled debater, the old priest then asked, "Is self-defense allowed?"

The answer to this challenge is clear: While the Roman statesman Cicero and the pagans agreed that killing in self-defense is justified, this too is not a Christian position. It is better for us to ask, "Is defense by immoral means allowed and is it obligatory? Is killing ever the only alternative?"

My next stop in Brazil was the city of Recife. Before boarding the plane bound for Recife, all passengers in Rio were searched for guns. Officials were worried about planes being high-jacked to Cuba.

Recife, with a population of about one million people, had been controlled by Portugal for three hundred years until 1882. The architecture reflects the Portuguese influence.

At the airport I asked three officials, who were talking to each other, how to get to the residence of Dom Helder Camara, the Bishop of Recife. All three knew him. One was driving to the city and took me right to the large, Spanish-styled building marked "Bishop's Residence" or "Palacio Episcopal." A two-story building with heavy walls and high ceilings, this building, formerly the exclusive residence of the bishop, was now turned over to the people. As I entered, I saw people everywhere, all of them poor, many of them children.

There was a pleasant receptionist who told me that Dom Helder didn't live there anymore, but had moved to a small room in another part of the city. This added authority to his gospel preaching and his service to the poor.

When I finally met Dom Helder Camara, I was warmly greeted by a small man, about five-foot tall, with twinkling eyes, wearing a plain black cassock with no red or braid. Around his neck he wore a wooden cross held by a string — there was no gold chain. Bishop Camara had a charm and an attractiveness that added force to his words. To see him seated at the table in his office somehow undisturbed by the constant stream of people — like the poor woman with her child standing at the door — was to see a bishop in a unique setting.

When I came back the second day, I brought Susan Johnson, a twenty-year old Peace Corps volunteer who had been six months in Recife and was eager to meet him. We sat at a table talking with Bishop Camara about the nature of injustice. When I brought up that injustice is endemic to war, he commented that he was more concerned with the injustice created by the disparity between the rich and poor — globally, nationally and within local communities. He remarked that this type of injustice killed more people than war and indeed often leads to war.

Susan asked, "But Bishop, do you think that there is any hope of bringing justice without violence?"

He answered, "I am a man of hope. In every country you have people on the left and the right who fight and kill others. In every country there are people . . . who are striving for justice. If these people could be brought together, much might be done." He turned to her and said, "Look at what you are doing. You are away from your family; you are using a strange language in a strange culture, and you help us change by developing cooperatives. You are a young woman and look at how much you do. My work is not just with one religion or with one culture. I think it is my mission to convince the university centers to work to correct the injustices that are done by the rules of trade and commercial interchange between the rich and the poor countries."

Then he listed an impressive account of invitations for the months ahead: Salzburg, Paris, Lyons, and then to Berlin where Buddhists, Muslims, Protestants and Catholics worked together on a program to develop world peace. He also planned to go to Ireland, Holland, New Zealand, Australia, and the United States.

I wondered what his ideas on pacifism might be, so I asked him, "Does the gospel demand that there be no killing? Does the gospel demand that Christians take no part in war or in the economics of war? Do the problems of the Church today — authority, lack of faith, the alienation of the young — have anything to do with the failure of the Church to oppose killing and war?"

He answered that there are various schools of interpretation of the Bible and that in his heart he felt that the New Testament allowed no killing. But he added that he was not a scripture scholar, and the Old Testament ordered the killing of some people. "I sympathize with your view, but there are other views, and it is a mystery to me."

"But is not the central teaching of the gospel that God is the Father of all, so killing is wrong," I insisted.

"My people suffer so much that I really believe that God is their Father. The poor are living in a state of violence." I took this to mean that God is the protector of the poor. Dom Helder continued. "I am often asked, 'Do you know any country where the structure has changed without violence?' and I reply with a question, 'Do you know any country in the world where the structure has changed with violence?'"

Our discussion intrigued and challenged me, so I was pleased to meet again with Dom Helder later in my trip: I was visiting the Catholic Seminary in Olinda, the twin city of Recife; Dom Helder was there for a meeting with the bishops. I gave him the answers to several questions he had asked me to answer. He had composed this list of questions during a recent visit to the United States. They were such questions as, "What can the people of the United States do for the people of Brazil?" and "How can nonviolence work with an oppressive government like Brazil's?"

He came out of the meeting to see me and to thank me for doing this work. "This will give me a good picture of your thoughts," he said. He told me it was very difficult to try to meet the minds of foreign audiences, but this was one of the ways in which he would try.

He had no difficulty with audiences in Brazil. Tom Bren, a Peace Corps volunteer, told me, "Anyone who can hold the attention of the poor, unlettered people for thirty-five minutes is very good, . . . and Dom Helder does it."

Every Monday he gave a radio address; he and his message were deeply loved by the poor. Since he was watched by the government, he was not able to say much politically. Even so, by 1977 the government halted his radio program. At age seventy-five Bishop Camara's resignation was accepted by Rome. He continued his world-wide lecturing even after retirement.

In 1976 at the Eucharistic Congress I again met Bishop Camara. In a small group discussion I asked him directly to say something about peace and justice. He refused. He said again that his sympathy was with me, but he didn't want to publicly agree or disagree.

After talking with some friends of Bishop Camara, I came to this conclusion: He did all he could for his people; he risked his life and risked persecution. His mission: to tell the outside world how badly the Brazilian government treats the poor and how the gospel requires that we all do something about the violence and oppression, an oppression for which all of us in the developed nations are responsible.

In our earlier discussion he talked about the problems faced by under-developed nations. They can be crushed by capitalism as well as by socialism. "Neither accepts a pluralistic system. They either impose their own models of materialism or they require blind obedience to the party. This is not the ideal. I would speak of political realism. North Vietnam is now getting help from China. Can China impose its brand of socialism? Can South America develop a type of socialism without oppressing human persons? The Cuban position is not the solution for us!"

He pointed out that conditions of trade must change. For fifteen years Latin America received three billion dollars in help, and then returned eleven billion to the United States. He continued, " In the United States the first time I said that the structure needed to change, I was told, 'If our countries are coming along, why change?' Despite the fact that many admit that the basic structure needs change, if you are rich, you are tempted to say, 'Why change?'

"My part is to visit the universities and to say that the developed countries must face their job. They need to help change the rules of international trade. With the union of all men of good will and all religions, justice and peace may be achieved. It is not impossible."

My time in Recife was one of the most pleasant parts of my trip. Much of my time was spent just relaxing in a hammock in the backyard of the Peace Corps Headquarters. Hammocks handmade in Brazil are so finely knit that they can hold water. Five or six of these hammocks were set up under a roof, open to the breeze. It was a good way to meet the volunteers as they came and went. They were good company.

The evening of April 9 I went with Bob Rosenbaum of the Peace Corps to his hilltop home on the outskirts of town. He lived in two rooms of a mud and grass hut, one of many located on the side of a large, steep hill. He worked with the people there to improve their water system. One room was just big enough for two small chairs and a suitcase. The other had a hammock. Bob told me, "I didn't even bring my trunk, I left it at the Peace Corps Headquarters. Still people think I am rich. They judge by the texture of my shirt and trousers. I don't even wear a wristwatch."

As we were talking, he directed my attention across the valley to an ordinary-looking structure: It was the church of a sect that originated in the time of slavery. The slaves combined their native religious practices with Catholicism. For instance, the Blessed Virgin was also prayed to as "the Goddess of Light." In the market, I had seen statues of the Goddess of Light sold along with the Catholic saints. Even with its adaptation to Christian faith, the practices of the native religion had been banned by slave owners It occurred to me that under the circumstances, these slaves would hardly have been convinced of Christian brotherhood and sisterhood. Of course they would persevere in their own religion and, in order to survive, tailor it to Christianity.

Accompanied by two Peace Corps volunteers, Josh Cobure and Dick Lawless, I traveled six hours by bus to San Caetana, inland from Recife. Their two-bedroom apartment, in a building constructed by the Alliance for Progress program, had a concrete floor, running water and electric lights. Although these apartments rented for only five dollars a month, one-third of the group's apartments were empty because people couldn't afford that much rent.

The Peace Corps volunteers also helped operate a marketing and consumers' cooperative which sold everything from seeds to hatchets to instant coffee. From them I learned something about the economy and working conditions — why people couldn't afford five dollars for rent. Cane cutters got about one dollar per day, plus a dollar bonus for work on Sundays. But if the worker missed one day, the day's pay, plus the bonus, were lost. If assigned work was not completed, no pay was received for any of the work.

The minimum wage was the equivalent of twenty-five dollars a month, but few got it. The average person worked piecemeal jobs and got about seventy-five cents a day, four days a week. Often wages were in the form of credit at the company store which charged high prices. Because one-fourth of the people were illiterate, they had little chance of finding or creating an alternative to this slave labor.

By bus I returned to Rio, a trip through the mountains that took forty hours. The narrow road twisted and turned, with hardly a half-mile of straight, level road. The bus had a noisy motor; exhaust fumes wafted through the windows. A shelf on the seat in front opened up for leg support, but there was no real place to stretch out. An ice-box packed with ice, soft drinks, and cold water free to passengers added a bit of comfort. Some people brought their own fresh fruit and other perishables and stored them in the ice-box until needed.

At one point the military searched the bus and asked everyone for a police pass. This was not a border crossing; the whole ride began and ended in Brazil. I asked one of the soldiers why he wanted to see identification. He said he didn't know; it was just orders.

— ❖ ❖ ❖ —

Argentina

I traveled on from Rio by bus to Buenos Aires on the Rio de la Plata. In the capital city my first stop was to meet the relatives of my friend Susanna of the Ark Community in France. Immediately, these kind people began to educate me on the situation in their troubled country: For the last four years Argentineans had lived under complete dictatorship; the federal legislature had been shut down and there was no movement toward elections. Even at the university, there was no freedom of discussion. Approximately half the of the Argentine population lived in the Buenos Aires region, so away from the capital, roads and bridges were in utter disrepair — a symbol of the lack of concern by the government for the people.

In summing up the many problems, my friends cited the United States as having a direct link to their country's difficulties with democracy and self-determination: "We are weary of the United States. All our industries are bought up by U.S. firms. But it's hard to prove because they keep the old names. The military permits it. It gives them more money from the United States."

My new-found friends joined me the next day on a visit with priests from an organization, led by eighteen bishops, called "Priests of the Third World." In 1967 the priests, most of them from Latin America, signed a manifesto on the conditions of the people in the Third World. Father Misomette and two other priests, with whom we visited, accepted violence as a possible last resort, but their sympathy was with nonviolence. In their view, under a military dictatorship, promoting "peace" meant working for the "status quo." Indeed, peace is not merely the absence of armed conflict.

After we left the priests, Oscar Fernandez, one of Susanna's kin, said, "These priests seem to be groping. They have no clear program." This confirmed my view that you need a firm base from which to build. My foundation: that God is the parent of us all. Therefore, we are all to behave as brothers and sisters. Complexities don't change this; bloodshed can't be a part of the program. With this base I never get confused — I never have to wonder if my support of violence is justified.

— ❖ ❖ ❖ —

When I visited the consular affairs section of the U.S. Embassy, I again experienced an institution in the grip of violence. Outside the building two Argentinean police officers with machine guns stood guard. As I reached the third floor, another man, armed with a machine gun, was watching the hallway. I asked him, "What are you here for?"

"I don't know. I just have orders." — the age-old answer of the mindless military.

When I reached the upstairs mail desk, I asked why they had armed guards. The receptionist said they were afraid of bombs or attacks on embassy personnel. I asked if it was not a violation of American sovereignty for armed Argentinean law enforcement officers to be inside the embassy. She said that there was no other way to protect the embassy. Why would we require such extraordinary security measures? Were we that disliked in Argentina too?

Chile

I took a plane to Santiago. As we flew over the Andes, the mountains looked like sand dunes covered with grass instead of mountains covered with trees. In less than two hours I arrived in Santiago and took the bus to the Jesuit Theological College. As I rode in from the airport, I saw election signs everywhere. Senator Tomec of the Christian Democratic party had his signs in red, white, and blue. You could almost tell the size of the candidate's following by the size of the signs.

During my time in Chile I discovered a tense political scene. I later learned that the CIA had much more involvement in the internal political affairs of Chile than had ever been acknowledged. If I had known this while I was in Chile, I would have understood more or what I saw and heard.

The upcoming presidential election had come down to a race between the centrist candidate of the Christian Democrats, the candidate of the right-wing Nationalist Party, and the eventual election winner, Salvador Allende.

My first evening in the country I talked to Father John Henry, rector of a Jesuit school in Osorno. He told me about a letter from the Jesuit provincial on the social formation of students. The letter put social development and an interest in applying Christian principles to the problems of the day as a priority for all educational work of the Jesuits in Chile. The next day I participated in that process by speaking about peace and morality to some of Father Henry's high school students.

On the evening of April 29, 1970 I went to the outskirts of the city to see a commune that included two Jesuits among it membership. One of the Jesuits, Father Arroyo, taught agronomy at the University of Santiago. Caspar Lobiondo assisted him. Their program aimed to raise the consciousness of the people, to educate and empower them. They saw that unless conditions are changed through education, violence may be the only choice. They also told me that they could not rule out violence as a last resort. I told them this was also the position of Presidents Johnson and Nixon. I quoted Johnson who, when he sent the first one-hundred twenty-five thousand combat troops to Vietnam, said: "I don't want to hurt a single person. There is nothing else I can do. It pains me very much to have a single person hurt at all."

I spoke with Father Poblete, director of the Jesuit-run Social Studies Institute in Santiago. He told me, "Before 1965 the Church was the largest organizer of rural workers — resulting in the creation of sixty cooperatives. Now the government has replaced the cooperatives as well as many of the cooperative leaders; now I've gone to work for the government."

He told me that a new militant socialist group, Movimento Izquierdo Revolucionario, (MIR) was implementing a strategy designed to weaken the communist influence amongst workers. MIR wanted to foment a violent struggle against the political right. Fr. Poblete's concern was that the resulting conflict would harm the well-organized communists who were working in more peaceful ways.

Accompanied by Francisco Diaz, M.D., I visited a slum, Jose Maria Care, named after a Catholic Cardinal who was very interested in the poor. Diaz worked there in a clinic run by the government. He got fifty dollars a month for his work. A few days later, Francisco's brother, Eduardo , a former Georgetown student, gave me a more extensive tour. The slum had developed paved roads, medical care and running water. A group of American sisters from Kansas worked on literacy.

Eduardo outlined the overall economic troubles. The per capita income in Chile was three-hundred and sixty dollars a year. About five percent of the people owned almost all the property and wealth in Chile. He supported the Christian Democrats because they had a program to change many of these conditions. However, he also pointed out that government programs often fell short because officials didn't want oppose the army; they feared, and rightly so, a coup d'etat. Eduardo used an example from town of Temuoco where he worked for the government. Near Temuoco, many poor people had built houses on the banks of the river. Now, erosion was threatening to destroy their homes. The government allocated funds to divert the river, with the condition that Eduardo secure permission from the army for the diversion. So he went to the Army Chief of Staff in Santiago who granted permission. But then a local general refused because the army owned the land and didn't want to give it up. This general, U.S.-trained, told Eduardo, "Those communists will soon want the entire shore." He viewed all poor people as communists. Eduardo then pointed out that this kind of refusal only pushed people toward communism. The general wouldn't budge.

As in so many cases, in fear of an army takeover, government officials would not override the general. They were skittish anyway about losing votes in the upcoming election, and if the current national government didn't roll over to the army, they would be labeled "soft on communism."

On May 1, a hacienda owner and his employees killed the chief of the land reform agency as he tried to enforce the land re-distribution law. They beat him to death with spike-studded wooden clubs before the police, only fifteen meters behind, could intervene. The land was being expropriated, according to law, with payment of the assessed price made by the government over a period of thirty years. The owner objected on the grounds that the assessed price was too low; although, for tax purposes, the owner had determined the assessed value.

The victim became a people's hero; President Eduardo Frei and his entire cabinet attended the funeral, as did I. Allende was also present. At the gate of the cemetery, speeches were made honoring the new martyr. A campesino said. "Your blood is our own; you led the fight for the campesinos." Then he turned to the living, "The campesinos of all countries have been persecuted; we must let the world know that we are fighting for a new society."

The crowd followed the body around the cemetery gate. There were shouts in chorus, "Who killed him?"

The crowd replied, "The monies," (a term used to designate the far right). Others shouted, "Long live the land reform."

Hugo Triendele, Minister of Agriculture, spoke for the Christian Democrats, "The sacrifice of life is the most powerful lever in history. The hands of mercenaries raised against this man have put an end to his bodily life, but they have made him a symbol, a new martyr. Let us not weep as if we have no hope."

A representative of the Federation of Campesinos said, "He died working for justice, for the campesinos; his name will live forever in the heart of the campesinos."

As the political oratory ceased, the coffin was carried to the cemetery. The wife and three children of the murdered man followed. Farm workers with banners walked behind the coffin. Some banners had the names of their farms and the dates the land had been re-distributed. Others carried Christian Democrat flags showing an arrow piercing two objects representing communism and capitalism. Some carried signs. One read: "Blessed are those who die for the land reform because they will be the redemption of the campesinos."

As we left the cemetery, Eduardo Diaz said to me. "Chile is one of the few places where we mention Christ's name in politics."

I soon learned more about politics in Chile: I entered the Senate chambers just as one of the Senators was carried out on a stretcher. A fight had developed after a Christian Democrat, Eduardo Sepulbedo, spoke out against the murder of the land reform worker. Someone had made a motion to send condolences to the dead man's wife. But Victor Zuniga, a rightist, said we should not console any family whose father and husband was a land-robber. Then he punched Sepulbedo; in the ensuing brawl, Sepulbedo, was seriously hurt and required hospitalization. The next day, the Nationalist Party expelled Zuniga for his violence.

I had the great fortune of meeting Pablo Tomas, president of the Senate, who told me that Chile had done much for social justice in the way of housing and benefits for the poor. "Latin America must find its own solution for its problems because neither the United States' system nor the Soviet system will work here." He stressed that the United States needed to work in cooperation with, rather than dominate, Chile. Democracy was the method; social and economic development were the goals.

Pablo Tomas resented hearing lectures in Washington about what to do and what to think. He didn't consider it worth the trip if there was no dialogue. He found that Kennedy had more interest in South America than any other official that he'd known. He gave Rockefeller as an example of "no-dialogue." Furthermore, Rockefeller was more of a problem than a help because of the additional security required. Johnson had no interest, and Nixon didn't know what he wanted.

— ❖ ❖ ❖ —

Just a note here about a very significant event that took place while I was in Chile: On May 5, 1970, as I passed through the University of Chile campus, I saw the student protest against the U.S. bombing of Cambodia. At the time of the invasion I thought right away of returning home, but when I read about the massive protests, their very size convinced me that I wasn't needed. Also, I was convinced this would be the end for Nixon. I felt that this time he had overplayed his hand.

In retrospect I think I was right about Nixon and Cambodia. Information leaks about the illegal bombing sorties into Cambodia led Nixon to actions like the raid on Dan Ellsberg's analyst's office. Though Nixon was re-elected, the damage was done; eventually, Nixon would be forced his resign.

Peru

From Santiago I flew up the coast to the resort town of Arica — a kind of dream town by the sea where it almost never rains. From there I bused into Peru, entering the country in the heat of the lowlands and ending in the cold of the mountains. Our bus made six stops. At each stop we had to show our passports to the military. When I wearied of this procedure and questioned one of the soldiers, he said. "You show it or go to jail." As he spoke, he pointed to a little cell in the back of the room.

I understood from the other travelers that all Chileans are suspect to Peruvians, and Peruvians are suspect to Chileans. They have not forgotten the bitter war fought between them over land and borders. Such hostility, as evidenced today in the former Yugoslavia, is one of the fruits of war that lasts for generations.

The next day I flew to Lima. My first stop was the church where St. Martin de Porres had lived for sixty years. The rector, Vincente Sanchez, showed kind hospitality during my time at this ancient cloister. We discussed peace, the faith, and racism. As I was making the usual charge of heresy against the Church for its blessing of war, Father Sanchez suggested that I establish a new religious order dedicated to peacemaking. He saw it as a real need for the Church. We agreed that the Catholic Church has failed to specifically promote peace — part of its commission by Christ.

In Quito I visited a home for shoe-shine boys. George Crane, an American Jesuit, established this home for them in the large tower of a Jesuit church. When I came in, they were celebrating a Eucharistic liturgy. As George showed me around, he expressed how difficult it is to get the boys in — they didn't want to be controlled. Bringing these wild children of the streets together to sing and pray was quite an accomplishment.

That evening I met with members of the Pastoral Institute for Latin America, a group of about fifty people, including priests and sisters. They showed a keen interest in the topic. "What Jesus taught about killing."

Colombia

From Cali I took a small seven-person passenger plane for Buenaventura. As we flew low over mountains, I had the sensation of going over a cliff, falling off the top of the mountain. We flew in the rain. As it grew heavier, visibility was reduced to zero. Our pilot even turned off the windshield wiper because the rain's intensity made the windshield opaque. I knew the mountains were just below; I knew we had to land on a small field. My mouth was getting dry. I could hardly swallow. My stomach knotted. Then we broke through a cloud bank. Below I could see the sea, but then the pilot had to turn back into the rainstorm to land. We couldn't see the runway, but felt the jolt as the wheels hit the ground. I departed a little weak-kneed, but much relieved.

A short car ride brought me to the residence of Bishop Gerardo Valenco Cano, one of South America's leading proponents of nonviolence. In his own residence he was dressed in ordinary lay clothes. "I am not a Romanist, but I know the Pope likes the Roman way and Roman style of things."

He also told me, "I am a socialist. Capitalism is like a nest of termites, it kills to live; it needs war." He added that capitalism is anti-Christ. The Church must identify with the poor if it is to be faithful to Christ. To explain his views on international relations he told me an intriguing parable of Fray Martin, St. Martin de Porres: The cat, the dog, and the rat all eat out of the same dish, just like the Black, the white, and the Inca. The animals symbolize Russia, the United States and China. The dog (U.S.) and cat (U.S.S.R.) are almost equal in strength: the cat fears the dog. The rat (China) has the cleverness which balances off its weakness. And yet God gives food to all. God does not decide this is mine and this is yours. Everything is in one dish, one world. God is not a nationalist.

In contrast to many other Catholic officials I had met, he agreed without hesitation that killing is not compatible with the gospel. Bishop Cano's central thesis is this: The great lesson that Christ taught is the unity of the human family which began with the first man and woman and includes all of us up into eternity, all united through Jesus. "A religion with a vertical sense, a religion only oriented toward God, has given rise to all kinds of paganism: a type of Christianity which has allowed and consented to wars and to inhuman vices such as racism, capitalism, and colonialism. Some will say these vices happened before Christ's time. That is true, but it cannot be doubted that the majority of its followers are Christian."

This statement of Bishop Cano represented not just a formal statement on the Christian in a revolutionary age, but also one borne out by the life he lived. (He was since killed in a plane crash.) He was opposed to war, to violence in general. He saw to it that the Church was involved with the poor and with their struggles.

On the road back from Buenaventura to Cali, I rode in a crowded bus and through another rainstorm. At several places water poured from the heights of the mountains like a waterfall. Most people in the bus knew it was coming and closed their windows. I didn't and got soaked. On this ride a drunk sat beside me. He gave speeches against America and yelled at me so much that many in the bus turned around to see my reaction. I just went to sleep, or tried to, and he did too.

Near Medellin, Colombia, I met with Fr. Gabriel Diez in his residence. This young priest was an admirer of Camillo Torres and even resembled him in appearance: strongly built with a full head of black hair. Diez was dressed in loose black clothes with a white shirt and no collar. Three years prior, Diez had been preparing to teach liturgy, but, because of Camillo's influence, he asked the Bishop to let him work in a poor parish. Following the murder of Torres, Diez was concerned that his murder would touch off a revolution in Colombia. He said, "No one had shown Camillo any other way than revolution." Diez himself was interested in a revolution of nonviolence.

Diez, as part of the liberation movement of the poor, took part in one of the first invasions of a barrio: All in one night a group of about three-hundred people who had no homes moved in and occupied an area of unused land. I asked why the police didn't stop the people from moving in. He told me the following dramatic story: Equipment to build simple houses was brought in very quickly, and the next morning when the authorities came, the people had already established residence. As soon as the owner of the land found that a priest was involved, he offered Diez the land as a donation. Diez turned him down because he wanted to be like the rest of the people — sharing whatever fate came to them. He felt this insecurity would be a cohesive act. If they could go to jail, he could go to jail with them.

After a few days the police came to clear the area. One family began to make a brick house, but the police said that only paper and cardboard houses were allowed because brick gave the impression of permanent possession. The police grabbed the arm of the woman who was building the brick house. They pulled her to the wagon to take her to jail. Diez stepped up to talk to the police. As he talked, the crowd of squatters pressed in close to hear. They yelled, "Take all of us if you take her. We are all invaders and we all intend to put up brick houses." The police called for back-up. Ten more cars arrived. The police fell in to formation — the people took up arms: sticks and rocks.

Diez, the peacemaker, announced over a loudspeaker that the people should drop their weapons and cross their arms, that all of them should be willing to go to jail. They responded. As they dropped their rocks, the commandant ordered the police to put the people in the wagons and take them to jail. As the order rang out, everyone turned toward a new sound: Another thousand people were coming down the road to join the fray. They had heard about what was going on. So many people got into one wagon that a tire broke. When that happened, the police ordered everybody out of the wagons. Ultimately, so many people had lined up to be arrested that there were not enough police or wagons.

After more discussion, the police agreed to leave on the condition that no brick houses would be built. The people set a condition of their own: that legal aid would be provided to help them procure "legal ownership" of the land.. Finally, a settlement.

Eventually, some of the land was declared available for building brick houses and a chapel. But then came another glitch: The owner said that the title was valid only for the first one-thousand homes. So the police came again and confronted twelve young men who were constructing a house. Three police officials and many police wagons arrived. Meanwhile, the Vicar-General of the Diocese, Victor Viderman, appeared and joined the discussion He tried to remain neutral.

One of the young men stepped forward and said that the police threatened to shoot him. The chief of police said, "You'll get six years in jail for calumny." The vicar-general stepped into the argument. He pointed out that the police were not the judges and could not give sentences. The people cheered, "Long live the vicar-general! Long live the clergy! Long live the Curia (the officials around the Bishop)!" The vicar-general was so pleased that he gave a speech in favor of the people. The police listened and left.

The next day I traveled to the barrio on the mountain-top where Fr. Diez had confronted the police. In the rain and the mud, it was immediately obvious how futile paper houses would have been. It was so sloppy that it was difficult even to walk along between the brick houses. The church also was built of home-made brick and had a tin roof. Bricks were also used to make the furnishings: the altar, lectern, crucifix and priest's chair. Boards across brick pillars served as pews. Everything was built by the people; it was truly a community-made church. On the wall beside the confessional was a picture of a man breaking out of chains; beneath was the inscription: "Break the chains that separate you from God and your fellow man."

Across the street from the church I saw the place where Gabriel Diez had lived for three years. Now the new priest, who lived outside the barrio, only came on Tuesdays and Sundays. The identification of the priest with the poor was lost.

From Medellin I took a plane to Baranquilla, then a twenty-mile bus ride to the old walled-in city of Cartagena. Here on the edge of the Carribean, near the harbor I found the Jesuit Church of St. Peter Claver. The Jesuits' residence was a three-story brick building with a walkway on the roof giving an impressive view of the harbor and the city. All the rooms looked out on the water. The church, with its bell tower, was a city landmark. The house's Jesuit Superior, Alfonso Jarmillo, aided the workers of St. Peter Claver Church who had organized schools, a workers' union, a cooperative. and medical clinics — all to help the poor.

One day in St. Peter Claver Church I met a young American couple just out for a walk and admiring the gardens. They invited me to a little get-together with some other Americans at the house of some marines. I accepted their offer. During the visit I found that the marines were divided on the issue of war and how to make peace. At least two of them agreed with me that the Vietnam War was ridiculous. Later I saw them on the beach. They were training the Cartegenians in underwater demolition.

St. Peter Claver church is kept as a memorial to St. Peter who aided the slaves in the early 1600s. From his window, St. Peter Claver could see the slave ships coming in. He, an angel of mercy, was the only white man who met the slaves with food, medicine, clothes and love. In his room he stored bags of supplies begged from rich white people. Every day until his death in 1654, worn out at the age of fifty-four, he worked in the swampy area near the dock where the slaves lived before being sold.

As I prayed in the room where St. Peter Claver had once lived, I was deeply moved.. His body, dressed in Mass vestments, rested behind a glass altar. His skull was clearly visible. The sight of his body gave me pause for reflection. Over three hundred years ago, Peter worked along with God against the slave system. He had no real hope of breaking it, yet in his short life, he did all he could. His witness continues to stir the consciences of all who visit his memorial at Cartagena. And so it is today — in the fight against militarism, the killing fields of war — one person working alone with God can do much. We should not despair if we are unable to see the fruits of our labor.

Cartagena was the home of the Inquisition, another scandal. The Inquisition had operated out of a building beside the church. The tour guide showed me a place where a Protestant had been imprisoned for twenty-four years before he was tried. I saw the spot where he was burned to death because he would not convert to Catholicism. On the narrow Spanish street outside the house of the Inquisition there was a small four-inch opening in the wall with a bar across it. I was told that this slot, six-feet above the street, was the mail box into which notes could be put for the Inquisition! The notes didn't even have to be signed. And denunciations were made on the basis of these anonymous accusations.

Cartagena saw tragedy again from 1811 to 1816. Many people died when the Spanish, with ten thousand men, laid siege to the city to crush an emerging independence movement. After the siege succeeded, the Spanish shot the independence leaders. Their memories are kept sacred on the "Plaza of the Martyrs" where statues of those shot line the front of the main gates of the city

Despite this human tragedy in its past, Cartagena is a most beautiful city with a warm climate, beautiful sea and friendly people. I took a bus along the curving shores of the Carribean. The bus was old and open, painted red, yellow and blue, with a bedroom size mirror for rear view. Pictures of saints were tacked up above the windshield. People were smiling and laughing. It was a microcosm of Latin America: old, and yet holding together and moving along; and in it all, laughter and smiles.

Central America

I left South America and flew to Guatemala where I met Peace Corps volunteers Jeanine Jarvis and Christine Murray. They had written a public letter to President Nixon to protest the invasion of Cambodia. By writing such a letter, they were risking reprimand because, like in Africa, the Nixon administration had filled the Guatemala Peace Corps with businessmen who opposed its spirit and its program. I was cheered to see their interest and all the support they were getting for the letter.

On the streets of Guatemala I met three young members of the Church of Jesus Christ of Latter Day Saints who had just finished two years of service. They started telling me about the Mormon religion and I asked them, "Would you go to Vietnam if you were told to?" They said they would.

"Do you believe the Bible allows killing?" I continued.

"Do you want the communists to take over the U.S.?" was their response.

In Mexico City I searched out Fr. Alex Moreller, a French Dominican and a nonviolent leader among the workers and students. He arranged a meeting with about twenty of his friends so we could talk about their program on nonviolent action. Among those present was Pablo Monroy Gomez, the young International Fellowship of Reconciliation secretary who worked primarily with students. He began the discussion with two questions: "What do we do in the face of repression that is so great that a hunger fast in the cathedral is stopped by arrests one hour before it starts?" Second question: "There was a forty-day fast in prison. The people outside of Mexico knew about it, but the people inside did not. There was no publicity about it. There was complete control of the press; the youth get disinterested in nonviolence. What can we do?"

Although I was surrounded by people with years of working on nonviolent action, they didn't give any answers — they wanted to know my opinion. I told them that I thought publicity was not the only aim of the fast. Through the fast one seeks to give witness to the truth. Gandhi maintained that if only one person gives witness to the truth, he can be successful in his witness. He said this can be done in all circumstances, even by the Jews faced with the gas chambers of Hitler. Suppression is never complete. As far as publicity goes: if very few people know or care, then another task before starting the fast is to get them to care.

Maybe the goal of the prison fast was not well chosen. Gandhi studied the situation, and after much reflection, chose the most universally disliked and most immoral law to act against. Many lesser acts of discipline should be gone through before going to jail.

It is possible in Mexico for people to work in other ways through their faith. Look at what the grape workers did in California. When Chavez and the United Farm Workers were forbidden to hold a strike march, they organized a religious procession in honor of the Virgin of Guadaloupe. This appealed to a greater group of people. Perhaps similar tactics could be used in Mexico.

One of the members of the group didn't like the idea of the Blessed Mother Mary being brought into it. I answered, "Then neither should the grape growers bring God and justice in on their side; these are religious concepts. Certainly if religion is to be brought into the discussion at all, or into the action at all, it should be brought in on the side of the poor."

By the time I crossed the border into the United States, I had spent three months in South and Central America. I had been around the coast everywhere except in Venezuela. In this vast area, I found vibrant cultures full of personalism. A typical Latin American would not think of breaking off a conversation to be on time for an appointment —the personal interaction is more important.

All of the countries of Latin America are nominally Catholic. But much of religion is associated with the ceremonies: baptism, marriage and burial. I found little understanding and knowledge of Catholic concepts of peace and social justice in the average Catholic (similar to the U.S. Catholic?). About ninety five percent of the people are poor. Maybe this is what makes them simple in their lifestyle, more loving and open to others and friendly to visitors, less worried about protecting their possessions.

However, a brand of violence grew out of their collective poverty. While never waging war as a group, the effects of armed conflict were pervasive, and advocates of pacifism were few. Yet, bishops such as Dom Helder Camara and Bishop Cano and others, were outstanding leaders of nonviolent action. Moreover, on the whole there was much more consciousness of social justice among Catholics than in the United States.

Everywhere I went, the influence of the United States was pointed out to me as supporting the rich and the military. I think that the best way that a North American can help the people in South America is to change our foreign policy to one which will support the poor and the efforts for social justice.

I now see a clear division in the U.S. Church that was not evident in 1970: a difference in opinion among the bishops about peace, about cooperation with the government, about identification with the poor or the rich. As my stories show, this division already existed in Latin America back in 1970 and persists in almost every country today. In the United States, due to a kind of managerial union among the bishops, the division was invisible until recently.

The clergy in the United States, in general, are not directly confronted with the global effects of disparity in the way wealth is distributed. Not so in Latin America: Into the 90s, Jesuits in San Salvador have been under threat of death. Yet they do not leave the country. They identify with the poor and their efforts at land reform. They are backed most by the bishops in their country. In Guatemala, Nicaragua and other Latin Countries the church leaders increasingly respond to the cries of the poor for justice. In paying this heavy price for their witness, they renew the life of faith in those countries. In most cases they have been the only voice to speak publicly about the injustice and cruelty of oppressive military governments.

On July 6, 1991, a four-thousand-word editorial in the official Vatican paper, *Civilta Cattolica,* said that the Just War Argument is outdated and that "all war is immoral." I have hope that the power of the gospel of Christ can and will be a force for justice and peace.

19 ❖ *The Holy Land*

This Holy Land — the place where Jesus walked and talked and preached among his friends — is sacred to all who believe that Jesus is God. To be in this place makes Christ's existence on earth more tangible. The joy one feels when visiting their hometown or the street on which they grew up — that's the kind of joy the true believer in Christ feels here.

Christians are often warned to stay behind their altar rails, to stay in their sanctuaries. But this is not the way Christ lived. He had no sanctuary. He had no home of His own; He had no real estate, nor did He call on Christians to possess any. He taught by word and by deed that we should love one another, even at the cost of our own life. We believe that He will strengthen us. We don't need to prop ourselves up with bricks and mortar to be sure of our faith. All the disputes over real estate, the history of lives taken in the Christian-Muslim wars, show how easily we humans are distracted from the teachings and message of Christ.

In the summer of 1969 I traveled to the Holy Land as assistant tour leader for a group of Americans. At each site I tried to imagine what the biblical characters must have experienced. While nothing can compare "being there," I try in this section to give a description of what I saw and learned, as well as the thoughts and feelings these sacred sites evoked.

Our journey to this ancient land began with a very modern sight. From the plane we could see Tel Aviv looking like any big city —Baltimore, Philadelphia, or Washington — etched against the dark of night by chains of light.

We took a bus from the airport to avoid the city-center of Tel Aviv and traveled forty miles to Jerusalem, arriving at the Palace Hotel near the old city. A few of us couldn't wait until morning to explore Jerusalem; so in the dark of night we walked the narrow, empty streets and felt a mysterious sense of the past

As I delved into the mysteries of this troubled land, I began to see it as a place of dynamic, living history., a place to witness not only Jewish and Christian roots, but also those of Muslims and pagans. We saw the place Abraham offered his son to God, now the site of a Jewish temple.. From the floor below the rock, we could see where a hole had been drilled so blood from sacrifices could flow into the brook below. Sometimes thousands of goats and heifers were offered to the Lord at one ceremony. Many historic events took place at this site: Solomon built his temple; Nebuchadnezzar captured the city and destroyed the temple; the Ark of the Covenant was returned here after the exile; Herod lived here and enlarged the temple; Joseph and Mary brought Jesus here to be circumcised; at the temple Jesus drove out the money-changers; Jesus, at only twelve-years of age, argued with the doctors of the temple; and, He preached on the portico a few days before His death.

This site has significance for Muslims as well as Christians. In 636 A.D. when the Muslims took the city of Jerusalem, they built a mosque here, which, despite its age, is still brilliant and beautiful. To Muslims this is the most important place after Mecca. As told in the Koran, Mohammed had a vision of himself arriving on a burro, and in a flash he had reached the Holy Mount. The vision concluded with his ascension to heaven.

From the heights of Jerusalem, our guide pointed out King Solomon's mountain on which now stands a small monastery. King Solomon once had his hundreds of concubines there plus a pagan temple in which they could worship. If Solomon could be so unfaithful yet be forgiven and loved by God, there is hope for all of us.

And while learning about ancient pagans, Muslims, and Jews, we also got a glimpse of a more modern world. On a hill in this area is the "Government House," the center for the United Nations' Mission. It used to be, in the time of English rule, the seat of British government in Palestine. The Jews called this mountain the "Mountain of Evil Counsel," where Caiaphas held the meeting at which he decided that "one man must die for the people." When the British had their headquarters here, the Jews still called it the Mount of Evil Counsel. And some — those who do not like the U.N.'s flag flying there — still refer to it as a place of evil counsel.

The new city of Jerusalem also had all the modern amenities. We visited the museum, saw the university, and stopped at the monument to the six million Jews killed by Hitler. After seeing actual historical sites, the museum, with jewelry and archeological exhibits, seemed lifeless and removed from reality. The museum had treasures of history stripped from their locale. These treasures mean much more when they are in the place of their origin where the impact on human lives can be dramatized in your imagination. For me, Jerusalem was like a stage on which my mind's eye could re-enact the drama and fire of the gospel story.

As we left Jerusalem and headed for Jericho, we got a better feel for the landscape: both physical and political. Half-way between Jerusalem and Jericho we passed the Good Samaritan Inn, a kind of check-point for the army and a point of conflict during the Six Day War. It was here that the Good Samaritan assisted the man wounded by robbers. It's still a desolate place with rocky and barren terrain — no water.

Jericho itself is an oasis in the midst of a desert. Father Gregory, our Franciscan guide, explained that Jericho only exists because of one large spring. With the intense sun and the steady supply of water, almost anything can grow. Date palms, oranges, and bananas grow in abundance. Jericho is one of the oldest cities in the world. In an excavation we saw ruins of a tower dating back six-thousand five-hundred years before Christ.

We moved on, away from Jericho toward the Jordanian border. We saw the remains of tanks here and there on the hillside. Along those hills, Bedouin nomads roamed with their sheep and goats. From Jericho a good road ran through the desert, down a gentle grade to the Dead Sea, visible for miles before we reached it. At the Dead Sea there is no escape for the water and, since the sun is very hot, the water evaporates and leaves salt and other minerals which have accumulated over the centuries. The Israeli government used minerals from the Dead Sea in the manufacture of fertilizer.

We floated in the water; its fifty-percent salt content kept us buoyant. The Dead Sea, eighteen-hundred feet below sea level, is the end of the Jordan River, which begins at the Sea of Galilee, seven-hundred fifty feet below sea level. The Jordan River, though not very wide, flows deep and green with cool water.

In the refreshment parlor right by the Dead Sea, we met General Oddboll, a friendly Swede. He had just driven up in a station wagon tagged with the flag of the U.N. observation team. He pointed out to us the shrapnel holes where the refreshment center had been recently shelled — an American girl was killed in the attack. A mortar shell had even pierced through the ceiling.

In order to hit one military vehicle, those guiding the artillery fire were willing to risk the lives of civilians. The rationale is that some "collateral damage" is inevitable in meeting military objectives: an old argument used by all governments including our own — a weak and false argument no matter where it is used.

In later travels, we visited Tiberius where officers of Rome had their homes by the sea. We saw the mansion built in Roman times for the empire's governor. It is still a place of beautiful villas and resorts. As we lunched by the Sea of Tiberius, we felt the intense humidity of the area around the Dead Sea. The ocean breeze provided some relief, but it was still oppressively hot.

By now we knew that in this country water is like gold: On the way to Hebron, an ancient city where Abraham is buried, we passed Solomon's pools. One of them supplied water to Bethlehem. Solomon also constructed the pools to supply water for Jerusalem. He must have done a good job of it, because one of them still worked. As we read stories from the Old Testament, children and women went past us and down the steps to get water in rubber and tin buckets which they then hauled on the backs of donkeys.

We also stopped at the point where the Apostle Philip baptized the Ethiopian eunuch who was returning to Egypt. (Acts 3:28 ff.) He was a Black African, an important man in his own country. He had the piety and the faith to come on a pilgrimage to the temple. On his return, as he was riding along in his carriage, Philip was urged by the Spirit of the Lord to go up and talk to him. Philip entered his carriage and spoke to him of Christ. I realized that, with the scarcity of water, baptizing with water was indeed a powerful symbol of a new life in Christ. Bishop Harold Perry, the only Black bishop in the Catholic Hierarchy of United States at the time, read the story of this baptism. He pointed out to me later that we need to emphasize the faith of a man on pilgrimage, not the fact that he was Black or an eunuch.

Hebron, also a city of great antiquity, was at one time the capital of a region that was part of Egypt. As we walked through the streets of Hebron, children begged from us and merchants tried to sell us their wares. This was the homeland of Abraham, Sarah, Isaac, Lot, and King David.. It was an important city because all of the caravans between Egypt and Jerusalem passed by. Herod built a temple here, St. Helena built a church here. In modern times there was a mosque open to all people since the Six Day War.

The Life of Christ

On our tour we visited all the significant places in Jesus' life. At each site, we read the scripture account and offered prayers. I was so moved to be in this Holy Land. I felt a deep, spiritual connection to Christ as never before. I was also amazed at how close together all the sites were, often within walking distance.

At nearly all of the important sites in Jesus' life, a church has been built in tribute to the event. For instance, the Church of St. Anne was located at the birthplace of the Blessed Virgin. This cave, converted into a church, is purported to be the home of Mary and her parents. This primitive cave, about ten feet in diameter, had a couch cut into the rock. Whatever truth there was to the story, it certainly gave us a sense of the poverty they endured.

John the Baptist

We visited a shrine at Aim Karim, the birth place of John the Baptist. On the marble altar in the shrine the Latin inscription reads, "Here the precursor of the Lord, John the Baptist, was born." Not far away on the hillside, the Church of the Visitation commemorated Mary's meeting with her cousin, Elizabeth, already pregnant with John.

Annunciation

In Nazareth we celebrated the Eucharist at the Church of the Annunciation where the angel appeared to Mary. Under the small altar in the church are the words inscribed in Latin: "Here the word became flesh." Much of the history corroborates this sacred site as the actual place of the Annunciation.

The population of Nazareth was about thirty-three thousand, almost equally divided between Christians and Muslims. Of the Christians, about nine-thousand were Catholic divided between the Greek and Roman Churches.

In Nazareth the big feast day is the Feast of the Annunciation. As we walked through the church built over the spot where Mary conceived of the Holy Spirit, we met two groups of Israelis on a tour. It was a hopeful sign.

The upper church, built over the place of the Incarnation was stunning even compared to the other beautiful shrines that were there. It was still under construction and was inviting decorations from many nations.

Nativity

As we saw Bethlehem in the distance, it was easy to recall the words of the shepherds: "Let us go over to Bethlehem." We entered the Church of the Nativity by a low door which we were later told was purposely constructed to keep the Turks from coming into the church on their horses. Sections of the church were covered with gold tapestry sent by the French Government.

To celebrate Mass, all five of us priests on the tour crowded together in the very small space at a level lower than that where the other members of our group surrounded us in a tight circle. It became evident how the body heat of animals could warm a cave like this.

We prayed the Mass of the Nativity, read the scriptures, and sang songs of Christmas. I spoke of how Christ had come to the world a poor child and chose to remain poor. And not even these golden tapestries — clearly an attempt by the rich to co-opt the example of Christ — can ever change that. He came as the Prince of Peace; He showed us that the way to peace is not by accumulating wealth, but by forsaking it. Identification with the poor and rejection of the power of the state, these lessons were illustrated by His birth.

After the Mass, we went to the side of the cave where the manger is supposed to have been. We kissed the spot. In this area there are several churches: the Greek Church of the Nativity, a church built by St. Helena; a church and a fortress built by Crusaders; and the Church of St. Catherine.

All these buildings, though interesting and marvelous, in some ways are also a structural record of our inability to fully follow Christ's teaching. Though they provide a place to praise God, they don't provide a structure for teaching peacemaking, for feeding the hungry, for clothing the naked, and for sheltering the homeless. Jerusalem has remained a sad record of man's divisions and armed struggles since the time of Christ.

After leaving the cave of the Nativity, we went into other caves nearby: where Joseph slept during the night of the Nativity; where the Magi rested overnight; and where Joseph was supposed to have dreamed that the child was in danger from Herod. We saw caves into which the bodies of the Holy Innocents were thrown and one where St. Jerome, the first bishop of Jerusalem and one of the first scripture scholars, lived for seven years translating the gospels from the Aramaic and Greek into Latin.

Along the hillside, a mile away, the shepherds had seen the angels. As in the days of Christ, shepherds were still grazing their sheep on this hillside and using the caves for protection. In a natural cave, large enough to hold fifty people, was the Church of the Shepherds. Our guide, said that his family came to the area in 1930 and that he was born in this cave.

Christ the Carpenter

Until he was thirty, Jesus worked with His hands as a carpenter: part of his work to change the world, to establish God's kingdom on earth. Carpentry, the fashioning of useful things by hand, would relate Him to the vast majority who work daily, making it possible for them to imitate His life. His early life was characterized by obedience to his mother and foster-father, simple living among poor people, and manual work — no direct effort to overthrow the empire of Rome or to influence the religious leaders of Israel. Rome would fall later when His followers began to practice what he taught. He would confront the religious leaders at the time and in the manner planned by His Father.

In what would have been the central part of Nazareth, we entered the Church of the Cave of the Carpenter Shop. Beneath was the basement of the house of the Holy Family. Certainly in Jesus' day this basement was below the street level. As we rode out of the city of Nazareth, the guide pointed out Mary's well to us. People were drawing water from it as we passed.

Mary and Martha

At Bethany, only a few miles from Jerusalem, we visited a chapel at the site of Mary and Martha's house where Jesus often stayed. The words, "I am the Resurrection and the Life" are on the top of the chapel. Nearby is the home of Simon the Leper whose house Jesus visited and where Mary poured ointment on Him.

At this site there is layer after layer of history — four churches built on top of each other from the second century to the twentieth century. The changes in architecture, still partially visible, tell a story of destruction and conquest. What would the place be like, I wondered, if the peace message of Jesus had been followed from the earliest times? Surely, all the destruction would not have taken place. Would there be a building for the hungry to be fed and clothed? Would there be another dedicated to peacemaking? Although churches are a recognition of Jesus' presence, a church often is built and maintained at great cost while all around it the poor suffer.

Near the ancient home of Mary and Martha we went to a modern home — one room in which seven children and their mother and father lived. This Jordanian family graciously greeted us. The woman, dressed a long blue and red robe down to her feet, evoked an image of how Mary might have looked. The children were in rags, but smiling and colorfully dressed. They had few possessions. A baby rocked peacefully in a wooden cradle strung across the corner of the room and tied to two walls. The entire sleeping apparatus for nine people, blankets and quilts, were stacked in huge piles along one side of the room. There was hardly space for that many to lie down.

As we left, I noticed most of the people in the area lived under similar conditions. The people — Arabs, most Muslim, some Christian — had been under persecution from Israelis.

Miracles Happened Here

We visited Cana where Jesus performed his first miracle. A church, built in 1863, was erected on the site of a fourth century church which was built on the site of the house where Jesus performed the miracle.

A well is in the center of the chapel at Cana; a water pitcher, the kind Jesus used, stands about two feet high and holds five gallons. Nearby, a picture depicts Jesus, standing near the well blessing the six water containers. Here we read the text of the gospel where Jesus said to his mother, "My hour is not yet come; what would'st thou have me do?" He yielded to His mother's suggestion and changed the water to wine. I was struck by the fact that he performed this miracle simply to bring joy to a feast. Yet, this does fit with His entire message of joy and love.

Also on our itinerary was The Church of the Loaves and Fishes, a chapel on a hillside by the sea. Behind the main altar, an ancient mosaic with the loaves and fishes is preserved. We also passed the place on the shore where Christ taught Peter how to fish.

Teaching and Preaching

At Capernaum we read the scripture of Christ's preaching in the synagogue. In the ruins of the synagogue we saw the remnants of a wine press. The present structure goes back to the third century, but was built on an earlier first-century synagogue, one where Jesus preached.

Up the hill from Capernaum, is a small mountain, the Mount of the Beatitudes, which has strong gusts of wind blowing across it almost all the time. The guide explained that Christ and His Disciples came up here to get away from the oppressive heat of the lowlands Here too is a chapel that was built in the form of an octagon — representing the Sermon on the Mount. Each of the beatitudes was inscribed, one on each of the eight sides. I was especially pleased to see the quote "Blessed are the peacemakers" (Matthew 5:9) engraved in the wall near the entrance to the church with a notice that it was donated by the Church of the God of Prophecy in Cleveland, Ohio.

Inside the chapel we sat around the altar with its octagonal rail and read the Beatitudes. I, and a few of the others, looked out the window to the sea while the words were being read. I imagined how Jesus might have looked out over this same vista as He said the words, "Blessed are the peacemakers." Here was the Gospel of Peace which in every phrase called for voluntary suffering in order to receive blessedness and, in turn, give it to others. "Blessed are you when you are prosecuted; blessed are you when men think ill of you." How different life would be if we really felt blessed when this happened! How far we are from the way to peace when we feel blessed because others praise and think well of us.

The Woman and the Well

Wells and water play a significant role in the gospel accounts of Jesus' ministry. For instance, at Jacob's Well He told the Samaritan woman, "I am the Messiah." She had already guessed it. "You must be the Messiah to know my secrets." Jesus told the woman that God is spirit and truth and those who worship Him must worship in truth.

On our tour we stopped at Jacob's Well ourselves. It's near a small town and surrounded by beautiful mountains. Our guide told us that the shaft is one-hundred forty feet deep and the well remains in use. This area, where Jacob settled, was once the Kingdom of Shikem between Mount Ibal, which means a curse, and Mount Garizan which means a blessing.

The Last Supper

Eventually, we made our way to the Cenacle, the site of the Last Supper. Down a steep hillside near here, Judas hanged himself.

The five priests in our group concelebrated Mass in the Catholic part of the complex of buildings. After Mass we visited the Upper Room. The complex itself told a story of the relationship between Catholic, Muslim and Jew. In one building there was a large Catholic Church; conjoined to it and up one story was the room in which the Last Supper took place, referred to by Jesus as the upper room. This section was owned by the Muslims. Catholics were allowed in for Mass only on Holy Thursday. Anyone could come as a visitor whenever it was open to the public. The Hebrew priests cared for the tombs of the Patriarchs in the basement of the building.

In the Cenacle again there was a series of architectural changes: a fourth-century church remnant, a seventh-century church, evidence of a crusader's church. In one corner of the Upper Room there was a Muslim prayer niche facing Mecca. The room was about forty feet wide and almost square.

After the meal, Jesus had walked down the hill to Gethsemane. As I listened to the reading of the story, I was impressed by Jesus' words, "You will be scandalized in me." The suffering that Christ would take upon Himself would separate Him from both the religious and the secular authorities. Even Peter would disown Him.

"I have desired to eat this pascal meal with you." He had a desire to accept suffering. He would teach this lesson by example to all who wished to learn it.

The Apostles met again in the Upper Room while Jesus was dead in the tomb. They met in fear of the authorities, fear that they too would be punished for association with this criminal. Yet all through the early Church, prison was part of the Christian scene. When we look on prison and prisoners as disgraceful, we depart from the spirit of Christ and the early Christians!

Gethsemane

The garden of Gethsemane, a garden of olive trees, is a square of about sixty feet. Two sides of the square are formed by the two sides of the Church of the Agony, and the other two sides by two roads. The olive trees are reputed to be two-thousand five-hundred years old. In the garden the three apostles had slept while Jesus went a short distance from them and prayed on the rock, now inside the church. Jesus prayed for strength for what He had already planned to do. This was no new decision.

To this garden Judas had come with the soldiers and priests to arrest Him. It was here that, after Judas kissed Him, Jesus said to the crowd, "If you seek Jesus of Nazareth, I am He."

I have been associated with those arrested for the sake of conscience — they fulfill intentions made in the spirit of Jesus. Just as Phil and Dan Berrigan knew what to expect after they were arrested, so did Jesus know. Jesus gave the example of being arrested — without struggle, without running away, without shame.

Above the garden, we could see the city. Below the garden were three cemeteries: Muslim, Jewish and Christian; the hill was so steep that stone terraces had to be constructed, and now run through the cemeteries like huge steps. On Palm Sunday Jesus had gone to the top of this hill to enter the Golden Gate. While we were there we saw some heavy gashes in the gate — the result of artillery fire during the June 1967 war when Israel took the city from the Arabs. Our Arab guide didn't tell us this. But one of the Franciscan priests who accompanied us, Father Godfrey, told us that the guide might have gotten into trouble if he mentioned it.

The Arrest

After arrest, Jesus was taken to the house of Caiaphas, the High Priest. Today The Church of the Crowing of the Cock sits on top of the old palace of Caiaphas. Part of the old courtyard was visible. It was in this courtyard that Peter denied knowing Jesus.

From here we could see Gethsemane and the steps Jesus walked up as a prisoner. Here, in this place, Jesus was condemned by the Sanhedrin and then taken to Pilate.

The church mosaics show Jesus in chains, looking at Peter after Peter's denial of Him. The central mosaic in the church depicted Jesus on trial standing on a small platform with a group of ten or fifteen Jewish priests around Him.

I listened to the scripture readings: "They sought false witnesses against Jesus;" and "This man said 'I am able to destroy the temple of God and in three days rebuild it.'" Here Jesus admitted that He was God when they asked Him His answer, "Thou hast said it," brought on the accusation of blasphemy. Here they spat upon Him, blindfolded and struck Him.

Near the courtyard we saw Caiaphas' prison; large enough to hold thirty people. While we were able to enter through a door, in Jesus' time there was no door; prisoners were let down with a rope around the waist — about a twenty-foot drop from a hole in the ceiling. The prisoner was raised up from the dungeon in the same manner.

First-century Christians made a door through which they could come to pray in this prison. Early Christians drew crosses, still faintly visible, in red on the wall. The Crucifixion, painted on the wall, was also faded, but visible. We read the 88th Psalm which describes the feelings of a man who was let down into a pit and called on God for help. I knelt down and prayed for all those who were in prison for conscience sake and for all who are faced with prison: Fathers Dan and Phil Berrigan, Reverend William Coffin, all those in the military prisons — American and Vietnamese.

Christ Condemned

The next day we began with a Mass at the Lithostratos, the place where Christ was condemned by Pilate. Bishop Harold Perry, the main celebrant asked me to say a few words:

"You are standing where the crowd stood . . . the crowd that yelled, 'Crucify Him!' Jesus stood approximately where I am. Here Pilate, the governor, said, 'Behold the man.' Jesus had already been crowned with thorns by the soldiers; He had already been scourged. Pontius Pilate thought that Jesus' condition was so worthy of compassion that, if He were shown to the people, they would be moved to sympathy and Pilate would be excused from his dilemma of either offending Caesar by letting Jesus go. or offending his own conscience by punishing an innocent man. The crowd, because of money offered them, were not moved to sympathy. Pilate, in order to please Caesar, buried his conscience and condemned Jesus to die.

"Throughout the centuries, Pilate's act has been repeated. In order to please the state, Christians, . . . not Roman governors, have buried their consciences and condemned Christ again in the person of other innocent men and women."

The historical sense of this holy place was intense; the audience was attentive and moved by my description. It gave fresh meaning to an old ceremony. Imitation of Jesus is the most clear and perfect definition of holiness. It is the Christian belief that Jesus came on earth and became human in order to show us how to live.

The truth that He was God was disagreeable to both the church and the state of His day. It conflicted with their power and their plans. Similarly, the Berrigans, Franz Jaegerstaetter, Dorothy Day and others have spoken truth to power through the ages and have been obedient to God in the very act of disobeying humans. This was also true of the apostles who were put to death. It was true of thousands of martyrs in the first three centuries. Jail and death were honorable to Christians in those days, a sign of faithfulness to God.

Why is it that Christians no longer talk of jail as honorable and as something we should expect as we attempt to imitate Jesus? Are we so far from His imitation now that we don't understand this anymore? Are governments today so attuned to God's will that they no longer punish those who teach and give witness to truth?

Our tour was a kind of liturgy — we saw the sites, but also integrated worship into our travels. Using the stations of the cross, we were able to follow the path of Jesus as He went from condemnation to the cross and to the grave. We paused at each station and prayed — reflected on the passion and the suffering of Jesus.

A station: We went to the palace which Herod built in 35 B.C. with a tower to defend the city. This temple was near the spot where Jesus was condemned to die by Pilate. Pilate was simply a soldier who was condemning a trouble-maker to death.. This was a small amount of death for a man connected to an army. Pilate did not see it as world-shaking! He saw it as a way of avoiding trouble. How often has this been done!

The next station: Below the surface of the Chapel of the Scourging, the stones were marked where the soldiers use the tip of their swords to draw games (similar to tic-tac-toe), a rough eagle and other emblems. Here Jesus suffered; He was condemned to die; He was scourged and crowned with thorns.

Another station: Below the Lithostratos (the courtyard) Herod had built large cisterns to hold water, and we climbed down a long ladder to see one. Near here, on a small road Jesus met Simon the Cyprian who was forced to help Him carry the cross.

The ninth station: A stone pillar sunk into a corner of the wall. Here Jesus fell to the ground for the third time. We entered the Church of the Holy Sepulchre for the last four stations. We stood in front of the altar where Christ was nailed on the cross, was stripped of His garments. A few feet away He was crucified. The entire drama took place within the space of thirty feet.

The last station: A marble slab on the floor of the church where the body of Christ was laid in preparation for His entrance into the tomb. People kissed the slab as they came by. At the tomb, we finished the stations.

Crucifixion

Next morning, July 20th, I offered Mass at 6:30 a.m. at the altar between the crucifixion and the nailing to the cross where Mary received the dead body of Jesus. Three feet to my left was the spot where He was crucified and three feet to my right, the place where He was nailed.

By request of the Franciscan in charge of the sacristy, the Mass was in Latin. I felt that this was appropriate since no one there, with the exception of our group, seemed to understand English. A group of seven or eight nuns did respond in Latin. During the Mass, I prayed for peace and for peacemakers. I prayed that they would understand that sacrifice and the acceptance of suffering is a way to peace. Peace does not come through inflicting suffering on others. This is the basic fallacy of those who strive to achieve peace through war or other forms of violent force.

Below the mezzanine floor of the Church of the Sepulchre to the left of the altar was the large church of the Greeks. Here at 7 a.m. a High Mass began. About twenty seminarians and young priests came out and formed themselves into choirs on both sides of the main body of the church. At the altar about six priests went about donning vestments, preparing the altar, opening the gate and checking the pictures and arrangements. Soon a Bishop came in, gave blessings and mounted the throne. A second official, apparently a subordinate, went to another throne. Two priests began the reading. It was a long ceremony, throughout which there was a great deal of chanting.

(That night, July 20, 1969, I listened to BBC radio reports of the first U.S.-manned spacecraft landing on the moon. In the very place where Christ lived and died we heard of humans landing on another celestial body.)

Resurrection

Behind the resurrection site, the Coptic Rite Mass is celebrated in a small chapel less than two feet wide. The intensity and the devotion of the crowd gathered at the door of this chapel was unmistakable. The veil of mysticism and strangeness of the Eastern rite was lifted as I recognized that this ceremony was almost identical to the Roman Catholic Mass.

In the sides of the church, some thirty feet from the resurrection site, were tombs — the burial caves for the family of Joseph of Aramathea. Joseph had given up his own tomb for Christ's body. In here, the Syrian Rite Mass was in progress. The cave was full of incense and people. Three priests were at the altar. The Mass was a deep confirmation of the faith that unites all Christians. Although the church itself had been divided into different chapels, each used by different sects, the expression of faith through the Mass continued to unite one nationality and custom to another.

In the Chapel of Angels, a tiny room in the center of The Church of the Holy Sepulchre, is the spot where the angel had appeared to announce the resurrection. From this small chapel, just three feet wide, you must stoop to enter the grave where a slab marks the place Christ's body was laid.

I prayed for the spirit of Resurrection; I prayed for blessings on all those of the peace community, for my family and friends. I asked that the spirit of victory over death and the spirit of peace might increase in all of us. I asked God to raise up peacemakers in great numbers.

My own experiences of so many wars, of so much killing, of so much danger, gave my visit to the place of the Resurrection a deeply personal and intense meaning. It is a mystery to me that Christ could look forward to the Resurrection and still suffer. The mystery is somewhat lessened by my own realization that the Resurrection is before me too; and yet, suffering is difficult for me to accept. It seems that the more certain we feel about the Resurrection, the less our fear of suffering can control our decisions.

As we left the church, we passed through the bazaars; surrounded by begging children who wailed tearfully and complained that they had no mother nor father and that they were very poor. I gave what coins I had in my pocket. The poverty of these children led to other thoughts. They were victims of the militarism of the State of Israel which spent so much of its public monies for armaments.

In the United States the effect of militarism is revealed in the games the children play and the things they make. Militarism, which is a part of their culture, has become a part of their lives. Even small children play with guns, with toy soldiers and war toys.

Ascension

On the Mount of Olives two chapels — the Ascension and the Lord's Prayer — stand side-by-side. There we saw the rock from which Jesus is said to have ascended into heaven. In The Chapel of the Lord's Prayer, we, of course, recited that prayer together. I felt anew the peacemaking call, "Forgive us our offense as we forgive those who offend us." Amazingly on the walls of the chapel was the Lord's Prayer in forty-five languages.

A Final Reflection

Throughout the trip there were many signs that the teachings of Christ had been overlooked, avoided, or heeded far too little. There was plenty of opportunity to think about what a different place the Holy Land (and for that matter the world) might be today if more people had followed His nearly two-thousand-year-old message.

For instance, our first guide on the tour was an Arab Roman Catholic born in Bethlehem. He was well-informed on some historical events, but insensitive to many of our Christian and pacifist interests.

He showed more interest in a town that had been built by the crusaders than in the sites of many biblical events. I asked him, "What did the crusaders do?" He replied that they took this town from the Muslims, but now it is all Muslim again. I asked him if he thought the crusaders had accomplished very much, if that was the best they could do. However, his interest in the crusades was shared by others we met. Shortly after we left Cana we passed Ateen. Here the crusaders were beaten by Saladin. I was pleasantly surprised that a few in the bus clapped as this was announced by our tour-guide.

Our visit with the Latin Patriarch of Jerusalem, Archbishop Albert Gori, O.F.M., illustrated the legacy of the crusades. His responsibility was to lead the Latin Rite Church in Jerusalem. This Franciscan was formerly in charge of his order's work to preserve shrines in the Holy Land. There were about three-hundred fifty Franciscan priests from around the world who spread out over the

Holy Land and were devoted to the maintenance and promotion of the shrines of our Lord's life.

Over fifty of us met Gori at his residence. Patriarch Archbishop Gori wore a gray dress signifying the special privilege of a Franciscan Bishop. The meeting was quite formal. Although Gori is Italian, he addressed us in French, translated by Father D'Rosseaux. In the large, stately room, we sat in nice chairs while the Patriarch sat on a throne at one end of the room. Around the walls hung banners which exalted the crusades. Beneath a portrait depicting crusaders going off to battle hung a banner that read, "God wills it." Pope Urban used this phrase as he encouraged Christians to go off to kill.

Later Bishop Perry came to confer with me and Father D'Rosseaux because one of the Patriarch's official asked us to take up a collection for the Patriarch. I gave Bishop Perry a strong, "NO!" Then added that we would only give funds if the Patriarch agreed to take the banners down; they were a disgrace. The bishop seemed happy for the excuse since he felt the people were burdened enough with contributions to the other shrines.

After experiencing a deep mood of intimacy with the historical Christ, the visit with the Patriarch seemed a sad contradiction. In the very land where Christ lived and taught that killing is wrong, these banners still promoted the crusades as glorious, just and good. The crusades contradict Christianity because they turn the cross into a sword and use the name of Christ to destroy other people. As in so many places, again the gospel is identified with war. The time of the crusades was one of the lowest points in church history, and all of Christendom still suffers from it. It's a scandal in the deepest theological sense of the word.

The Crusade's notion that "God is on our side" has impassioned many men and women as they prepared for battle and then participated in war and killing. This theme has run through many long and bloody histories. It is a co-opting of the force of good in the service of evil.

It begins in seemingly innocent practices: placing the national flag near the altars of our churches. People even pray before the flag, the ultimate symbol of battle and conquest. God, the source of infinite good and everlasting love, is not the source of competition, vanquishing, and killing.

Our relationship to God should be one of obedience, love, and service. At its best, the state is a group organized ideally for the common good. Compare that with the church at its best: a group called by God to promote love for God and for each other. In the ideal order, there would be no conflict between church and state. However, the ideal is not practiced; the state often seeks not the common good of all people, but the official good of the rich and powerful at the expense of the poor. It achieves this goal through war or the threat of war. This common tendency among states results in the build up of armies, abandoning God.

Through the centuries, churches have sided with kings and killers of all kinds, and the Church has consistently deserted Christian ideals.

It's quite clear that the state is not mentioned much in the gospel. As Christ said at His trial, "You have no power over me unless it was given to you from above." He asked for no special relationship to the state. His teaching focused on the individual's attitude toward God and others. It was clear that Jesus saw the state as a passing transitory arrangement; history shows that this is true of all states.

History also shows that when churches identify with a particular state, they also fall with that state. The church should remain separate from the state. This is especially crucial when the state disrespects human life, as it is so prone to do.

The proper relationship of church and state should be a constantly evolving process as we move toward the Kingdom of God that Christ foresaw. Since each member of the state is also a human person with this same divine destiny, the state should be related to our religious goals and subordinate to God's plans: each person fulfilling his or her destiny to be united with God. Everything individuals do should further this goal. Anything that hurts or separates the human beings from their divine destiny is harmful.

The Church, though it has an institutional component, is an expression of the divine on earth The state without its institutional form is nothing. Nationalism makes the state superior to the individual. This runs counter to the Christian way.

In the history of Israel, the prophets dealt primarily with God, giving us an example of how the individual person should relate to God. The state of Israel with its internal and external conflicts, is a mixture of religious and racial hatreds festering within it. This reflects the world of our time. We are in a war-torn world. The Christian pacifist should not be an aberration, something unusual, but instead a sample of what God intends us to be. Because acceptance of wars has been so prevalent, we tend to see wars as status quo, as inevitable. We fail to see that they are a dissent from Christ and His teaching.

When Leo Tolstoy first saw that the gospel centered around the theme of "resist not evil," he wrote *My Religion.* Twenty years later in another book, *The Kingdom of God is Within You,* he described the process of discovering that the gospel forbids killing. Instead it demands love of enemy. Tolstoy found that others had taken this path, but their writings on pacifism had been buried. Now, his writings on pacifism are also ignored.

Thomas Merton, the Trappist mystic well-known for *The Seven Story Mountain,* began to write about peace in 1964. He condemned the war in

Vietnam and the use of nuclear weapons in *Confessions of a Guilty Bystander*. Yet this work is hardly known by many Merton admirers. The same is true of other well-known writers like Mark Twain who wrote a scathing condemnation of war, *War Prayer*, and Herman Melville, author of *Moby Dick*, whose criticism of the American navy in *White Jacket* led to naval reforms.

The war psychology is so pervasive that it leads us to believe, as Gandhi said, "that all history is the history of wars." War consumes every perspective: history, psychology, faith, literature, economics, technology, and business. It has to take in religion or else it is not complete. We must instead bring peace to every perspective.

Everything that Christ did on earth can be seen as an effort to inspire faith in humans — faith in God, faith in God's love and therefore, faith in each other. A living faith leads to action: the public expression of that faith. Intelligence is the steering force that directs the action. Political analysis is necessary; that's where research or intelligence comes in. Faith by itself isn't enough.

Some say that the United States is an instrument of God and that some other nations are instruments of the devil. When political analysis or research is used in examining such a statement, it can easily be seen as false. Political analysis is needed to decide where our efforts for peace are best directed. But you don't need much political analysis for your basic program: a program of love, a program that rejects violent force and fear.

While the Holy Lands are replete with a history of turning away from peace, little is recorded of those who embraced peace. Jesus reconciled us with God and broke down the barriers that divide us. We are all one in Jesus through the wood of the cross. Peace is also the simultaneous reconciliation between God, my neighbor and myself — a triangular relationship, a trinity of reconciliation.

In Jerusalem the divided population of Muslim and Christian is easily recognized in the architecture as I've illustrated in my descriptions. Christian temples are on top of Muslim mosques; each group is protective of its religious sanctuaries. In 1095 Christians killed Muslims to take back what they thought was their land, and since that time Muslims have struggled to get the land back. The on-going division has caused war, which has fed new wars, and will continue to cause war until it is resolved. This situation exists even though both the gospel and the Koran forbid killing.

In Muslim cities when I asked individual Arabs on the street, "Do you think that Christians allow killing?" they answered, "Of course, just look at what they do."

Then I asked, "Does the Koran allow for killing?"

They answered, "No."

Christians look at Muslims and say, "Look at the way they kill."

As we look at the history of division, we can trace the failure of church and state to engage in a proper relationship. When Christians began their accommodation to the state, the Emperor Constantine, even their buildings took on new forms — assumed the character of imperial architecture. The so-called holy part of these early Christian basilicas was only accessible after going down a long nave built with arches and columns to impress the visitor. A great arch separated the worshippers from the presbytery. It was called the triumphal arch and was clearly derived from the secular tradition.

By failing to follow the gospel message of pacifism, both on the individual and state level, the whole of the Christian message is distorted and for many, remains an unsolved puzzle. If a person can't see that peace is a part of the gospel, then their picture of Christian life is fragmentary and mixed up.

Deep inside each person and beneath the layered and shifting sovereignties in Bethlehem and Jerusalem lies the idea of love struggling to be reborn. Despite the inroads of profit-making and wars and armaments, this survives.

The questions of who owns the land, who shall control it, use it, profit from it, control the people who live on it, continue to be debated as the United States tries to persuade Israel to make peace with its neighbors, especially the Palestinians. Love between Israelis and Palestinians is not on the agenda, yet that is the solution taught by both the Bible and the Koran. Should enemies decide to cease being enemies, everything is possible.

One night in Jerusalem I heard the cries for prayer over the minarets, towers located all over the city. Equipped with loudspeakers, they sound a wailing cry for the Muslims to come to prayer. The Israelis do not interfere even though one of the cries comes at about 3 a.m. and can be heard for quite a distance.

When Abraham asked God to spare the city, he said to Him, "If there are only fifty just men, would you spare the city?" God says yes. Abraham asks again, "If there were forty-five, would You spare the city?" God keeps yielding to Abraham's request until Abraham gets it down to ten just men, and God says, "Yes."

Now this is something to think about in regard to the peace message of the gospel. God would be able to work with just ten of us. "I will not destroy you for the sake of the ten," God says and then uses them as leaven to change the whole mass of the city. In fact, this is the way that God did work when He came on earth in the form of Jesus and collected eleven faithful apostles and sent forth the good news in the form of the eleven, the Mustard Seed, the Word of God that was to change the world. The numbers are not as important as the link with the divine.

Certainly much is being done by peacemakers to bring nations, groups and individuals together. For every peace effort that is recorded — the witness of

Franz Jaegerstaetter who refused to join Hitler's army, the early Christians who were put to death, St. Francis of Assisi who gave witness with his rejection of property — there are that many more that go unrecorded..

Those who witness for peace often feel lonely, but their effect is great because it is the power of God that works through them. Peacemaking is never truly a lonely task because we are never without God's help.

— ❖ ❖ ❖ —

20 ❖ *Behind the "Iron Curtain"*

The Berlin Wall

In June of 1972, I served as tour leader for a group of forty-two Americans bound for Eastern Europe. We departed from JFK airport, and after a seven-hour flight across the Atlantic Ocean, over England and the Channel and above the pastoral French countryside, we arrived in Frankfurt. From there we were bused to West Berlin.

The deep divisions between East and West became apparent even before we crossed the border into the German Democratic Republic. For example, there seemed to be a general confusion and ignorance about the currency situation. Our West Berlin tour guide instructed us to not take money into East Berlin because we would have to make an elaborate accounting of our affairs and might be harassed. Later, outside my hotel I talked with a West German about my plans to go to East Berlin. He told me, "Well, they're very agreeable. You don't have to worry, that's no special problem."

I told him that I understood that changing money would be a problem. He said, "No, there's no difficulty about that. I've been there many times."

When I checked with the man at the hotel desk, again I heard that we'd have to give a strict accounting for everything we bought. The advice: we'd better be pretty careful.

Early the next morning we went by bus to Checkpoint Charlie. We asked our East German guide, a university graduate who spoke fluent English, why the East Germans did not allow travel to the West. Her reply touched on the deep problems of division which stretched over many years. "In the beginning we were at a great disadvantage because of the Marshall Plan. It helped West Berlin, and they were rich compared to us. The people would have left if allowed to do so. We could not allow that or we would never have been able to rebuild. It is not so necessary now."

"Why then can't people leave now?"

"In all struggles," she answered, "the ideal cannot be lived at the start. Our ideal would be to have open communications. We have diplomatic relations with thirty-four nations. We will not allow our people to visit where there is no diplomatic representation." She seemed very sure of herself and was forceful in her arguments.

Later she got involved in a discussion with one of our group concerning the existence of God. She said, "I don't believe what I cannot prove. The Creator, if there is one, would also need something to create him, so there's no explanation in that."

It seemed to me that she had read or heard most of the arguments for God's existence and also learned to find the loopholes in the arguments. In listening to her, I reflected that I could never convince her and wondered if arguments ever convince anyone. What does reach people is love. Love's force cannot be denied; it has no loopholes.

At Checkpoint Charlie we visited a museum in honor of those who defied the wall: the dozens who were killed trying to scale the wall and others who succeeded. Though a small building from the outside, the story of tension told within fills quite a dimension. Upstairs, a documentary film on some of the escape attempts was running. Some of the actual instruments of escape were displayed: a little automobile, a hammer tied to a rope. There were many newspapers and pictures; it was a physical record, a history and summary symbolic of the division between the East and the West. If you can begin to answer the questions that arise here, then you can better understand the differences between East and West.

Why was there a wall here? Why did the East Germans shoot to kill people when they tried to escape? These were the questions that repeatedly filled my mind. In the days ahead I hoped to get some answers.

I thought of many reasons why the East Germans needed to build the wall. Kenneth O'Donnell in *Johnny, We Hardly Knew You* dealt with some of them:

> "He [Kennedy] couldn't be very upset about them building a
> wall because he knew very well that so many capable citizens,
> so much of the talent, was escaping into the West. The East
> could have been drained of its most valuable citizens if it didn't
> do something. There was nothing much they could do in the
> way of enticements because of their oppressive form of

government, so they built the wall. From the East German
point of view the wall was built to keep their treasures in, their
talented and capable people.''

If you probe a little deeper, you see that these people wanted to leave because
they wanted freedom. Freedom to make money, but also freedom to live as
their conscience directs, to worship God as they choose. They couldn't just be
told what to believe by the government.

These thoughts converge in the symbolism of the wall. Walls divide people.
Hate and desire for money divides people. But love unites, and there seemed to
be a proportional relationship between the amount of division and the lack of
love or between unity and the presence of love.

I thought about the other "walls" separating East and West: The economic
wall which the East German guide had mentioned. The West with all their
wealth and their Marshall Plan wouldn't share with the East. While the United
States helped to build-up West Germany, it stopped short at East Berlin. So
when the East Germans fled, they did so partly because the West denied them
certain benefits in their own land. While the physical wall was very visible to
the West, the economic wall was equally visible to the East Germans. It was a
division and a barrier that is the result of our long-term reluctance to trade or to
have diplomatic relations with the communist regime in Moscow.

Even as we tried to show the love of God to the West Germans, we denied it
to the East Germans. We were being very definite about whom we would help.
We didn't do it based on the love of God. To promote our own power, we
helped our particular friends and built alliances. This policy completely denied
the principle that we are all children of the one God.

Later, after I returned home, I learned more about the history of the divisions
between the United States and the Soviet Union. The more I learned, the more I
understood Soviet distrust — fueled by our own paranoia. After all, there is
scarce evidence that our country's foreign policy (then and now) can be defined
as Christian: reconciliatory and dedicated to the relief of suffering. Nor does it
demonstrate any understanding of Russia's past — brutal rulers who touted
Christianity, not to mention the German invasion of World War II that left
twenty million Russians dead. In this atmosphere of suspicion, we unleashed a
brutal arms race which made nearly impossible any true understanding of the
Russians. Even with the end of the Cold War, we continue a one-sided arms
race that threatens "any prospective enemy."

— ❖ ❖ ❖ —

Poland

We flew via Polish airlines from East Berlin to Warsaw. I walked from our hotel at night alone with the hope of more easily meeting people. As I looked in the window of a bookstore, a man introduced himself in English. He was a professor of modern languages and a private tutor. Although he spoke twelve foreign languages, there was not much demand for his work in the schools.

A little later I met nineteen-year-old Mirac who came up to me as I stood on the street corner and asked about the possibility of changing money. When he noticed my peace pin, he called over his two friends Jerzy and Wieslaw. Jerzy took off his shoe and stocking and showed me a peace sign in ink on the sole of his foot. I asked him why he didn't wear it openly. He said that it would only cause trouble; it was considered a Western peace symbol.

I talked with these three for many hours over the two days I was in Warsaw. Mirac was class D in the army, the only classification which exempts military service based on physical or mental health. He had left college. When I asked him what he would do, he answered in a dejected voice, "Go to the fabrica." (factory) I learned that the ordinary worker got about the equivalent of fifty cents an hour for an eight-hour work day. Although wages were low, other benefits were enjoyed by the people: Education was free. Each month every student received an allotment — the equivalent of twenty dollars — from the government. Trolleys or trams were so cheap they were almost free; often the conductor did not show up to collect the fare.

Some people in communist countries did get rich. Many of these were the professionals who made about four hundred dollars a month and could have a servant, a car and a small house in the country. Mirac explained that this was possible because of the low cost of living.

I went to visit Mirac at his home in a ten-story apartment building. His apartment had only two rooms, and he shared it with his mother, father, and sister. His mother was an office worker and his sister was an airline stewardess. Mirac told me that such small flats were common and were rented and allotted by the government. He added, "I know of a twelve-person family in the same size flat." Often there was no increase in the size of the flat as the size of the family increased.

Mirac, his mother and sister stayed in one room because his father had a drinking problem; they preferred not to be with him when he had a drunken tantrum. Although sparsely furnished, the apartment was immaculate. There was no storage space and very little to store. They did have a glass-topped table with postcards from various countries encased in it.

The unadorned building was straight and box-like. The elevator was a control point through which you could access the upper floors. To reach it, you had to go through a hallway such as I found later in the hotels in Moscow. These places were controlled by a floor supervisor, a government employee. In this way the government controlled the building and monitored the comings and goings. It was even a risk for this young student to invite in a visiting American. Later when I tried to write him, my letters had no success getting through though I did get letters from him. This was further evidence of how tightly-controlled everything was in his world.

Mirac told me there was little hope in life. He seemed to have centered a great deal of his thought on money. To him that seemed the only way to secure liberty and a better quality of life. If at age twenty life seems so drab and hopeless, it's little wonder that in middle life a man turns to drink.

Our group visited Cardinal Wyczinski, the primate of Poland. We met him in a formal reception room with a stage where he could greet the crowd. The forty-two of us pretty well filled the room. A vigorous-looking man of seventy with a full head of gray hair, he made no effort to be formal, but walked among us and gave a talk in French which was translated. He told us of the difficulty of the life he was leading. He welcomed us as Christians who came in faith and cautioned us on realizing that repeating what he said could be used against the faith. We became united in our admiration for him. Despite all the difficulties, he told us, "We are not confounded." He quoted the psalms, "We have hope in God, our hope is in the Lord." He broadened that hope to include other Christians and other religions.

In a way Mirac and Cardinal Wyczinski had much in common; both were frustrated in their hopes and both faced a dim future with few prospects of having their hopes fulfilled.

However, much has certainly changed since my last visit to Poland. For example, a church was consecrated in a post-war industrial town that was built to "be a city without God, without a church." A twenty-year struggle with the state authorities had ended. For many, a step toward the church has become a step away from full acceptance of the political and moral authority of the state — an effort to gain personal theological independence.

Russia

We went next to Moscow. Customs gave us a difficult time over religious objects in our possession and allowed each person only one item. The practice struck me as somewhat similar to the old days of the Catholic seminary where everything was censured. There the given reason for censorship was to cut down on distractions that might make union with God more difficult. Here the censorship was to keep God out.

It was a strange situation as the search of our belongings went on. The Russian guide was friendly and spoke English. The officials were cold and distant; they spoke only Russian. The search took an hour and a half; we were not even allowed to go to the rest room. They looked at all my belongings very carefully: my book *Kill for Peace?*, the New Testament, and a chalice. It seemed curious later in the trip to hear government guides describe religious art as myth when immigration officials seemed to have seen it as something of a danger.

Because of trouble with our hotel reservations, we continued on a midnight train to Leningrad. We slept in compact cars with compartments of four berths each: steel trays with two-inch mattresses. With some difficulty we got clean sheets and pillow cases. It was very crowded; there was no separation by sex and very little place to put our heavy luggage. It was hard to sleep. We realized as we traveled north, that we were getting into the all-night light. At 11:30 p.m. the sky was still dusky, and at 1:30a.m. the sun began to rise. Seven hours after our ride started, we left the train to a bright sunny morning in Leningrad where we went to our hotel located on the shore of the Neva River.

Leningrad was a somewhat spectacular city on a river that includes a hundred islands of the Neva delta, crossed by three hundred bridges. Government buildings and the palaces of the Czar border the river. The beautiful setting explains why the czars chose it for their summer palace.

We visited the fortress surrounding the church of Peter and Paul with its dramatic gold spire. Inside, Czars Peter I and Peter II are buried in marble vaults that lie inside the altar railing. The architecture and the artifacts all speak dramatically of the union of church and state and a practical ownership of the church by the Czar.

This place was called the Hermitage. It was cut off physically from the people by the water and by walls, but the edict of the czars, its usage, its smallness, and its wealth all cut it off too.

Such walls and boundaries separate both churches and governmental bureaucracies from the people on which they depend. As time passes, the separation becomes more and more fixed. The people are not listened to, but eventually they prevail; empires topple and bureaucracies die. New ones rise from their ashes.

When this happens in a church, which should be open, the Holy Spirit continues to guide both those inside and outside the group. When the Spirit prevails, people will unite. There is nothing in the gospel which is compatible with this separation of the leaders from the people. When the church allies itself with the state, as it did in Czarist Russia, it alienates the church from the people. In every land where the church becomes closely allied or in marriage with the government, it's in danger of a divorce from the people and from its own ideal.

What was once the Czar's church in Russia is now a museum owned by the state. Ironically, it is more open to the people today than it was when it was a church.

I talked with a university student and asked him what life was like. "It is difficult to disagree with parents or officials. We are the people who set up communism. It is very difficult to object. The police will grab you."

I asked him about living without God. He answered, "God is from the people."

It seemed to me that this statement could be taken in many ways. He might have meant that the state cannot take us from God because God is with the people. The state can neither make God nor do away with God. If this is what he meant, it makes good sense. But if he meant that everything flowed from the economy and the people, and God is limited to what the people can do, then such a theology allows little room for a transcendent God.

When the oppressed call to God for help, they call to a God who has the power to intervene in human history. God works through people, but people are not the limits of God's working. The fact Soviet officialdom continued to fear the influence of God was demonstrated in the actions of the customs officials who tried to stop our icons and Bibles from entering the country.

Religion was still free in the sense that people could go to the Russian Orthodox Church. A state church, it was allowed to have a seminary and about thirty churches operating in Moscow alone. Roman Catholic or Protestant Churches were not allowed except for a chapel connected with an embassy. Such was the chapel of St. Louis used by U.S. Embassy personnel. How hard to find, it was! Even with directions written in Russian, I did not find it though I spent several hours trying.

In the ordinary sense of the word freedom, meaning you can join the church of your choice and have public worship and other public expressions of your faith, there is no freedom. Each day of the tour I had a Eucharistic liturgy with the tour group. I took the opportunity during each day's homily to comment on what we were seeing: the memorials which identified the czars and the wealthy with the Russian Orthodox Church, how this added to the corruption of both church and state, and how it alienated both from the masses of poor. Furthermore, was religion free in the time of the czars? Within the walls of the Kremlin there were six chapels, former chapels of the Russian Orthodox Church. One was a private chapel for coronations and burials of the czars. It was small, packed with icons and tombs, obviously never intended for the people. Five other chapels close by were all within the Kremlin walls, all small. All of this says it was for the use of the czars, their friends and servants, and not for the masses. The communists kept them as museums that exhibit the jewels, golden religious ornaments, expensive household trappings of the czars — a historic witness to the wealth of state and church while the masses lived in great poverty. The communists didn't need to say that the czars and the Church were corrupt. The museums said it for them.

Curious to know the outlook of the average Soviet citizen, I asked one of the women who worked at the hotel, "Do you think there can be any purpose that would make life worth living if you eliminate God?" She hesitated to agree and told me that the goals of life are to work, to marry, and to have a family. I asked her if there would be any purpose to life if these things were denied her. There was no reply. She asked for evidence of God's existence, and I told her how the existence of created, limited, changing things speaks of the existence of a changeless and unlimited being. Although she did not refute me, neither did she agree.

Our flight back to Moscow ended with a view of the Kremlin encircled by its high, forbidding wall. Outside the wall was Red Square, which from the plane, looked the size of three or four football fields. We checked into the Ukraine Hotel, constructed in a type of architecture known as "Stalin Gothic." Towers at the top widen at their base to include the whole of the building. Against the skyline these towers create the image of a suspended medieval city that has mysteriously been hydraulicly raised.

In the afternoon we visited a world's-fair-like exhibition designed to showcase Soviet economic development. Space and agricultural exhibits dominated the fair, but industrial production was also represented.

I got a better idea of economic development one early evening: I walked down Gorky Street, one of the main streets, and past Moscow City Hall. Near 9 p.m. I went into the enormous Gum's Department Store. It was closing time and when the bell rang for closing, police locked the gates immediately and the sales people quickly put everything away. It looked more like the last day of school than the kind of last minute effort to please a customer that occurs in our consumer economy. There was a large supply of all sorts of goods in the huge store, but prices were high.

After noting the high prices, I wondered how far out of reach these items were for the average Soviet citizen. I questioned our guide about job positions and their salaries: The rector of the university got the highest salary paid in Moscow, but he turned much of it back to the university since he didn't need it. A senior teacher got two-hundred and fifty rubles a month, about the same as a bus driver. A doctor got one-hundred and fifty rubles. A street cleaner got the lowest salary, seventy rubles. Taxes began at one-hundred rubles, and checks were paid from the Supreme Soviet. Although the guide's pay was low, she said she kept this job with its small salary because she liked the work.

We took a trip seventy miles outside of the city to the town of Zagorsk, the center of the Orthodox Church in the Soviet Union. The head of the Church was involved with the Soviet government as part of the Ministry of Religious Affairs. We visited the old Orthodox seminary of Zagorsk where there were about two-hundred and fifty theological students.

On the way back, one of the buses suffered a flat tire. This occurred on a country road near a collective farm. An old man who could speak no English showed me around the farm; he knew the word "peace" as I knew the Russian counterpart, "mir". He showed me his home and his garden. Even in a collective, each person had a small piece of land — a few acres which they were obliged to cultivate. His house was simple, but it did have electricity and an icebox. He proudly opened his closet and showed me his clothes. He also showed great pride in his treasure box where he kept various lapel pins. He gave one to me; I took it as a token of friendship.

The collectives were organized in communities with elected leaders. Their wages came during the harvest season and depended on their productivity. Products were sold in a state store. Some collective farms were owned by the state which also owned the farm machinery. Independent collective farms bought their own machinery, but received help from the state in the form of loans for machinery and buildings. When I was in the country, about twelve-thousand state farms, each with several hundred members, were in operation.

This unscheduled visit was our first glimpse of country people. They were noticeably more friendly than the city people; they laughed and smiled more easily. They seemed more independent of the state with their own food supply which included chickens and other livestock. They lived in the great outdoors, away from the sterile high-rise flats with their controlled elevators. Here, a river flowed nearby; their gardens grew around their houses. It seemed to me they had more room, more freedom, more self-reliance.

When we left Moscow, we were told that the icons and other items which were taken from us at our entry could not be returned because the manager of the airport was away. Later, when I returned to the United States, complaints were to no avail.

In Russia I felt the heavy control of the government over its people. The state was the only employer; it blocked most news from the outside world. It restricted travel abroad, denied religious freedom. Yet this was hardly an excuse for threatening them with nuclear disaster, goading them into an ever more insane nuclear arms race. I had gone to Russia at the urging of Bishop Taylor, an American bishop in Stockholm. During the Second Vatican Council he was one of the foremost church leaders opposed to the nuclear arms race. When I encouraged him to broaden his work for peace by helping U.S. deserters from our unjust and immoral Vietnam War, he told me that none had asked his help. "Why should they? You've given no public sign that you disapprove of this war. How can they expect help from you?" In response to my challenge, Bishop Taylor proposed a deal: He agreed to seek out and help deserters if I would go to Russia for a first-hand look at life there. I suppose he thought it would temper my strongly expressed views about the insanity of our nuclear arms race; it might teach me that the fault was not all on our side. I agreed to go to Russia.

What I observed in Russia in no way justified our nuclear deterrence policy, the arms race nor what we were doing in Vietnam at the time. Of course, I witnessed the almost total control that the Soviet government exercised over its people. But that made me even more interested in building solidarity with them, rather than target them for destruction.

Hungary

Our next stop was Budapest where we found ourselves in a much more informal atmosphere. Customs workers were all smiles, and they didn't even search our baggage.

At the hotel we had a fine supper accompanied by gypsy music, and then we walked the few blocks to the banks of the Danube. As we came to the edge of the river, we could see a castle — illuminated in such a way that it appeared suspended in air. The high mountainside on which it stood was hidden by the night. The castle was a monument to freedom, erected to commemorate the Russian liberation of the city during World War II.

The next day we toured the church of St. Stephen and attended Mass in the chapel that stands on the site of his grave. A statue of Stephen — sword in hand — towered over the tabernacle. The inscription read that Stephen brought Christianity with the sword. It seems that he is the Constantine of the Hungarians. Later, in another part of the city, I came upon another statue of Stephen. On horseback, the universal symbol of the warrior, he had a cross in his hand and a sword by his side.

I met a student from Sudan, Maghoub, who showed us more of the city and told us about life there. He himself was a communist and thought that most of the Hungarian students were either communists or supportive of the government. We went together to a nightclub where he explained that all the employees were on government salaries. This included the manager, the servers, the pianist and other musicians, and the women dancers. It was hard to believe because it looked and felt so much like a nightclub in the United States.

Work, as in other communist countries, was a requirement in Hungary. If one refused employment over a three-month period, they went to jail and stayed there until they agreed to take a job.

One evening I went with a group of young people from the university to an outdoor music park where hundreds danced on a plateau above the Danube. The music was good and the beer was cheap. The evening was beautiful. Compared to those we met in other Eastern Bloc countries, the people of Budapest seemed more content with the government and with communism. Much of life seemed easy and pleasant.

The churches were open and easily accessible, unlike in the Soviet Union. Although, identical restrictions on religious education and meetings of religious groups outside of church buildings were in place.

Czechoslovakia

In Prague we were given an uncertain welcome and a long wait by soldiers who handled the passengers. They seemed suspicious and intent on finding smugglers.

Our first stop was the Cathedral of St. Wenceslas and the adjoining Hradcany Palace, the residence of the President of Czechoslovakia. Nearby was the residence of the archbishop. However, the house stood empty — due to the tension between the Church and the state, the position had not been filled even though there were a large number of Catholics in the country.

The palace had a large auditorium. Knights used to ride into the auditorium on horseback. The palace, although plain on the exterior, was stunningly beautiful on the inside: a fitting setting for the celebrations and assemblies held there over the centuries. It is unusual for a building to be constantly in use for a thousand years. War or natural disasters often destroy such sites. In this historical treasure, we saw the throne room of the Hapsburgs and the courtroom where they met. Archbishops and bishops had reserved seats. The room was too small for a parliament or for representatives of the people, just large enough for nobles and churchmen. Another church we saw, St. Vitus, emphasized this caste system. There were seats near the altar for the nobles, but the people had to stand.

The physical arrangements of the courtroom and church illustrated the close association of church and state during the middle ages. The cross and the sword were almost always linked. No wonder the church was so affected when Europe divided into nation states. No wonder that as the nation states evolved into an international world, the peace teachings of the gospel were diminished.

We crowded into the palace balcony to look down over the city. Our guide pointed out one church after another. "A city of one-hundred forty spires," she said. When I asked her to show me the Jesuit Church, she said there were no Jesuits. I insisted that there must be Jesuits here somewhere, but she was adamant. When I got the chance to talk alone with her, she admitted that there might in fact be some Jesuits in Prague, but there was no recognized organization. All religious orders were banned by government orders in 1950.

Back at the hotel, I asked the desk clerk for the phone number of the Jesuits.

"What are Jesuits?"

"Priests."

"What are priests?"

I ignored what seemed to be feigned ignorance and requested the phone number of Monsignor Tomasek, the Apostolic Administrator of the Prague Diocese. The Monsignor's secretary provided me with a phone number which she assured me would put me in touch with a Jesuit. Finally, I made contact: I caught a trolley and was soon at a building like the Gesu in Rome. The Jesuit motto, Ad Majorem Dei Gloriam, For the Greater Glory of God, was imprinted on the front of the building. Inside I felt at home; it had all the familiar items of a well-kept Catholic church: the statue of the Sacred Heart in a shrine of red marble at the left front, Immaculate Conception on the right.

A man cleaning the red rug in the center aisle showed me the way to the sacristy and called the priest. A small man in a gray shirt and gray trousers entered. I told him in Latin that I was a Jesuit priest from Washington, D.C. He invited me to his office upstairs. "No one lives here. This is not a parish. We can baptize and preach and administer the sacraments. Only two of us are here."

He had been teaching in a Jesuit seminary in 1950 when the government banned all religious orders. He and others continued for six months, defying the ban. Sixty of them were rounded up and jailed. His crime, "Enemy of the state and traitor to his country." His sentence: Twenty-three years — nine years in solitary confinement, the rest at hard labor in the coal mines or glass factory. He had worked long hours that left little time for reading or anything else. He was allowed one family visitor each year, one letter each month.

In 1968, after eighteen years in prison, he benefited from the amnesty granted to all political prisoners who had served more than eight years in jail. He and many other Jesuits were released. Unfortunately, some had already died in prison.

At the time I spoke with him, he was an employee of the state and received sixty-three dollars a month for administering sacraments in the church. He lived in a flat nearby with a friend, also a former prisoner. I asked why the government allows him to function at all. He answered, "We have laws here which say that religion is free, and we want to impress the rest of the world."

In 1969 he went to Rome as a pilgrim, but since then, he had not been allowed to leave the country. When I asked if there was anything we could do for him, he told me, "We don't need material things; what we need is spiritual strength." Books in quantity were not allowed, but individual copies could be sent to him. I learned that although many young men wished to become Jesuits, they had to be trained individually; no group instruction was allowed, nor could they live together. Despite these great restrictions on faith, there was much interest. Baptism of university students was common.

This Jesuit was fifty-nine years old, with a difficult life, but the strength of his faith was not diminished. He told me that he knew of the Berrigans and thought well of them. This brought to my mind a discussion I had with the Berrigans: I told them of my belief that by staying out of jail, they could better voice their opposition to the war. They answered that their example would speak to the whole world, especially where oppressed people need to stand against persecution. Now I was talking to one of those people. The witness of this brother Jesuit inspired me. His ability to persevere under the circumstances could only be explained by his deep faith in God.

The next evening I attended a Mass, delivered in Bohemian, by my Jesuit friend. The church was half-full. The people responded, singing parts of the Mass. I found it a rich and full religious experience.

Before leaving Prague, I asked my new friend, "Do you have any hope?" His face lit up with a bright smile. "It is the only thing we do have. God does not desert us." His answer stays with me. I recall that after my return from three years as a Japanese prisoner of war, I found it next to impossible to convey the experience to others: the uncertainty of the future, the daily struggle to stay alive. My experience, while extremely difficult, paled in comparison to the length of time this Jesuit endured persecution.

I shook hands with him on the pavement outside the church. He instructed me not to mention his name in public for fear that he would end up back in jail. His parting words to me: "Give my love to the brothers!" As I flew back to the United States, I compared my life with his and wondered what I would do in his shoes.

International Peace Conferences

Soon after I returned to Georgetown, an association of lawyers opposed to nuclear war invited me to speak at an international conference in New York. While there, I joined the International Peace Bureau at the request of Sean MacBride, a Nobel peace prize winner from Ireland and president of the Geneva-based Bureau. Some time later I was elected as the Bureau's Vice President.

At the suggestion of Sean MacBride, the Committee on Peace and Confidence Building in Europe invited me to attend one of their meetings in Vienna. I chaired and drafted a report from the Ethics portion of the meeting. MacBride asked me to call Armand Hammer with my report when I returned home because Hammer had funded that part of the meeting. MacBride added, "Also ask him if he will fund your next trip to the International Peace Bureau meeting." In New York I reached Armand Hammer by phone. He was pleased with my report and agreed to my funding request.

Because of these contacts, I started attending many of East-West peace conferences, about two or three each year. We usually met at Geneva, Vienna or Helsinki. At the meetings I met peace leaders from all over the world The International Liaison Forum, which hosted annual international conferences attended by non-governmental representatives from ninety-five nations, elected me as one of the permanent U.S. observers. As part of this honor, I could invite one or two friends to attend with me and have their expenses paid. I invited Father Angelo D'Agostino, a psychiatrist interested in peace, Father John MacNamee, and John O'Rourke of the Catholic Peace Fellowship in Philadelphia.

A coalition of peace groups funded the forum. In the United States, it was commonly thought that the forum was fully funded by the Soviet Union and that anyone participating was a dupe of the communists — ideas I considered U.S. propaganda.

One morning at breakfast in Vienna, Appolinario Diaz-Collegas a well-known journalist and a former Minister of Culture in Colombia, asked if I would join with him and a Soviet writer in putting together a book that would give perspectives on the common problems of peace such as nuclear disarmament, intervention in Central America and Afghanistan, and the effects of armaments on Third World nations. Together we would represent views from the two super-powers and one Third World country, Colombia. I was thrilled by this invitation and excited about the project.

A month or two later I met the third author: Sergo Mikoyan from the Soviet Union. He was a small man of slight build with bushy black-gray hair. His fluent English made the logistics of the project much easier. As we began our collaboration, the first task was to iron our differences. Sergo said to me, "I know from your writing you are opposed to all war. I almost agree with you. But I think sometimes there is an exception. You write just what you think, then I will write where I agree and disagree with you. The same with Appolinario. We will give our views on various peace topics. . . . We can all submit manuscripts on the topics we want to treat. Then we can come together to discuss what we want to add or change."

With the process settled, I initially sent seventy-five pages to Appolinario and received much more from him. A couple of months later we all returned to Moscow for additional work on the manuscript. During this time, I got to know Sergo better: In the two-story office in a residential section of Moscow, he and his small staff published a magazine on Latin America. Sergo was head of the Latin American branch of the Soviet Academy of Sciences. I also learned that his father, Anastasio Mikoyan, was once President of the Soviet Union.

One day, during my time in Moscow, Sergo offered to drive me around. This was fortunate because I couldn't read the Cyrillic street signs and had been unable to find St. Luke's Catholic Church. Sergo not only knew where it was, but insisted that we wait the half-hour for Mass to finish so that I could talk with the priest. The Lithuanian priest and I conversed in Latin, our only common language. On the way back, I told Sergo, "I didn't recognize the hymns they were singing; it wasn't Russian or Latin."

"No. It was Polish. The church is attended by Polish people. I must tell my mother about it. She is a believer. She likes Polish hymns." That surprised me because of the major role his family played in Soviet politics.

After the three of us submitted our manuscripts, we were ready to work out common themes and fine-tune our points. Sergo supplied us with tea and cookies while we waited for interpreters to arrive. I spoke only "tour-book" Russian, but had enough Spanish skills to converse with Appolinario who spoke Russian, but no English. Sergo spoke no Spanish. Soon the interpreters arrived: an Argentine, who spoke Spanish and Russian but no English, and two young Russians who spoke English. None of us could speak all three languages.

We sat around a table with a tape recorder between us. We took turns proposing topics and offering comments. Sergo planned to transcribe the tape and translate it into the three languages. After our edits, he and his staff would publish a version of the book in each of the three languages. After much work, our book *Peace Prospects From Three Worlds* was published in 1989.

I was curious about how the interpreters viewed the discussion, so after one of the session, I engaged one (who spoke English) in conversation. He said this was the first time he ever interpreted for a Catholic priest and he didn't know many of the words such as penance and reconciliation. When I asked him about his religion, he said he was an atheist.

I replied, "Well, if you were to ask me, 'What's your work?' and I answered, 'I'm not a carpenter,' that wouldn't tell you very much. When you say 'I'm not a believer in God,' it doesn't tell me what you do believe."

He said, "What do you mean?"

"Why are you interested in peace?"

"Because I don't want to be hurt and don't want to hurt others."

I continued to press him on the question, and finally he was able to say something about the value of people above all else. I responded, "As long as you believe that, you do believe in God because if people have value, they have to get it from somewhere; that 'somewhere' is God. You're just a theoretical atheist and a practical believer." He seemed to accept that. I wondered if he said he was an atheist to remain secure in his government job.

Later, as part of a speech delivered to an audience that included nearly fifty communists, I used this anecdote to make a point about atheism. I started by saying that "if you shoot an arrow and want it to hit the bull's eye, you have to aim a little high. If you want to work for peace, you have to aim a little higher than the humanitarian programs you've been hearing about today. That higher target is Jesus' teaching that we should love one another and love God." I could feel a kind of chill in the room. I continued with the atheist interpreter story, "Theoretically you can be an atheist by simply saying so, but your life will tell your friends and your enemies what you really are. You're interest in peace, you're belief that people are more valuable than the ground they stand on, this is the value of God, and in that sense, all of you are believers in God." Some of the Buddhist priests didn't agree with my analysis, but most there seemed to understand my point of view.

The chairman told me there had been a recent meeting in the Kremlin in which Graham Greene made a similar point. Greene admonished Gorbachev, "You are losing opportunities. All of you have a passion for justice as Marx had, and you don't recognize that same passion exists among Christians. For example, you have right now in Nicaragua two Catholic priests who are in the cabinet of a communist country, and you just ignore this asset . . . this desire for justice in both believers and atheists."

I learned much during my time in the Eastern Bloc countries. I hope that I was able to contribute to the "thawing" of the Cold War and thus further the cause of peace.

Medjugorje, Yugoslavia

Sometime in 1985 the director of the Catholic Travel Agency in D.C. asked me to lead a tour to Yugoslavia where the Blessed Mother was appearing daily. Since I knew nothing about such appearances, I needed convincing. After viewing a video supplied by the travel agency, I agreed to the proposal because the message of the Blessed Mother was peace. This message coming from a communist country was enough to arouse my interest.

In my eight days at Medjugorje I became convinced. I talked with the young visionaries and found their assertion to be true: The Mother of God was appearing there daily. I did not think it was a hoax because they were too young, uneducated, and unskilled to articulate such a theologically-sophisticated and profound message of peace. In addition, all these young people came from different families; they spent three to four hours a day in prayer; they fasted on bread and water twice a week. This life of holiness had been sustained for five years without any compensation from visitors. All this was done despite opposition from the government and the local Catholic bishop.

The peace message of Our Lady: "I come to make known the peace of Christ. The way to that peace is to believe what my Son says, especially his commandment that we should love one another, including our enemies. To do this is difficult. It requires that we convert entirely to God and entirely away from all sin. You will find the energy to do this through constant prayer and regular fasting."

A year later I returned to Medjugorje. My conviction was re-affirmed: Our Lady was appearing there and that her message was an epiphany for all. All of the programs of Gandhi and King — marches, boycotts, and civil disobedience — could and should be rooted in love of enemy and energized by conversion, prayer and fasting.

I had the opportunity to reflect on Our Lady's peace message and then preach in the parish church of St. James at Medjugorje. After hearing me preach, Heather Devish of Arizona asked me to write a book emphasizing the peace message and offered to pay the expense of publishing it.

I returned a third time to Medjugorje — this time with a tape recorder to interview the visionaries, priests of the parish of St. James, and the pilgrims. I asked each one of them these five questions: 1) Is the peace of Christ the focus of all the Blessed Mother's messages? 2) Does she say we must believe what her Son taught that we should love everyone including our enemies? 3) Does this mean that we should love atheists? 4) Does this love mean we cannot kill anyone? 5) Could a believer in the messages of Our Lady conclude from the messages, that one should not prepare for, take part in, or pay taxes for war? The answers I received made up my book titled, *Medjugorje Speaks Peace.*

I found that not all who heard the message were ready to accept it. One day, just after an interview with Marija, one of the visionaries, I asked the group of over a hundred Americans who were visiting Medjugorje with me if they wanted to hear the questions I asked Marija and her answers. We had just finished Mass and were assembled out in front of the church to plan our daily program. Most wanted to hear what I had to say.

When I got to the question, "Does Our Lady mean we should not kill anybody?," one of the pilgrims yelled out, "That's a political question. You're dividing us. You're suppose to be our spiritual director."

"You don't have to listen," I answered. "I told you that before I began."

"We don't have to love communism to love people who are communists or atheists," yelled out a peacemaker in the crowd.

The discussion almost ended my talk. It illustrated the unwillingness of many devotees of Our Lady to understand or to accept her peace message when it is concretely applied. Our Lady's message clearly directs us to oppose war and militarism.

Through these experiences, I began to believe the message at Medjugorje could build bridges between Marians who typically neglect peace, and those committed to peace and justice, but who ignore the example of the Blessed Mother. The gift from Our Lady at Medjugorje is a model for both groups.

VI

Living the Beatitudes

21 ✣ The Community
for Creative Nonviolence

In September 1970 after my sabbatical, I resumed teaching at Georgetown. I returned full of encouragement and inspiration from all the people of peace I met throughout my global travels. I resolved to turn this inspiration into concrete action. So I decided that, as long as ROTC was on campus, I wanted my salary withheld from the Jesuit community's annual gift to the university.

When I made this request, the Jesuit rector, John McGee, replied that I had taken a vow of poverty and therefore could not determine how the money should be spent. I told him that I was not asking for money, but only that the money not be used for something I considered immoral. I also informed him that I was not the only one in the university community who opposed ROTC.

He attempted to leverage me by pointing out that the community had allowed me to go on sabbatical. Sensing the manipulation, I responded that if I had known that sabbaticals were given with strings attached — granted in exchange for not "rocking the boat" — I would have refused sabbatical. I added that it was too late for blackmail.

He must have taken this as an affront, and he told me that I didn't belong in the community, that I should leave.

At the advice of Jesuit friends, I wrote the provincial, Jim Connors, to ask if he would allow me to live outside the community, to send him my paycheck, and in return receive what I needed each month. He agreed because it was a matter of conscience.

About the same time I learned that Ed Guinan, a newly ordained Paulist priest and a campus minister at George Washington University, had helped to start the Community for Creative Nonviolence: a radical Christian community. I had met Ed at several peace rallies.

Ed had asked the pastor of Luther Place Memorial Church in Washington, for the use of some church property located on N and 14th Streets, N.W. to house the community. The pastor, who had a deep interest in social justice and peace had Ed make his plea before the parish board. They agreed to give him the property for use as housing for the homeless, for Vietnamese refugees and as a halfway house for those released on personal bond by the courts.

Ed Guinan was joined by Kathleen Thorsby, Rachael Linnor, John Shiel, Dick Dreter, and Maggie Lourdes. Soon the Community for Creative Nonviolence (CCNV) quickly grew to occupy additional houses, one in the 2100 block of N Street, N.W., the other, on Thomas Circle and 23rd Street. I moved from the Georgetown Jesuit residence into the community and joined them — in protests against the Vietnam war and the draft, in daily home Mass, and in service to the hungry and homeless.

Ed believed that the community should not be ruled by a "boss," but should be governed by consensus; a style of anarchism where everyone did what they thought best. He believed the community should be religious, but interfaith. He believed that admission to the community and other important decisions should be made by consensus and at community meetings.

All of this sounded good, but it was in strong contrast to the Jesuit community life where authority is clearly vested in a superior, where everyone had to be Catholic, where all lived on a common economy and where all members were men committed to lifetime service.

Although I had use of a car if I wanted it, I generally rode a bicycle the twenty-five city blocks back and forth to teach at the university. My ride brought me from one of the poorest sections of Washington into the wealthy section of Georgetown. The contrast was unbelievable.

I told one of the Jesuits that I estimated we lived on about a dollar per day per person at CCNV. He couldn't believe that was possible. I pointed out that we paid no rent and we got most of our food from begging. I urged him to come for a visit to see for himself. He still couldn't believe it and he never did visit.

At 14th and N Street we lived in the center of the red-light district. Hookers and police were in evidence day and night. This often led to interesting interactions. For example, one afternoon I was walking along 14th Street toward the house. A woman walked up alongside me and asked, "Are you dating today?"

"I don't believe in sex for money."

"Neither do I. Just give me the money. . . . Do you live near here?"

"Yes."

"Let's go to your house and have a beer."

"I don't drink."

"Could you give me a cigarette."

"I don't smoke."

"You don't drink and you don't smoke and you don't want sex. What do you do for fun?"

"I try to enjoy the deep adventure of the union with the infinite God."

"Oh, pardon me. I didn't know you was one of them."

Another Sunday morning out in front of the house I overheard a very loud conversation between a hooker and a man. He was standing about ten feet away from her and yelling, "You good-for-nothing bitch, I'll go home and get a gun and blow your head off."

"Leave me alone, I ain't askin' you for nothin'."

After the man left, I went up to the woman to ask what that was all about. "He was screaming at me because I said I wanted twenty-five dollars for a trick, but he wanted it for ten dollars." I told her she shouldn't have to take insults like that and I asked her why she didn't get out of the "business." She replied, "I have three children to support. I'm Black and I have a record of drug abuse."

I couldn't think of what to say. Here was a mother supporting her children by selling herself. Jobs in D.C. were scarce. Her record and her color were major strikes against her. It gave me a lot to think about.

My contact with the poor continued to challenge me: Generally, at the soup kitchen we prepared and served one meal a day, usually consisting of thick soup containing whatever vegetables were on hand, tea without sugar, and bread without butter. Sometimes we had more; most days we didn't.

One day after serving until the crowd of three-hundred was finished, I got a bowl of soup and sat down beside an old woman. She was already on her fourth bowl of soup. I commented, "You must really be hungry."

"Yes, I'se hungry."

"Don't you get anything to eat at night?" I asked.

"No, I don't get nuthin'," she replied. Then, after a pause, she asked, "Do you get something at night."

I felt embarrassed to answer. She took me to be one of the poor. Her compassionate interest in my well-being touched me deeply. "Yes, I get plenty at night," I finally answered.

One day while I was serving, an old man had a heart attack while eating. I asked someone to call an ambulance, but was told not to bother because no ambulance would come to our soup kitchen. They had refused before.

The man, still holding his chest, somehow managed to walk with me across the street to the police station. There I asked the policeman at the desk to call an ambulance. After some "run around" at the station, the ambulance finally arrived. It was clear to me that even the personnel at the police station would have refused to call for medical assistance if I had not been there to insist. It was a small insight into the everyday life of the poor.

Though I was a man with a variety of experiences, I still had much to learn from those around me. Laurel was one of my "teachers." A young woman of twenty, she was an activist who worked part-time in my office at the Peace Center. As a live-in community member who worked regularly at the soup kitchen, she got to know many of the homeless poor.

Once, as we were bicycling from the university to the 14th Street house, she saw one of her friends from the soup kitchen sitting on the sidewalk. She stopped to talk with him as I continued on a bit without her. But I turned around and went back. The old man was so happy to talk with her — neither of them appeared in any hurry. But I was impatient; I didn't want to be late for supper. Finally, she told me to go on without her.

The next day she asked me, "If George were a rich man, would you have ignored him like you did? I tried to explain that supper at the community was scheduled for a set time, and if we weren't there, it would make it difficult for others.

"You didn't answer my question. Would you have treated George that way if he had been a rich man?"

Reluctantly, I answered, "No, I wouldn't have."

"Then don't you see that you treat the poor differently than the rich? . . . If your schedules don't have room for love, there is something wrong with them."

She made an impact on me because she lived as she spoke: honoring the poor. At the soup kitchen the homeless could see the love in her eyes, and they constantly asked her for help.

(Laurel died suddenly at age twenty-one of a heart problem — a great loss to the community and to the poor of the city.)

In 1976 the Community for Creative Nonviolence split apart. Mitch Snyder and others started an independent branch several blocks away. He began raising funds in the name of CCNV and rented several adjoining houses on Euclid Street.

To this day that branch of CCNV continues. Throughout the 1980s Mitch and CCNV earned national recognition for their efforts on behalf of our sisters and brothers who are homeless. In 1984, Mitch engaged in a nearly sixty-day fast to force the Reagan Administration to renovate and release to CCNV the crumbling Federal City College building. Just days before the '84 Presidential Election, Reagan acquiesced. Eventually, the building was renovated and opened as a model shelter. For the last ten years the community has operated this two-thousand-bed shelter, serving the homeless in the shadow of the Capitol building.

It was a blow to the entire movement for peace and justice when Mitch took his own life in 1991.

Following the community split, the situation back on 14th Street was deteriorating. Ed was feuding with the pastor of Luther Place Memorial Church. We held the lease for the three houses we occupied, but the pastor asked him to vacate the house in which he was living. Ed refused. The pastor hired a lawyer to settle the matter, but before evicting him, the pastor called for several meetings with the community to settle the differences. Ed refused to attend the meetings, but most of the rest of the community attended. I kept a record of the proceedings.

Consensus had broken down. Most of the community members were in favor of staying even if Ed and his family had to leave. The division showed itself in many forms. People from each one of the three houses tried to meet the mail carrier first with the hope that there might be checks in the mail that they could cash. The daily liturgies were so mixed up that I stopped attending. Instead of following the guidelines for the Mass, various people were assigned to design a liturgy according to what they liked. When Ed finally left (before he was summoned to court), I also decided to get a fresh start.

22 ✣ *The Catholic Worker*

I asked our landlord if I could have the use of the house to start a Catholic Worker House. Two of the community members, Robert Teske and Anne Lado agreed to help me. We began with hospitality to a few of the homeless people already there as guests of CCNV. I phoned Father Marvin Mottet, who was director of the Campaign for Human Development program for the U. S. Bishops Conference. He had helped to start three Catholic Worker houses in Iowa. I asked him to join us in this new endeavor.

"I have a full-time job and spend about three months of the year traveling, but if you still want me to come and just sleep there I will. . . ."

He was a great asset because I had no experience running a Catholic Worker, but he did. He suggested we should call it St. Benedict Catholic Worker named after Pope Benedict who fed the starving people of Rome.

One day the four of us were at dinner and Anne started crying.

"What's the matter?" I asked.

"This is too much for Robert. He comes home tired from his law studies. He's not well and there's always some emergency to take care of when he gets home."

They took a walk, and returned a half-hour later. As I feared, they announced that they were leaving.

I didn't know what to think. I was sure I could not run the house by myself. I was teaching full-time at Georgetown and Marv was always gone all day. I asked the Lord to give me a sign of what He wanted me to do. Next day I got a phone call from Phyllis Shepherd. She had been advised by her spiritual director to look for work that would be more supportive of her faith. She was ready to volunteer at the Catholic Worker.

I knew Phyllis and enthusiastically accepted her offer — truly a sign from God. She was an invaluable asset to us. The pastor of Luther Place Memorial Church liked her so much that he asked her to help open and staff a women's shelter in an adjoining house. He and I were both surprised when, after she was asked for her resume, Phyllis produced a diploma from Loyola University Law School.

After six months Marv suggested that we should move to a new place — one where we could set our own guidelines and not impose on the generosity of the good people of Luther Place church. We were able to rent a three-story house on the corner of 6th and M Streets NW, not far from our original location. Marv also appealed to Archbishop Hickey to pay the rent for us. There, we were joined by Paul Magno, Marcia Timmel, John and Polly Mahoney. Marv, an expert farmer, grew a successful garden in the front yard. The garden won us the goodwill of the neighborhood.

It was still a dangerous section of the city. Marv got held up at gun point in sight of the front door of the house. He lost some money but persuaded the thief to drop his empty wallet in the snow as he ran away.

After about six months at M Street, we made a deal to buy an empty three-story house about a block away. The house had no front door, its plumbing and heating pipes had been stolen, and the two houses on either side were empty. Because of these factors, the asking price for the house was only fifty-five thousand dollars. The owner agreed to charge four-hundred dollars rent per month, allowing us to spend the rent money on repairs and also count it toward the purchase of the house. Within three years, primarily due to Marv's efforts, the community had secured enough grants and the house was ours.

While these changes were taking place, romance was in the air. In 1980, nineteen-year-old Monica Siemer came from Columbus, Ohio where her father was a well-known peace activist. She came to work at the Center for Peace Studies and lived at the Catholic Worker. By the time the Worker had moved to M Street, Pat Cassidy, a twenty -year-old student of theology at Catholic University contacted us. Because he was interested in service to the poor, he asked if he could live at the Catholic Worker while he was going to school. Pat moved in and soon Monica and he fell in love. Before long, they decided to get married. Her mother thought Monica was too young to get married. I assured her that Pat was as good a man as she was likely to meet. Both of them were interested in serving the poor and both were strong in their faith. She finally agreed to the marriage — Pat and Monica were married in Columbus on December 19, 1981. I was honored to be the officiating priest.

After their marriage Pat and Monica were the first staff members of the new Catholic Worker at 503 Rock Creek Church Road, N.W. That house had been the residence of the staff and students of the Trinitarian fathers who attended Catholic University.

One day I got a call from one of the Trinitarians who asked if I would be interested in having the house as a gift for the Catholic Worker in honor of Dorothy Day who had often made retreats there. Dorothy loved the Trinitarians because they would send their students to work on farms as part of their education. I went up to the house at 503 to see it and found that it was a fine large house with ten bedrooms and seven baths, wall-to-wall carpeting and storm windows. It was much nicer than most Catholic Worker houses. The rambling structure became known as the Dorothy Day House

While the wedding was going on in Columbus, Paul Magno stayed behind to take care of the house. He invited Marcia Timmel to come and help him keep the house going. Their work there developed into a friendship, and they were married in December 1983.

Shortly after a second child was born to Monica and Pat Cassidy, they decided to move out of the Catholic Worker because they found it hard to raise a family in that context. When they returned to Columbus in August 1986, the whole Catholic Worker community, including myself, missed them greatly.

The Dorothy Day Catholic Worker continues to provide the works of mercy: feeding the hungry, clothing the naked, comforting the afflicted.

— ❖ ❖ ❖ —

VII

Return to Georgetown

23 ✤ The Center for Peace Studies

Once I was resettled in the Jesuit residence at Georgetown, I did indeed become focused full-time on peace activism. As in the previous decades, I continued to participate in nonviolent direct action. In June 1982, during the U.N. Special Session on Disarmament, I joined in the national effort to shut down the embassies of the five nuclear powers: the Soviet Union, the United States, England, China and France. In New York I joined hundreds of others in blocking the entrance to the Soviet Embassy. After New York City Police told us to move and we refused; they arrested us. Because of the size of the demonstration, the police had to take us to jail in city buses. The police carried those who refused their order to board the buses.

In our bus one police officer stood in the middle aisle, another at the front door. I was near the middle of the bus. In the seat ahead of me, Father George Kuhn from New York, called out to the police in a loud voice, "When we protested against the Vietnam War, you policemen told us to go tell it to the Russians. Now you arrest us for trying to tell it to the Russians. What's the matter with you?"

"Are you a priest who has a parish in mid-Manhattan," one policeman asked.

"Yes, that's right. How do you know?"

"I think you're my cousin."

"Then I will tell your mother that you arrested your cousin. But I will forgive you if you will say five Hail Marys."

When the bus arrived at the precinct station, the police ordered us to produce some identification and to fill out an information form in the bus — we would be released without going to jail. Most of the protesters, including me, got released that way. Although most of us chose to cooperate and were released, we were too far from the embassy to rejoin the blockade.

In May 1983 Sojourners Community organized a protest against the U.S. installation of cruise missiles in Germany. We picketed on the steps of the U.S. Capitol. Then about a hundred of us went into the Rotunda of the Capitol for a public prayer. In the Rotunda, a public place, visitors are allowed to stay until closing time. But after we had been praying for about an hour, police arrived and told us we would be arrested if we didn't leave immediately. We continued to pray while one by one we were handcuffed and led out to police buses.

After receiving a series of messages about the availability of a judge, we thought we were headed for arraignment. But we finally learned that we would have to wait until Monday for our court appearance — typical of the confusion of the D.C. Government.

Meanwhile some of the prisoners started singing, "Give Me That Old Time religion," and "Onward Christian Soldiers " and many more songs. We were good singers and we shook the rafters. We were crammed into two large holding blocks. Each cell, one for men and one for women, held about fifty people, but only had one commode. Although we were hungry and overcrowded, we were people full of talent. One fellow put a napkin on his forearm pretending to be a waiter in a French restaurant. With a notebook in his hand he would come up to a prisoner and ask, "Can I take your order?" The merriment must have been contagious because the police even joined us in singing and passed around pitchers of water.

After awhile somebody decided that those who lived in the Washington area could be released on personal recognizance provided they fill out information forms. Since the majority of us were from D.C, that's what happened. I got out after about four hours.

In 1986 many people were arrested for demonstrating against South Africa's racial policies. I went to the South African Embassy with a group of about a dozen Georgetown students. Before going to the embassy, we received a legal briefing: The law forbade demonstrations within five-hundred feet of any embassy. We could be arrested for just standing there with signs. We also knew that demonstrators typically were released after arrest without being charged because the embassy did not want to bring attention to its racist practices.

On the way to the embassy one of the students said to me, "This will be my first arrest. It's probably a piece of cake for you."

I replied, "Every time you get arrested, you have to accept the risk that you might spend some time in jail. You have to be willing to put yourself in their control." Fortunately, true to form, we were released after processing at the police station.

In November 1989, six Jesuits were killed by Salvadoran police. Father Joe Mulligan, S.J. came to Washington two weeks after the murders to organize a demonstration on the White House sidewalk. After parading on the sidewalk we went across the street to Lafayette Park to hear speeches denouncing U.S. support of the Salvadoran Government which was persecuting the campesinos and killing priests.

Afterward, a group of us went back to the White House sidewalk to pray and to risk arrest; the law stated that demonstrators had to keep moving on the sidewalk. Arrest was assured when some in our group sprinkled the White House gate house with blood. I never felt more sure that I was doing God's work than when I saw that blood on the fence posts, the blood that represented my murdered Jesuit brothers. Joe Mulligan marked the gate house with his own blood mixed with soil stained by the blood of the slain Jesuits. After a few hours in jail we were processed and released.

(See Chapter 24 Jesuit Martyrs of El Salvador.)

In addition to these actions, my time was filled with speaking, writing, and organizing. In the 1980s the Center for Peace Studies presented an annual award for peacemaking called, the "Pacem en Terra Peace Award." Among others, it has been presented to Bishop Walter Sullivan of Richmond, Virginia; Daniel Berrigan, S.J. of New York; Sister Mary Lou Konacki, O.S.B., coordinator of Pax Christi, U.S.A. in Erie, Pennsylvania; and to Soviet President Mikhail Gorbachev. At the suggestion of my friend Dan Duffy, the Center gave Gorbachev special recognition with an award naming him "Peacemaker of the Decade." In 1989 the award was presented to Gorbachev by Georgetown University President Reverend Leo O'Donovan during a banquet at the Soviet Embassy. I had never expected the Peace Center to be involved with anything this public.

When the U.S. Catholic Bishops began to debate the morality of nuclear war, I was there in support of their dialogue. In 1982 I went to the annual conference where they debated the first draft of their peace pastoral. I had sent many suggestions to dozens of bishops and was pleased to see some of them implemented in the first draft. Thus, I was very disappointed when the second draft came out — clearly, several bishops had been influenced by General Haig and President Reagan. Yet, I continued encouraging the bishops to take a strong stand.

I was present again in 1983 when the third and final draft was released. As I listened to their debate, I rejoiced that we had Bishop Gumbleton as a peace representative on the bishops' peace committee, and I rejoiced that Bishop Bernadin was chairman of the conference for part of the time. I gave news briefings and distributed my book, The *New Testament Basis of Peacemaking* free to any bishop who wanted it.

At the final debate in November 1983, I was in Chicago for a demonstration to encourage the bishops. The night before the final debate I was honored by an invitation from Bishop Hunthausen of Seattle, who was the leader of the bishops' peace caucus: I was able to join him, his chancellor, and several other bishops in their effort to fine-tune the final draft.

Tom Siemer persuaded me to cancel my classes so I could stay longer. Fortunately, Georgetown was able to get a substitute. And from the balcony of the auditorium, I witnessed this historic event: the final debate and vote — three-hundred nine bishops voted in favor of the peace pastoral and only eight against it.

Although the pastoral didn't include all that I wanted, it was much more than I had expected a few years before. Never in the history of the bishops' conferences has the world and the press been so interested in their voting and writings. Despite the Reagan Administration's efforts to soften the bishops' stand, the document spoke strongly to the world. I was disappointed that some bishops approved of some sort of conditional deterrent, but I was glad that they spoke on nonviolence as an alternative to war and the approval they gave to conscientious objection.

In 1985 Guitso Sato, a Buddhist monk, invited me to come to India for a peace conference. Because I had already committed to lead a peace tour to Medjugorje, I turned him down. But he pressed me further and offered to pay all my expenses. With assistance from the Catholic Travel Bureau I was able to leave the tour in Rome and go to India.

With Rome as my starting point, I could go around the world for the same price as returning to the United States from India. So I also booked a flight to the Philippines.

I landed in New Delhi at 3 a.m., not sure if I would be met at the airport. I was relieved to see Guitso smiling and waving. Guitso is Japanese and had been a major in the Japanese Army. When the emperor called a meeting of the military to demand their resignations, Guitso stood and said they would never resign, and he was arrested for disrespect for the emperor. As punishment he was sent to India to serve under a Buddhist teacher in a peace community.

After several years in that community he went to Hiroshima where he saw the shadow marks on the wall caused by those who had been incinerated by the atomic bomb. There he took a vow to work for peace for the rest of his life. As a Buddhist, his assigned mission was to reconcile the East and the West. We first met at an international peace meeting in Europe, and later I invited him speak to my class at Georgetown.

From New Delhi we traveled to Bihar where we were among the many foreigners who were guests of the government of India. We were treated royally: We stayed in a government lodge and had use of a government auto. From Bihar we went to the mountain where Buddha used to teach. It is so steep an ascent that pilgrims could only access it by cable car. I knew some of the people who were there including Jim Douglass, now of the Catholic Worker in Birmingham, Alabama.

One day while waiting for transportation, I was approached by an Indian official who said, "I am the minister of education in the Province of Bihar. I have this letter I would like you to read." The letter was an invitation for me to accept an honorary degree from the Nalanda Mahavihara University, at the site where Buddha, himself, taught in four hundred B.C.. The honorary degree would be conferred the next morning. I accepted with joy.

I went by car to this university at the bottom of the mountain. There forty or fifty Buddhist monks in saffron robes were chanting as we entered the auditorium which was a very large tent with a colored roof. The officials were up on the stage. The honorary degree, printed in Fari (a language used by Buddha), was conferred, "For making peace in the West." As a gift they gave me the saffron robe I was wearing.

I was asked to give a speech. In English, I spoke of the New Testament principles that mandate Christians to oppose to all wars. I never expected such an honor; my guess is that it was arranged by Guitso.

In 1985, at age 70, I was required to retire from teaching because the law allowed universities to insist on retirement at that age. (Today the law is changed so they can never use age as a reason for retirement.) After spending so many years diligently promoting peace — usually in a climate of tension, whether from lay people, my peers, my superiors, my government — I began to receive awards in recognition of my life's work.

In 1985 I received the Distinguished Teacher Award, the Bunn Award (bestowed by vote of the Georgetown alumni). When I left the theology department, I was awarded a plaque for teaching justice and peace. It was at this time that I also received an award from the National Interreligious Service Board for Conscientious Objectors, NISBCO, for having served on their board of directors for fifteen years. In 1970, Monsignor George Higgins of the U.S. Catholic Conference had asked me to serve on NISBCO's board. They wanted a bishop, but no bishop was willing to serve, so I was the first Catholic on a board primarily composed of members of the Traditional Peace Churches: the Mennonites, Brethren and Quakers. I found that all the meetings dealt with vital topics of conscience.

In 1991 my book, *It's A Sin To Build a Nuclear Weapon* (Fortkamp Publishing / Rose Hill Books) was honored with the Pax Christi, USA book award. The award was presented to me by the president of Catholic University, William Byron, S.J. I had served on the national board of Pax Christi, USA for six years. Shortly after I retired, Pax Christi also gave me the title "Ambassador of Peace," a title awarded to only four or five others who have been associated with Pax Christi from its beginnings.

I consider all these accolades to be an honor to peacemaking, to the life I have lived in service to God.

24 ❖ *Jesuit Martyrs of El Salvador*

November 16, 1990 — I sat on the ground near the spot where their blood was shed. Here, six Jesuits, all younger than I, finished the martyrs' blood course on this earth; they went home to God. They were the top academic officials of the University of Central America in San Salvador.

On the first anniversary of their death, thousands gathered to reflect on their call for justice and peace; a constant stream of pilgrims came to this sacred place — here red rosebushes were planted at the site of their suffering for the sake of Christ's poor. Here Jesus' words come to life: "He who loses his life for my sake shall find it." The Jesuits continued to call for justice for the poor and for an end to the war even after they had been warned to stop and threatened with death. The bullets that forced the blood out of their bodies and onto the earth still did not silence them.

"If you are going to shoot us, do it outside, not in the house," one of the martyrs cried out to the murderers. So it was done. Like Christ they died outside. Like Christ their place of death is now a permanent memorial. Like Christ their deaths speak the same message as their lives.

Together they lived here. They were the highest officials of the university, yet they lived in small rooms along the same small hallway. At one end of the hall, I saw the combined library and community room with seven chairs around the table, chairs now empty, resembling the emptiness of Christ's tomb. At the other end of the hallway a door leads out to the lawn where they died.

As I looked over on their graves that sunny morning, I saw the sunlight forming a moving cross as the light filtered through the trees onto the white wall of the Jesuit residence. Four young boys about ten years old stood near the fence and pointed to the place where the Jesuits died. Students from the University of Central America, with books in their hands, stood at the fence. They talked. They took photos. A television crew arrived to report on the anniversary with the murder site as background.

Their deaths attracted the attention of the world more than their lives. A student approached to show me a poem he had written about the Jesuits who came to El Salvador not to exploit the people or enrich themselves, but to enrich the country by teaching and, if necessary, by dying as Jesus did.

Their deaths tell me that if your faith leads you to promote justice and peace, you may pay a high price for it. For the Jesuit university officials, the price was their lives. They knew that price might be asked of them. Through their work at the university, they identified themselves with the cry of the poor: a cry for food, medicine, education, and basic human rights. And the poor of the country recognized the voices of the Jesuits as their own. The army also recognized their voices as the voices of the poor crying for justice and peace. The army feared the influence these six Jesuits might have with the government.

Perhaps the military decided that the only way to stop them was to kill them. A guerrilla attack on San Salvador could be used as a shield: The security zone set up to protect the headquarters also included the whole university area. Classes were closed, the university emptied except for the Jesuits who lived there. What an opportunity to both get rid of the troublesome Jesuits and to pin the blame on the guerrillas. No one could report the crime except the government security forces allowed in that area.

Whoever these attackers were, they were brutal; they shot up the reception room and offices, fired flame-throwers at computers once used to promote peace and justice. They sprayed machine-gun fire on the large portrait of the late Archbishop Oscar Romero, whose heart had been pierced by an assassin's bullets while celebrating Mass nine years prior. He was killed because he pleaded with the army to stop the killing.

The soldiers continued their rampage through the Jesuit residence, machine-gunning the library that was once used to research the roots of poverty and oppression. Their bullets cut thick books in half. They lunged onward, rousting the six Jesuits from their beds and ordering them to move outside where they shot them with so many bullets that witnesses first thought they had been tortured. One Jesuit, who did not go out, was shot in his room.

To the killer's surprise, two other people were in the residence. The Jesuit's cook and her fifteen-year-old daughter had remained in the house that night to escape the danger of travel. These two could not be left behind to tell the tale. Quickly, machine guns left them in pools of blood in their bedroom. The killers departed leaving eight bodies in their wake. They left the house riddled with bullet holes and blackened by fire.

No doubt when they left, they thought it was a job well-done. Reports are that the military radio immediately proclaimed "Ellacuria and Montez have fallen. Let's kill the other communists."

One year later, the murderers may not have thought they were so successful. The university welcomed thousands to celebrate a Mass commemorating the martyrs. Salvadoran Archbishop Arturo Rivera Damas and twenty-one other bishops from around the world were there along with two-hundred and fifty priests, many of them Jesuits like myself.

The Mass began on a large outdoor stage on the university's parking lot. Above the altar hung a large banner reading, "Central American University Celebrates Its Martyrs." Beside the banner a large white sign with bold blue letters was inscribed with the names of the six Jesuits.

The audience listened as the bishop representing the Episcopal Conference of El Salvador read a statement:

> "We have come here today to show our solidarity with the Society of Jesus which today celebrates the martyrdom of six of her best sons. We come also to show our solidarity with the anonymous martyrs, the campesinos, workers,

catechumens, religious men and women of the Church who have given their lives for peace in El Salvador.

"We come with a firm desire that our voices will contribute to the search for peace. As pastors, we beg that all sides use every energy to put an end to war and to seek the removal of the causes of war. We ask a negotiated solution of the war, but a solution from which the poor of El Salvador will benefit."

The Jesuit Provincial of Central America then gave a homily praising the martyrs as faithful followers of Christ. "We celebrate the martyrdom of eight persons who gave witness with their lives to a synthesis of faith and justice, of academic excellence and service to the poor, accompanied by the generous outpouring of their blood."

At the end of the Mass, the university's new president expressed gratitude to the slain Jesuits' family members, many of whom had come all the way from Spain. During the Mass, they carried glass urns containing the earth mixed with the blood of the martyrs gathered from the garden where they had died.

What do the murderers think of their crime today? Through organized Jesuit efforts and international pressure, one year later the U.S. Congress reduced by fifty percent its daily million dollar subsidy to the Salvadoran government.

If I could talk to the murderers today, I would say:

"You killed my Jesuit brothers because you saw them as affecting the promotion of peace and justice which interfered with your plans. You were right, they were enemies of injustice and war. You were wrong to kill them, but God forgives you and I forgive you. You did not know what you were doing. The blood shed by your bullets now flows in the veins of the six new Jesuits who took their place.

"When they heard of the murders, Jesuits from all over the world volunteered in large numbers to take their place. Do you know that the six selected are among the best Jesuits in the world, the most devoted to the principles of peace and justice? Do you know that the example of the six martyrs cries out to other Jesuits like me, calling on us to live life like them and die like them?

"Do you remember that the soldiers who killed Jesus thought that killing him would stop his message of love?

Jesus' death, instead of silencing the message, became the loudest way of proclaiming it."

I stayed for ten days after the celebration. With some of the families of the martyrs, I visited churches of the poor parishes where they had labored. Late one night while I was staying at the Loyola Retreat House near the university, I was awakened by bombing. It went on for a long time. A new group of men had arrived the day before to begin a retreat. Suppose they were guerrilla soldiers? This place could be bombed on suspicion. What would I do if soldiers started searching the room? I might hide in the bushes outside my window or on a patio nearby. What must be the terror of the campesinos during the bombing? Their homes, their children have no protection

I made an act of contrition. Again the deep roar of the bombing awakened me. Poor people may be dying at the hands of a government that should be their helper. North American money probably paid for these bombs — our way of promoting "democracy."

The next morning I asked where the bombing took place. The men working in the Retreat House told me the bad news: Five cities were hit including one near the airport.

"Were many killed?"

"We are the last to get the news. Foreign countries learn about it first."

I recalled my experience under Japanese bombing in the Philippines; we learned more from the Voice of America in San Francisco than from the Philippine news. "It is a crime that cries out to heaven for punishment," I said to my companion. "The poor are the main victims."

The Salvadoran government, claiming the need to wipe out the guerrillas, is unjustified because they kill innocent people. In the parish of Madre de las Pobres bombs were dropped on the church to deter guerrillas. After the murder of their loved ones, many people joined the guerrillas. A government that kills its own people creates guerrillas. Military minds never seem to learn that killing people does not stop war nor bring peace

✤ *Afterword*

I have now traced, as well as I can remember, my path to peace and justice — a path that began in early family life, led to racial justice and onto the peace of Christ. This is not the story of my sins and failures; those I leave to God's merciful judgment

Along this path I have struggled with what the word "justice" means: Justice is giving someone their due whether on a individual or group basis. By group basis, I mean social justice. I first became acutely awareness of the need for social justice — justice for the group — in Ridge, Maryland. As a pastor, I dealt with two communities in separation: white and black — separate and certainly not equal. At the time, none of my studies had prepared me to respond to this situation. But by vicarious experiences, I came to understand, at least in part, the suffering of Blacks at the hands of the white community. And I realized that I was not only a part of that white community, but also a leader within it and a racist myself. This racism was keeping me, and the people I led, from a perfect union with God.

Before going to Ridge, I had a very narrow definition of injustice: When God created me, he obliged me to seek the necessities of life: food, water, clothing, shelter, health, education and skills to earn a living. I felt that if I was blocked in these efforts, then I was experiencing injustice, individual injustice. After all, didn't God want me to have all these things? And perhaps more?

But I learned to expand my definition of injustice. The sin of segregation opened my eyes to social injustice. I also made another leap: the connection of one type of injustice (segregation) to another (war). However, I didn't gain these insights by myself. I was greatly helped by the examples of Aloysius Butler, my mentor in the Black community at Ridge; Martin Luther King, Jr.; Dan and Phil Berrigan; and many others who traveled the same path before me.

Especially through Dr. King and the Berrigans, I learned to see the Vietnam War as a massive act of injustice — not only to the American soldiers who were forced to be a part of it, not only to the Vietnamese who died in it, but also to the whole American public who were forced to pay for it and to the world that saw the brutality of a large country attacking a small one.

It took me some time to come to a satisfactory definition of peace, the peace of Christ, but I found it in Ephesians. (2:13-15) There St. Paul says,

"But now in Christ Jesus, you that used to be far apart from us have been brought very close, by the blood of Christ. For He is the peace between us, and has made the two into one and broken down the barrier which used to keep them apart."

To put Paul's words in Americanese, I define peace as a three way relationship: a relationship of reconciliation between God, myself and my neighbor. Reconciliation means we are at home with each other, we are communicating with each other. It is a step short of loving each other. It is the antechamber to loving one other. God is the central part in the three way relationship, but all three parts are essential. Peace can be more fully understood by contrasting it with war. War separates me, either from God or from my neighbor. But peace is not just the absence of war.

I began to see that these two main currents, peace and war, were flowing through our lives and through history. I came to define peace as anything that brought me together with my neighbor and my God. Thus, I began to see peace in many ways, in marriage, friendship, church. An act of economic justice or racial justice would be an act of peace. And peace, fed by hope and love, leads to new life.

In contrast, I see war as anything that separates us from God or neighbor such as racism, economic oppression. extreme nationalism and military operations. They are fed by fear and they lead to death, both physical and spiritual.

It took some time for me to clearly understand how justice and peacemaking are acts of faith, or at least require such faith as an essential component. In this way I came to realize that everything that had helped my faith, had also been the energizing force that helped me walk along my path to justice and peace. I saw that whatever I did for justice or peace was my way of doing God's will.

The example was clear to me: the life of Jesus, who taught that above all we should love others and practice justice. Should there be any doubt, He gave the example not just with his words, but also with his life. He did this by shedding His blood on the cross. When He completed this work of reconciliation, He said to His followers, "Peace I bequeath to you, my own peace I give you, a peace which the world cannot give, this is my gift to you." (Jn. 14:27)

Instead of inflicting suffering on others, He accepted suffering Himself. This is His way to peace and justice. The last steps on His journey were bloody ones, but the journey did not end with the cross. He went on to His kingdom in heaven which He promised to share if only we will walk with Him.

When we defend God's image in human beings, we also do His will. This is well illustrated in the life and teaching of Archbishop Oscar Romero of San Salvador. Some quotes from him are a good way to end this story of my path to peace and justice. I am sure I do not walk the path as faithfully as he; but our paths are parallel and his views are an expression of my own.

February 18, 1979, within a year of his death for preaching the liberating gospel of our Lord, Romero said, "Many would like a preaching so spiritualistic that sinners are unbothered and [that] does not term [as] idolaters those who kneel before money and power."

On March 11, 1979 he said, "A church that suffers no persecution, but enjoys the privileges and support of the things of [the] earth — beware — [it] is not the true church of Jesus Christ."

A week later, he said, "I look at you, dear friends, and I know that my humble ministry is only that of Moses, to transmit the word — 'thus says the Lord' — and what pleasure it gives me when you say in your intimate hearts or at times in words and letters I receive what the people replied to Moses, 'what Yahweh has ordered.'"

And again on June 2, 1979, he said, "When they tell me that I am a subversive, that I meddle in political matters, I say 'it is not true.' The church's mission, which is a prolongation of Christ's, must save the people and be with them in their search for justice, also, it must not let them follow the ways of hatred, vengeance, or unjust violence. In this sense we accompany the people, a people that suffers greatly. Of course, those that trample the people must be in conflict with the church."

And on March 20, 1979, he said, "It is wrong to be sad. Christians cannot be pessimists. Christians must always nourish in their hearts the fullness of joy. Try it, brothers and sisters: I have tried it many times and in the darkest moments, when slander and persecution were at the worst, [I try] to unite myself intimately with Christ, my friend, and to feel a comfort that all the joys of the earth cannot give: the joy of feeling oneself close to God, even when humans do not understand. It is the deepest joy the heart can have."

✤ Index